Freedom of Information:
Law and Practice

D1313019

Freedom of Information: Law and Practice

Edited by

ESTELLE FELDMAN

Published in 2006 by
First Law Limited,
Merchant's Court,
Merchants Quay,
Dublin 8,
Ireland.
www.firstlaw.ie

Typeset by Gough Typesetting Services, Dublin.

ISBN 1-904480–43–8

A catalogue record for this book
is available from the British Library.

Printed by Westside Press

For

Elaine Feldman

*whose lifetime of achievement
exemplifies vision, principal and dignity.*

Preface

"to enable members of the public"

The Freedom of Information Act 1997 is *sui generis*. It is one of a kind for a number of different reasons, but most especially because of its peculiar relationship with the public. It appears to be the only Act on our Statute Book that has in its Long Title a directive "to enable members of the public", more specifically to enable the public access to recorded information "to the greatest extent possible consistent with the public interest and the right to privacy". What is equally remarkable is that those who administer the freedom of information (FOI) regime on a daily basis are also members of the public: they are not members of the legal profession; they are not required to have any legal or other professional training. The sole qualification they have to administer the Freedom of Information Act is their employment by a public body that comes within the Act's ambit. What is unremarkable is that the Act is not distinguishable from many other pieces of legislation that have been drafted in turgid and well-nigh incomprehensible language. Possibly spurred by this knowledge, the expert contributors accepted an invitation to write for this book with alacrity.

It is hoped that anyone will find in the contents material that is both interesting and easy to read. The first Information Commissioner, Kevin Murphy, reflects on the early years of the FOI Act and the current Information Commissioner, Emily O'Reilly, takes the opportunity to further develop a call for legislative change first heralded in her recently published Annual Report for 2005 (Chapter One). Specific topics covered are health care records (Chapter Two), commercial information related to the public tendering process (Chapter Six), and accessing environmental information (Chapter Seven). At a very practical level there is a clear exposition on how the system works (Chapter Three), and the pros and cons of using the FOI legislation as a litigation tool (Chapter Four). There is also a comprehensive evaluation of the High and Supreme Courts appeal judgments (Chapter Five). The book concludes with a broad approach to the primary aspirations of FOI, openness, transparency and accountability (Chapter 8).

This is the first general publication on the workings of the Freedom of Information Act. It is directed at all practitioners. These include the Freedom of Information officer with no legal training whatsoever, the legal professional who may become involved in court appeals under the Act, the superior court judges who must decide those appeals, the public servants who may be inclined to involve the public in greater depth in governmental decision-making, the public servants who may wish to restrict public access to their recorded actions, and the journalists who use the Act to access information not otherwise readily available; It is also directed at the politicians who by their legislative actions have opened the door to greater public access to the workings of public bodies and who, by their actions in passing the Freedom of Information (Amendment) Act 2003, have slammed that door most tightly on the workings of central government. All of these people, and anybody outside these groupings, are also the members of the public, specified in the Long Title, who are entitled to make requests under the terms of the Act.

In some respects the contents may be viewed as practical guidance for navigating the freedom of information regime. However, in no respect does this book purport to give legal advice. Each contributor is responsible for any errors or omissions in his or her own chapter. The law is up-to-date as of early July 2006.

Estelle Feldman, Editor
July, 2006.

Acknowledgments

Westminster was where I first met the Information Commissioner and Ombudsman, Kevin Murphy, and the Director General to both Offices, Pat Whelan. Kevin had been a keynote speaker at a conference considering the UK Freedom of Information Act. It is not a secret, it is not even confidential, but very few are aware of the positive influence that the Irish Commissioner has had on Scottish and UK legislation. From that first meeting (to be truthful, we went to a pub), a relationship has developed which has been extremely fruitful from my viewpoint and, I believe, is viewed favourably by the Offices of both the Information Commissioner and the Ombudsman. So, when Kevin retired, his successor, Emily O'Reilly, inherited me. I am appreciative that both Kevin and Emily have contributed to this book and it would be remiss not to thank Pat, Fintan Butler, Sheila McCarthy and all the staff in both Offices.

Merely expressing thanks to them and to the other contributors does not really seem adequate. All were extremely busy during the period when the submission deadlines for their chapters, and then for return of proofs, loomed. Each has an expertise without par and their individual contributions combine as a comprehensive study of Freedom of Information. No one else would presume to write about environmental information once Áine Ryall has agreed to participate; Maeve McDonagh took time off preparing the 2nd edition of her seminal work, *Freedom of Information law in Ireland*; Sinead Byrne and Niall Michel were initially concerned about writing in the company of academics, an anxiety that their chapters on practice clearly dispel. Ciaran Craven brings to healthcare issues knowledge and experience from medical as well as legal practice, and is both a colleague and a friend; Gerard Hogan, also a colleague and friend in the Trinity Law School, in his modesty does not seem to realise the extent to which his contribution adorns any publication. To all my sincere gratitude.

I would not be in a position to write this were it not for a serendipitous meeting during the 1995-1996 academic year with William Binchy, Regius

Professor of Laws in Trinity. He accepted me as a Research Associate in the Trinity Law School and more significantly, agreed to be my academic supervisor for a proposed PhD. We still have not cracked the doctorate, he keeps me too busy writing on other topics and participating in study trips to sub-Saharan Africa, but under his expert guidance I began publishing in law within my first year attached to the TCD Law School. He is a particular friend whose hospitality knows no bounds and whose legal knowledge across a broad spectrum of law is always imparted and shared in an objective and captivating manner. I still disagree with William about two things. To my other colleagues and friends in the Trinity Law School, forgive me for not mentioning you by name; each of you has always been unconditionally willing to assist me and to fill in the huge gaps in my legal knowledge whenever I have asked. Again, without your support I would not be writing this.

Clearly, I have undertaken a career in law upside down. It was not until 2000 that I began studying for an LLB, this the University of Wales accredited Irish law course in Portobello College. My colleagues in Portobello are a wonderful group of people to study and to work with. Most particularly, John O'Keeffe and Tomás Clancy shepherded me through the degree in two years and then invited me back to teach constitutional law. They, too, I count as friends. The excellent librarians, Jane Buggle who kindly proofed my chapter, together with Joan Colvin are amazing in their ability to satisfy every query especially as the library is not rich in resources.

I have been involved in other publications with Therése Carrick; as commissioning editor, she is so easy to deal with and, as always, does the lion's share. Shane Gough typeset with masterful rapidity. Bart Daly, by accepting this book for publication, has hopefully advanced the fortunes of the freedom of information regime. All, not forgetting the unnamed staff of FirstLaw, deserve our thanks.

Ruth O'Reilly has always protected my back and Dermot Canavan might now appreciate how much his immediate interest and approval meant. Finally, to my family and circle of non-legal friends, you have been forbearing and supportive as ever: all will understand if I single out our cousin Ivor for special mention. This book is dedicated to my Ma, now in her 91st year, to whom all pupils of Stratford College, past, present and future, owe gratitude for her foresight, courage and tenacity.

REFLECTIONS

KEVIN MURPHY*

When the Government announced early in 1997 that it intended to nominate me for appointment as Information Commissioner under the Freedom of Information legislation, a former colleague of mine in the Civil Service sent me an e-mail with the caption "Definitely Gamekeeper Turned Poacher". He attached a copy of a circular headed "Official Secrecy" which had issued in the 1980s over my signature drawing the attention of civil servants to the need for strict compliance with the requirements of the official secrecy legislation. What my colleague did not appreciate, however, was that, during the 1980s when I was Secretary General of the Department of the Public Service, freedom of information had figured in our proposals for the modernisation of the public service.

The late John Boland became Minister for the Public Service when a Fine Gael/Labour Government was formed under Taoiseach Garret Fitzgerald after the general election at the end of 1982. He was, as is usual, given a number of brief position papers on the important issues then facing the Department. In relation to one aspect of the Department's work – the "reform" or modernisation programme – we gave the Minister a one page list of possible initiatives. These included the immediate appointment of an Ombudsman, radical changes in the promotion procedures at senior levels and a White Paper which would propose legislation to facilitate greater devolution of functions from Departments to executive agencies and which would, for the first time, prescribe the management duties and responsibilities of senior civil servants. The list also included a somewhat tentative suggestion that freedom of information legislation be considered. A number of these initiatives had been foreshadowed in a speech I had given in January 1982 entitled "Raising Productivity in the Civil Service".[1]

The first Ombudsman, Michael Mills, was appointed in 1984; the

---

* Former Information Commissioner and Ombudsman.
[1] Raising Productivity in the Civil Service: *Seirbhís Poiblí* Vol.3, No.1 (1982).

Ombudsman Act had been passed in 1980. In December 1983, the Government approved the setting up of the Top Level Appointments Committee to recommend who should be appointed at Secretary General, Deputy Secretary General and Assistant Secretary General levels. The conditions of appointment of Secretaries General under the new system were changed to limit their tenure to seven years and to require retirement at age sixty. John Boland must get the credit for pushing these radical proposals through Cabinet and the continued operation of the new system for the last twenty years or more under a variety of Governments is a memorial to his achievements. So too is the White Paper *"Serving the Country Better"* which was published in 1985. This received much greater recognition among foreign civil services then it did at home. Its implementation was put on the back burner in 1987 when, because of the extent of the country's public indebtedness, reducing the cost of the public services through a combination of arbitrary cut backs, voluntary redundancies and retirements and reductions in staff numbers became imperative.

I had a number of conversations with John Boland in the period 1985-1987 about freedom of information. He had an impressive capacity to get Departmental proposals through Cabinet but his assessment was that freedom of information was not a runner because of the Northern Ireland situation and certain opposition from a friend and colleague who was then Minister for Justice and who would have been a formidable adversary to any proposal. While I was never convinced that John was sold on the idea anyway, in fairness he raised no objection to my airing the matter publicly in 1986[2] nor indeed did Bertie Ahern in 1993[3] when he was my Minister at the Department of Finance. I mention these events to demonstrate my long held belief that freedom of information has to be an essential ingredient in the mix of measures necessary to ensure good governance. When the economy began to recover in the early 1990s, it was possible once again to give attention to modernising the public service.

Three year Administrative Budgets were introduced for civil service Departments and Offices and a start was made in providing incentives for good performance. An Efficiency Audit Group was set up with private

---

[2]   A Changing Civil Service?: *Administration* (1986) Vol. 34, No.3.
[3]   Managing the Irish Public Service in the 1990s :*Seirbhís Poiblí* (1993) Vol.14, No.2.

sector involvement and amending legislation was passed which, inter alia, extended the role of the Comptroller and Auditor General to value for money auditing.

In the period 1993 – 1997, during which there was a Fianna Fáil/ Labour Government followed by a Fine Gael/Labour/Democratic Left Government, many of the building blocks on which good governance rests were put in place. The Strategic Management Initiative was launched in February 1994 and a new Co-ordinating Group of Secretaries General was set up "to recommend management changes, including legislation, if such is needed". I left the civil service to become the Ombudsman in November 1994. In 1995 the Ethics in Public Office Act was passed and in 1996 the Co-ordinating Group published an excellent report *"Delivering Better Government"* setting out an ambitious agenda to ensure a public service of which we could be proud. Freedom of information legislation was seen as an essential part of this agenda. A raft of ground breaking statutes followed; the Electoral Act 1997, the Freedom of Information Act 1997, the Public Service Management Act 1997 and the Committees of the Houses of the Oireachtas (Compellability, Privileges and Immunities of Witnesses) Act 1997. Three ad hoc Referendum Commissions were also set up in that period which I chaired as Ombudsman and a statutory Referendum Commission was set up in 1998. All of these measures were designed to bring greater openness and transparency to the workings of the public administration, to provide fuller and better information to the public and thereby ensure greater public accountability.

Eithne Fitzgerald, as Minister of State at the Department of Finance and at the Tánaiste's Office, was responsible for the Ethics and the Freedom of Information legislation and guided both Bills through the Houses of the Oireachtas. Apart from my general interest in the two initiatives, I had particular interest in their implications for the Office of the Ombudsman. So far as FOI was concerned, the crucial question was whether or not the Ombudsman would be involved in appeals when requests to public bodies for access to information were refused. There were a number of different models operating in other countries. In the Nordic countries such as Norway and Denmark, citizens could complain to the Ombudsman about a refusal to release information and New Zealand had adopted this model. The UK had also given the function to their Parliamentary Ombudsman although access to information there was provided for in a non-statutory code of practice. In Ireland the Ombudsman had been handling for some years complaints against refusals under the Regulations on Access to Information on the Environment. An essential characteristic of Ombudsmen worldwide is that they make recommendations rather than binding decisions but, of course, they can seek the help of Parliament and the public when a particular recommendation is not being implemented. In Australia, on the other hand, both the Federal Government and State governments had, by and large, opted for a separate office of Information Commissioner who made legally binding decisions. The practice was, however, that the office would be held by the Ombudsman. In Canada, however, the office was sometimes combined with that of Privacy Commissioner (roughly equivalent to our Data Protection Commissioner). There were, of course, other models e.g. appeals to an administrative tribunal or, as in the case of the United States, directly to the Courts.

We saw advantages in the Nordic and New Zealand model because it would enable us to continue with the informal, flexible and problem solving approach which making recommendations allows rather than a more formal legalistic approach which making binding decisions would require. We were conscious that the majority of administrative appeals bodies, e.g. the Employment Appeals Tribunal, have been captured by the legal profession and that the Courts have a tendency to view the making of legally binding decisions by bodies other than the Courts themselves with some disapprobation. At the same time, we recognised that Nordic public administrations had a long tradition of openness and transparency whereas ours had an ingrained culture of secrecy. There was the possibility of frequent rejections of FOI recommendations and we accepted that there would be difficulty in enlisting the support of TDs and Senators, the media and the public at large to having such rejections overturned because the issues would often be technical and legal. Given the stated commitment at the time by most of the major political parties to the principles of Openness, Transparency and Accountability, we were hopeful the approach would be more liberal than restricted. An informal meeting which I had with Eithne Fitzgerald at the time confirmed these hopes although I was unable to ascertain what appeal model was envisaged!

When the FOI Bill was published, our expectations were exceeded because, in my view, it was the state of the art so far as FOI legislation went despite the complexity of its wording which seems to be a feature of our parliamentary draftsmen compared to those in the New World. A colleague remarked that "the Department of Justice must have taken its eye off the ball." Unfortunately, it recovered ground some years later! Equally impressive was the commitment, enthusiasm and hard work of the staff in the Office of the Tánaiste (and subsequently in the Department of Finance) in getting the legislation up and running. Excellent information and training initiatives ensured that all civil servants and later other public servants were well informed about the requirements of the Act and that those who would be involved in its operation were well versed in its intricacies and complexities. The logistics of setting up the Office of the Information Commissioner were handled with his usual expertise and efficiency by the Director Pat Whelan in addition to his normal work as Director of the Office of the Ombudsman. There clearly was an air of excitement among public servants generally that FOI could be a watershed in the process of adapting the public service to the needs of a modern, educated and sophisticated society.

The progressive nature of the Irish legislation did not go unnoticed in other jurisdictions. Over the next few years, I was asked to address a major conference on FOI in London, to give evidence to a Committee of the House of Lords which was considering proposals for the introduction of FOI in the UK and to talk to a group of backbenchers in the House of Commons. It was after one of those meetings that I got the first hint that, here at home, the Government – now a Fianna Fáil/Progressive Democrats one – was growing more hostile to our FOI Act. I enquired of a British official as to the reason why the draft FOI legislation introduced in Westminster was significantly more restrictive than that envisaged in the original White Paper. He replied that it was partly due to the "bad mouthing" of the Irish Legislation by Irish Ministers to their British counterparts. I found Scottish Ministers and members of the Scottish Parliament, on the other hand, determined to have robust FOI legislation which mirrored the original Irish Legislation much more closely than the British one. I also found it particularly interesting to be visited by the Parliamentary Ombudsman of Norway and the Ombudsman for the European Union to discuss the Irish FOI initiative.

During 1997 and early 1998, Pat Whelan and I spoke to very many different groups about the requirements of the legislation. In my contacts with Secretaries General of Government Departments, County Managers and Chief Executives of the Health Boards, I stressed that the Act gave the public a statutory right of access to records held by their organisations.

It would be my job, as Information Commissioner, to uphold this right proactively or as the Long Title of the Act puts it " to the greatest extent possible consistent with the public interest and the right to privacy." Section 34(12) of the Act makes it clear that the onus of justifying a refusal of access lies squarely on the public bodies and they would have to satisfy me that a refusal was justified. This would apply to official information and to personal information where that personal information related to the requester. Where, however, personal information about a person was requested by another person, section 28(1) of the Act provides that the request should be refused. This is subject to section 28(5)which provides for release where there are strong public interest considerations in support of access which outweigh the public interest in upholding the right to privacy or where release of the information would benefit the person to whom the information related. In my many subsequent decisions as Information Commissioner, these two principles were very much in my mind; where the arguments for and against release were evenly balanced, I should, as a general rule, favour the release of official information and personal information about the requester but not personal information about an individual requested by a third party.

As requests for reviews began to reach my new Office, I was faced with a particularly difficult problem. The Act required the Information Commissioner to make decisions within four months of a review being received during the first three years up to 21 April 2001 and within three months thereafter. If I were to ensure that all the early decisions were to be legally proofed against appeals to the High Court, it was likely – as occurred in some other jurisdictions – that decisions in significant cases would take a considerable time and might prove very expensive if draft decisions had to be referred to outside legal counsel. The volume of applications.for review to the Office was, in any event, much greater than estimated and the Office could be brought into disrepute if decisions were not made reasonably quickly. I decided to rely on the competence of my investigating staff, a few of whom were legally qualified and most of whom had broad public service experience which, almost invariably, involves implementing the provisions of primary and secondary legislation. Staff had, of course, access through the Internet to the decisions of Information Commissioners in other common law jurisdictions and, where particularly complex legal issues arose, to an external solicitors' practice contracted to the Office.

It is not for me to assess the efficacy of the approach I adopted. It would provide very useful feedback to the Office if an expert analysis of the decisions made in individual cases over the first five years or so were done. Indeed, I should particularly like to see an expert analysis, involving a legal expert in FOI from abroad, of the twenty or so appeals to the High Court against various decisions by the Information Commissioner. I would be surprised if such a study did not find that the overall approach of our Courts to the legislation has been noticeably less supportive than that adopted in other countries and has, in relation to interpretation, demonstrated many of the defects to which the Law Reform Commission drew attention in its Report on Statutory Drafting and Interpretation: Plain Language and the Law.[4] It seems to me that, at times, the Courts seem isolated from the changes that have occurred and are continuing in Irish society and the need for public bodies to keep pace with those changes.

I remain still somewhat bemused by the extraordinary change in the Government's attitude to FOI which resulted in the Freedom of Information (Amendment) Act 2003. I had received vibes, from time to time from both political and official sources, that I was seen as pushing out the boundaries a bit too much. But I had never received any indication that any specific decision of mine had been a cause of serious concern to Government. One or two may have caused some small embarrassment to individual Ministers but more embarrassment was caused by the release of records by Government Departments themselves without any involvement by my Office. The 1997 Act had very strong provisions protecting key state interests such as security, law enforcement and foreign relations and, as one might expect of someone who spent most of his working life in the civil service, I was scrupulous in observing these protections. I suspect that one or two cases, where I had decided to release records because they were so innocuous as to be harmless, were used by Departments, more particularly the Department of Justice, Equality and Law Reform and the Department of Foreign Affairs, to "wind up" Ministers about what I might decide in future cases. But I believe that the main reason for bringing in the amendments was to protect Ministerial decisions and more especially the process of making those decisions, from public scrutiny. The great political slogan of the 1990s – Openness, Transparency and Accountability – has become nothing but a shibboleth.

---

4 Law Reform Commission December 2000 LRC61-2000.

Ironically, the change in the Government's attitude occurred at a time when the benefits of greater openness in relation to services provided by private interests, e.g. crèches, nursing homes, restaurants, building sites had been demonstrated with the release of inspection reports under FOI.

The Government's attempts to limit or stifle any informed debate on the amendments either inside or outside the Houses of the Oireachtas betrayed a reluctance to have them considered on their merits. The same attitude was adopted by the Government to the decentralisation programme. The essence of a modern democracy is that there should be open, frank and informed discussion about all aspects of governance and that it should take place in a calm and professional manner especially in the Dáil and Seanad which have the sole and exclusive power of making laws for the State. When I decided to give a written commentary to each Deputy and.Senator on how the proposed amendments to the FOI Act would affect the practical application and operation of certain provisions of the Act, I was accused, by the Minister for Justice, Equality and Law Reform, Michael McDowell, of getting involved in an area which was the preserve of the politicians. My commentary was, however, strictly in accordance with the provisions of section 39 of the FOI Act. And when the then Minister for Finance, Charlie McCreevy, who had responsibility for the amending legislation, was queried by a journalist about the need for rushing it through, his response was that the Government had made up its mind, did not intend to change it and, if people did not like it, they could show what they thought at the next general election. Shades of old Stormont and majority rule! To cap it all, a month after I had retired, a €150 fee was introduced for appeals to the Information Commissioner: an action likely to encourage public bodies to incline towards refusal rather than release and to discourage requesters from appealing even when their statutory right to information had been wrongly denied. As a result of this rather cynical action, my successor, Emily O' Reilly, has had to work in an environment in which public bodies are much more antagonistic to FOI. Emily continues to highlight the adverse effects of this excessive fee and of the other amendments to the Act.

In the eleven years I spent as a Secretary General, I worked with eight or more different Ministers from a variety of political parties. I noticed over that time a growing reluctance on their part to record or have recorded any decisions or discussions where it could be argued that short term political interest took precedence over the longer term public interest.

The absence of a paper trail has operated in recent years to the disadvantage of civil servants and the advantage of Ministers. A Secretary General as Accounting Officer for the Department has a right to insist on a written direction from the Minister where there is a question mark over whether expenditure of public money in a particular case is correct but many Ministerial decisions do not fall into this category. The failure to make and keep adequate records is wrong in principle; there should be a statutory obligation on all public bodies and public servants to keep adequate records and to record all important decisions. There is, however a more fundamental issue involved because political attitudes to the civil service have undoubtedly changed. What is the role of the civil service? Is it now simply to provide an excellent service to Ministers and to Government and simply do what it is told? Or has it the responsibility (and the general public seem to believe it has) of trying to ensure that the wider public interest is taken into account when decisions are being made? And if the latter, how can this role be formally recognised across the board and what procedures should apply when problems arise especially if the process is no longer open to public scrutiny? In the past the civil service has contributed significantly to the national interest; if it is to be allowed to continue to do so, then these questions need to be addressed.

Table of Contents

Table of Cases

D

Table of Legislation

Freedom of Information Act 1997—*contd.*

Statutory instruments

CHAPTER 1

Access to Records of Deceased Persons under Freedom of Information

EMILY O'REILLY*

I have been invited to respond to Ms Estelle Feldman's very interesting contribution[1] and, in particular, to her conclusions on how the Freedom of Information (FOI) legislation regulates access to records disclosing the personal information of deceased persons.

The FOI Act makes explicit (if limited) provision for the release of the personal information (including medical records) of a deceased person. Section 28(6)(b) of the FOI Act provides for the making of regulations for the grant of access where "the individual to whom the record concerned relates is dead". Regulations in this regard have been made by the Minister for Finance in the form of the Freedom of Information Act 1997 (Section 28(6)) Regulations 1999 (the 1999 Regulations).[2] Consider the following situations and how you might expect the FOI Act to apply:

CASE ONE

Mr Brown died recently at the age of 78 years. He had been separated from his wife for the last 40 years of his life and during that time had no contact of any kind with her. In fact, on their separation, his wife returned to live in Britain taking their young daughter with her. His daughter has had no contact with her father since moving to Britain. In his last years,

---

* Information Commissioner.
[1] See p.177.
[2] S.I. No.47 of 1999.

Mr Brown was cared for by a niece (his sister's child) and her husband and he nominated this niece as his "next of kin" when hospitalised. Mr Brown's estranged wife and daughter have now sought access, under the FOI Act, to all of his hospital records.

CASE TWO

Mrs Smith and her husband separated some years ago. Relations between Mrs Smith and her husband were very strained and there were several court hearings regarding custody of their child (granted to Mrs Smith), maintenance and other family law matters. Mrs Smith contracted a terminal illness and had several lengthy hospitalisations. Shortly before she died, and in the knowledge that she was dying, Mrs Smith gave written instructions to the hospital concerned that, following her death, on no account was her estranged husband to be given any access to her medical records. Mr Smith has now applied, under the FOI Act, for access to the hospital records of his late wife.

CASE THREE

Ms Black was a successful business woman. Following a failed personal relationship, she displayed symptoms of a severe psychiatric disorder. She had a number of periods of hospitalisation and, unfortunately, she took her own life. Her sister has now sought access, under FOI, to Ms Black's hospital records which disclose very sensitive personal information about, amongst other things, that personal relationship.

CASE FOUR

Mr White and his wife drifted apart after five years of marriage. The parting was relatively amicable though Mr White and his wife did not have any contact or communication over a period of several years. During this period, Mr White's wife formed a new relationship and she and her partner now have a young child. Following an accident, Mr White's health deteriorated and he had a series of hospitalisations. During this period of ill health and hospitalisation, Mr White was supported by his mother and his siblings. When not hospitalised, he lived with his mother. He had no contact with his estranged wife during his illness. Following his recent death, Mr White's wife has now made a request under the FOI Act for access to all of his medical and hospital records.

CASE FIVE

Mr Green is helping his now elderly mother to piece together details of her family background. She had been raised in an orphanage and with a number of foster families and has no contact with, or real information on, her family of origin. She knows her own date of birth and the maternity hospital in which she was born. Mr Green has now applied to that hospital, under the FOI Act, for all information it holds on his mother's birth and on her mother. He assumes that his grandmother is now dead but cannot be certain of this. Mr Green's mother says that, before she dies herself, she would like to know about her mother – her age when she (Mrs Green) was born, where her mother was from, whether her mother had other children and so on.

These cases are based on actual reviews dealt with by my Office, though I have changed some of the details in order to avoid possible identification of the people concerned. It is noteworthy that all five cases concern medical records as opposed to other forms of personal information. It is almost invariably the case that, where applications to my Office concern the records of deceased persons, the records sought are medical/hospital records.

I think we can all agree that these cases raise fairly complex issues and require that competing interests be balanced. Amongst the issues raised in these cases are:

- whether deceased people have any right to privacy;

- whether the express wishes of a person, concerning who may access his or her personal information, should be given any recognition after that person's death;

- whether medical confidences must be protected after death;

- whether there should be a hierarchy of access rights as between the various parties with a family or other connection to the deceased;

- whether, in such cases, one party should be recognised as being the "guardian" of the deceased's privacy and access by others would require that "guardian's" consent;

- whether, in the case of individuals raised apart from their natural families, their need for information on their "origins" should be given priority over other considerations.

On the face of it, one might expect that a decision to grant or refuse access to records in any of these five cases should involve a rigorous assessment of the circumstances of the individual case. On the basis of Ms Feldman's analysis, however, each of the requesters in the five cases above would have their requests granted almost as a matter of course.

Ms Feldman's Analysis

I believe Ms Feldman's arguments may be summarised in the following terms:

- Deceased persons do not have any right to privacy and the FOI Act does not create any such right.

- Section 28(6) of the FOI Act (which creates a potential right of access to records of deceased persons) is free-standing in terms of the overall provisions of section 28 of the FOI Act; this is because it opens with the words "Notwithstanding sub-section (1) ...." and this can only mean that section 28(1) does not apply alongside section 28(6). [Section 28(1) is the provision which provides exemption for personal information.]

- Under the 1999 Regulations, spouses and next of kin have an unqualified right of access to the personal records of a deceased person.

- Whereas the 1999 Regulations provide for decision makers having regard to "any relevant guidelines drawn up and published by the Minister [for Finance]", no such guidelines have been drawn up and published by the Minister. (The Department of Finance's website has published guidance notes in this area but they are described as "approved by the FOI Interdepartmental Working Group - March 1999" rather than as guidance drawn up and published by the Minister.)

- While records of deceased persons are likely to be releasable under section 28(6) and the 1999 Regulations, it may nevertheless be that, in some cases, they will be exempt under one or more of the other exemptions in the FOI Act, for example, under section 24 which protects security information.

In broad terms, I accept that Ms Feldman's analysis is likely to be correct in most instances. In essence, Ms Feldman's contention is that a literal construction of the relevant provision in the 1999 Regulations does not admit of any interpretation other than that a requester, who is a spouse or a next of kin, has an unqualified right of access to the deceased's personal information. The relevant provision is that at article 3(1)(b) of the 1999 Regulations which specifies the following classes of persons, for the purposes of section 28(6)(b) of the FOI Act, as requesters to whom access "shall" be granted:

(i) "a personal representative of the deceased acting in due course of administration of his or her estate...,"

(ii) "a person on whom a function is conferred by law in relation to the individual [i.e. the deceased] or his or her estate acting in the course of the performance of such function,"

(iii) "the spouse or a next of kin of the individual or such other person or persons as the head considers appropriate having regard to all the circumstances and to any relevant guidelines drawn up and published by the Minister".

The particular issue raised by Ms Feldman concerns sub-paragraph (iii) above. In past decisions, I and my predecessor have taken the view that the qualification *"as the head considers appropriate having regard to all the circumstances and to any relevant guidelines drawn up and published by the Minister"* should apply to each of the three classes of person mentioned in sub-paragraph (iii). My Office has always recognised that the most obvious reading of sub-paragraph (iii) is that the qualification applies only to the final of the three classes identified; however, in order to avoid outcomes which seemed to offend against the spirit of the FOI Act, my Office felt entitled to depart from the literal construction of the provision and to treat the qualification as applying to each of the three classes (including spouses and next of kin). Of particular concern here is the fact that the 1999 Regulations adopt a definition of "spouse" which is very wide indeed.

The 1999 Regulations define "spouse" as including "a party to a marriage that has been dissolved" and also as including "a man or woman, as the case may be, who was not married to but cohabited as husband or wife, with the deceased individual". This means that former spouses and former partners are recognised as "spouses" for the purposes of the Regulations. In addition, the reference to "next of kin" is to "a next of kin" rather than to "the next of kin". I am advised that this wording is capable of being read as a reference to any party capable of being included in the class and not just, in any particular case, to the party regarded as the most immediate next of kin.

Legal advice I have received suggests that, in most instances, my Office does not have good grounds for departing from the literal construction of sub-paragraph (iii) of article 3(1)(b) of the 1999 Regulations. This is the case notwithstanding that the outcome may be at odds with the spirit of the FOI Act as well as being at odds with the presumed intentions of the Minister for Finance in making the 1999 Regulations. (The Minister's intentions may be gleaned from the guidance on the matter published on the website of the Department of Finance. Whether or not this guidance is what is envisaged in the 1999 Regulations - Ms Feldman contends it is not - is not something I deal with here.) However, my advice is that a departure from the literal construction of sub-paragraph (iii) of article 3(1)(b) may be warranted where reliance on the literal construction gives rise to an outcome which is likely to offend against the Constitution.

Adopting the literal construction of sub-paragraph (iii) of article 3(1)(b) could have the effect, for example, that a former (unmarried) partner would have the same right of access to the deceased's records as would the deceased's widow or widower with whom the deceased had been living prior to death. It is hard to envisage that such an outcome would be constitutionally sound given the provision at Article 41.3 of the Constitution whereby the "State pledges itself to guard with special care the institution of Marriage ... and to protect it against attack".

There may also be an argument, in certain circumstances, that an adult "child" of a family would have his or her constitutional family rights infringed where the personal records of a deceased parent were being disclosed to someone outside the family.

If Ms Feldman is correct, as seems likely, it is a relatively simple matter for the Minister for Finance (should he so wish) to amend the 1999 Regulations in order to provide for a situation in which the rights of access of spouses and next of kin would be qualified rights rather than unqualified rights. Indeed, I have already expressed the view in my 2005 Annual Report that the Minister should put the matter beyond doubt by way of an amending regulation. However, there is a more fundamental matter at issue here, namely, whether it is at all appropriate that the legislative ground rules for FOI access to the records of deceased persons should be set by the Minister for Finance, in secondary legislation, rather than by the Oireachtas itself, in primary legislation.

OTHER JURISDICTIONS

I cannot claim to have conducted anything like a comprehensive review of the law and practice in other jurisdictions in the area of accessing the health and other personal information of deceased persons. However, on the basis of limited research, it does seem to me that in many other jurisdictions these matters tend to be legislated for in considerable detail. Furthermore, such legislation tends to be primary legislation rather than secondary legislation.

In many cases, access to personal records is regulated under specific privacy legislation (as in New Zealand and Canada) rather than under FOI legislation. In some jurisdictions privacy and FOI are provided for in the one piece of legislation (as in the Canadian provinces of British Columbia and Ontario). And in several instances there is specific primary legislation dealing with health information as opposed to other forms of personal information; this is the case in the United Kingdom as well as in the Canadian provinces of Ontario and Saskatchewan.

What is interesting, even on the basis of a limited review of the law and practice in other jurisdictions, is the level of detailed provision *in primary legislation* in relation to accessing deceased person's records. For example, Ontario's Personal Health Information Protection Act 2004 makes access to the health records of a deceased person dependent on the consent of:

> "the deceased's estate trustee or the person who has assumed responsibility for the administration of the deceased's estate, if the estate does not have an estate trustee."

In the case of the United Kingdom, its Access to Health Records Act 1990 has been overtaken by the Data Protection Act 1998 in so far as the health records of living persons is concerned; but it remains in force in relation to access requests for the records of deceased persons. This Access to Health Records Act 1990 has some interesting provisions in the case of the records of deceased persons, including:

- the potential right of access to a deceased person's health records is limited to "the patient's personal representative and any person who may have a claim arising out of the patient's death";

- where the request is made by a person "who may have a claim arising out of the patient's death", any records disclosing information not relevant to such a claim are excluded; and

- access "shall not be given ... if the record includes a note, made at the patient's request, that he did not wish access to be given on such an application".

Queensland's FOI Act of 1992 protects "information concerning the personal affairs of a person, whether living or dead" though this protection may be set aside where to do so is, on balance, in the public interest. However, in Queensland the public interest override in relation to personal information must be preceded by a consultation with the person, the subject of the records. In the case of deceased persons, the Queensland Act requires consultation with an "eligible family member" and the Act establishes a hierarchy of such family members (spouse > adult child > parent > adult sibling etc.). Similarly, the Australian Commonwealth Freedom of Information Act 1982 requires that, in considering whether personal information of a deceased person should be released, the views of the deceased's "legal personal representative" should be ascertained. And in the case of the FOI Act of Western Australia, the personal records of a deceased person cannot be released without a consultation with "his or her closest relative".

I note that in some jurisdictions (for example, in the FOI Act of the Commonwealth of Australia) the protection of the personal information of deceased persons is expressed to be based on the right to personal privacy rather than simply on a generic exemption.

The law on privacy in Ireland is, it would appear, in a relatively undeveloped state. It is true that the Supreme Court has recognised privacy as one of the unenumerated personal rights under the Constitution; it is true, also, that the Data Protection Act applies and that there are certain common law protections for privacy as well as certain rights arising under the European Convention on Human Rights. However, taking all of these together does not amount to a comprehensive statutory code on privacy. In particular, it appears that there is no right to privacy in Ireland at present in the case of deceased persons; for example, the Data Protection Act applies only to the personal data of living persons. I understand the Minister for Justice, Equality and Law Reform has recently announced the Government's intention to propose new privacy legislation to the Oireachtas. At this stage it is not clear whether the proposed legislation will deal with health and other personal records in general terms, or at all, or whether it will focus primarily on media intrusion on privacy rights. Furthermore, it is not clear whether the legislation will deal with the privacy rights of deceased persons.

CURRENT IRISH ARRANGEMENTS UNSATISFACTORY

I have to say, with the benefit now of eight years' experience of the operation of FOI in Ireland, that the specific FOI Act provisions for dealing with access to the personal information of deceased persons are far from being satisfactory. There are two particular difficulties, as I see it. The first has to do with the *mechanism,* provided for in section 28(6), whereby the Minister for Finance is delegated to deal with the matter by way of regulations. The second difficulty has to do with the *content* of the Minister's 1999 Regulations; even if the Minister were to amend these Regulations to overcome the specific difficulties identified by Ms Feldman, I am not at all sure that the formula in sub-paragraph (iii) of article 3(1)(b) represents an adequate basis for dealing with the type of complexity raised, for example, in the five case studies outlined at the start of this piece.

Mechanism

It is well settled by the Courts that secondary legislation involves a delegation by the Oireachtas to a public authority (usually a Minister) to fill in, by way of regulations, the details of a provision of primary legislation (an Act of the Oireachtas) in a context in which the parameters of what is to be done are set down in that Act. What is involved is the putting into effect of the "principles and policies" set out by the Oireachtas in the parent Act. The Oireachtas envisages, in section 28(6)(b) of the FOI Act, that the records of deceased persons may be released where the requester "is a member of a class specified" in regulations to be made by the Minister for Finance. As matters stand, it is a matter for the Minister to specify classes of requester to whom a deceased person's records may be released.

However, in specifying such classes in his regulations, the Minister must not go beyond the "principles and policies" set down by the Oireachtas in the FOI Act. The difficulty is to discern what are the principles and policies set down by the Oireachtas in this regard. The FOI Act contains two explicit references to the personal information of deceased persons; the first is at section 28(1), which exempts such information from release, and the second is at section 28(6)(b), which provides for the making of regulations to derogate from the exemption in the case of requesters who belong to a class specified by the Minister. Other than these two references, the FOI Act contains no principle or policy concerned explicitly with the records of deceased persons. Indeed, insofar as I can establish from checking the Dáil and Seanad debates, there was no reference of any substance to the matter of deceased persons' records when the FOI Bill was dealt with by the Oireachtas in 1996 and 1997.

If one seeks out those principles and policies informing the FOI Act as a whole, one looks primarily to the Long Title which identifies certain key items such as:

• access is to be provided to the greatest extent possible;

• access is a matter of right;

- access is to be consistent with the public interest and the right to privacy;
- access rights are to be restricted by "necessary exceptions".

Within the body of the FOI Act, it may be argued that the Oireachtas has established relevant principles and policies insofar as it seeks to protect information obtained in confidence (section 26) and personal information, including that of deceased persons (section 28). Furthermore, section 29 establishes the principle of consultation with the third party concerned where confidential, personal or commercially sensitive information is proposed to be released in the public interest.

In the case of deceased persons, and as argued by Ms Feldman, it would appear that there is no right to privacy. If so, then the principle of respecting privacy is not relevant to the Minister's regulations. In the case of confidentiality, there is also a problem in that it is unlikely that a duty of confidence could be owed to a deceased person. If a duty of confidence may be owed to the dead, how can the Minister frame regulations which will circumvent such a duty?

It does seem to me that, in setting about the task of specifying classes of requester to whom a deceased person's records may be released, the Minister for Finance has very little to go on in terms of principles and policies contained in the FOI Act itself. It is arguable that of the principles and policies within the FOI Act, as identified above, the two of immediate relevance are (a) the use of a public interest test and (b) the desirability of consultation with whoever may be regarded as the "guardian" of the records of the deceased person. Interestingly, this approach appears to be that provided for in Queensland's FOI Act (see above) where records of a deceased person may be released but only on the basis of a public interest test and following consultation with the appropriate "eligible family member".

A further matter of some concern is that the delegation given to the Minister, under section 28(6)(b), is to specify classes of persons to whom records of deceased persons may be released. What the Minister has actually done in article 3(1)(b)(iii) of the 1999 Regulations is to prescribe classes of persons by reference to a test of being *"appropriate having regard to all the circumstances..."* and to guidelines which do not form part of the statutory instrument itself. Whether this is a valid prescription of classes, as envisaged in the primary law, may be open to question.

Overall, my conclusion is that the present FOI Act, insofar as dealing with access to records of deceased persons is concerned, does not contain a sufficiently clear statement by the Oireachtas of those "principles and policies" to which the Minister should have regard in making regulations. Furthermore, in confining the role of the Minister to one of specifying classes of persons to whom such records might be released, the FOI Act appears not to authorise the Minister to prescribe the circumstances (or to set conditions) in which such records may be released to specified classes. I appreciate that one could indulge in endless legal argument on these perceived shortcomings in the legislation. Rather than encourage such argument, I suggest that the matter is best dealt with by an amendment to the FOI Act which sets out a comprehensive approach to accessing the records of deceased persons and pays particular attention to the health records of deceased persons.

Content of 1999 Regulations

It will be clear from my comments above that I do not regard the content and approach of the 1999 Regulations as amounting to anything like the kind of comprehensive and clear-cut provision which this very sensitive area demands. While I appreciate that any comprehensive arrangements in this area are likely to continue to involve some level of assessment and exercise of judgement by the decision-maker (and by my own Office), the current Regulations are too general by far. I would like to make it clear that I am not making any specific recommendations as to what might be contained in any amended set of provisions. Rather, my intention is to draw attention to matters which should be given serious consideration in the context of drafting amendments to the FOI Act.

Article 3(1)(b)(iii) of the 1999 Regulations identifies "a next of kin" as a class with a potential right of access to the records of a deceased person. There is a difficulty with this in as much as the reference is to "a" next of kin rather than "the" next of kin. Indeed, even were the reference to be to "the" next of kin, this might not improve matters given that the term is not defined in the FOI Act, nor in the 1999 Regulations, nor is there any single agreed definition, generally. While the dictionary definition will define "next of kin" as the nearest blood relative, general usage is frequently at odds with this definition. Many married people regard their spouse as their next of kin. Furthermore, hospitals generally have a practice, when recording patient details on admission, of asking a patient to nominate next of kin. As I understand it, this is not intended to identify that person who is the closest blood relative; rather, it is intended to identify that person whom the hospital should contact in case of an emergency; this might be a spouse, a sibling, a more distant relative or simply a friend. The main criterion, it appears, is that the nominated person is someone whom the patient is happy to have contacted and who is authorised by the patient to take decisions on his or her behalf, should this be necessary.

It seems to me that if next of kin is to be used as an identifier for a class of person to whom a deceased person's records are to be released, much greater clarity and definition is needed in the use of that term. Even more so is it true that the reference to such "other person or persons", in article 3(1)(b)(iii) of the 1999 Regulations, is problematic.

As already cited above, the 1999 Regulations adopt a very broad definition of what constitutes a "spouse" for the purpose of the Regulations. While the principle of recognising the rights of non-marital spouses and of former spouses may be laudable, it seems to me to be essential that the rights of such spouses should be set within a statutory framework. Furthermore, the principles upon which access will be granted to such spouses should be contained in the primary legislation. In particular, there is a need for a hierarchy of rights as between the various sub-classes which constitute the current class of "spouse"; and this hierarchy should be set down in primary legislation. There is also the difficulty, referred to earlier, that purporting to afford a right to a non-marital spouse may in some cases be at odds with the protection of the "institution of Marriage", as provided for at Article 41.3 of the Constitution.

I think it is important to recognise the very genuine concerns of hospitals and medical practitioners arising from the release of the medical records of deceased patients. Unfortunately, neither section 28(6) of the FOI Act nor the 1999 Regulations address these concerns in any adequate way. By definition, where a public body holds the personal information of a deceased person, it is invariably information obtained or created in confidence. However, section 28(6) envisages that such confidential material will be released and, to this extent, appears to be at odds with the protections provided for at section 26 (information obtained in confidence). I take the view that, where release of records is found to be warranted under section 28(6) and the 1999 Regulations, then this amounts to an authorised release. In this situation, where disclosure is not unauthorised, one of the key requirements necessary to establish a breach of a duty of confidence - and the activation of section 26 - is missing.[3]

I acknowledge that this approach is cumbersome and lacks transparency. I believe it is very desirable that there should be a clear set of statutory provisions governing access to records of deceased persons and, in particular, governing access to the medical records of deceased persons. Not least of the advantages flowing from such a situation is that patients would be aware of what might happen to their medical records, after death, and doctors and hospitals would have the benefit of a clear statement of the law on the matter. As matters stand, some hospitals and doctors are very uncomfortable with the release of deceased patients' records as they fear, amongst other things, that it will affect the level of trust of current patients.

---

[3]   In the case of medical records of a deceased person, and where it is argued that they are protected on the basis of confidentiality, such an argument will generally be based on section 26(1)(b) of the FOI Act. For this provision to apply, it must be decided that release of the records would "constitute a breach of a duty of confidence provided for by a provision of an agreement or enactment ... or otherwise by law". Typically, the claimed duty of confidence will be based on the law of equity rather than on the provisions of an agreement or enactment.

The correct tests to apply in deciding whether there is a breach of an equitable duty of confidence are set out in the case of *Coco v. A. N. Clark (Engineers) Limited* [1969] F.S.R. 415 (which is accepted as reflecting the Irish law on the subject - see, for example, *House of Spring Gardens Limited v. Point Blank Limited* [1984] I.R 611) in which Megarry J. stated as follows:

"Three elements are normally required if, apart from contract, a case of breach of confidence is to succeed. First, the information itself...must have the necessary quality of confidence about it. Secondly, that information must have been imparted in circumstances imposing an obligation of confidence. Thirdly, there must be an unauthorised use of that information to the detriment of the party communicating it."

If the disclosure is authorised, then one of the essential tests for establishing a breach of a duty of confidence will not have been met.)

CONCLUSION

While I appreciate the difficulties of drafting amending primary legislation in this area, I am convinced that it is necessary. I do not believe that it is appropriate that key decisions as to the rules for access to records of deceased persons (particularly health records) should be left to the effective discretion of the Minister for Finance. I would hope that the Minister will undertake a comprehensive review of the whole issue of access to deceased persons' records (and medical records in particular) and, following that review, bring forward detailed amendments to the FOI Act for consideration by the Oireachtas. In the short term, I would hope that the Minister will amend article 3(1)(b)(iii) of the 1999 Regulations to overcome the difficulties highlighted by Ms Feldman.

CHAPTER 2

Freedom of Information and Health Care Records

CIARÁN CRAVEN*

INTRODUCTION

It is axiomatic that the Freedom of Information Act 1997 applies only to access to information that is held, by a public body, in the form of a record. That much is clear from the Long Title to the Act. In turn, the definition of "record", in the Act itself, is compendious and, whatever about its component parts, it obviously includes clinical records (and, indeed, diagnostic images and their reports) in the sense in which that phrase is ordinarily understood. It follows, inexorably, therefore, that if clinical records are not maintained, access legislation is wholly irrelevant. Obtaining clinical information held by a health care provider, in such circumstances, would present its own, self-evident difficulties. In order to contextualise the statutory position under the Act of 1997, the question of access to health care records at common law, and the relevance of the European Convention on Human Rights (in that context) merit discussion. However, before proceeding with that discussion, more basic questions might usefully be addressed, *viz.* why keep clinical records and other notes, in the first instance, and what do they establish? It is this topic that will be the focus of the first part of this Chapter, before moving on to the more substantive questions of common law and statutory rights of access.

---

* Dr. Ciaran Craven is a Barrister. He lectures on medical law in the LL.M Degree Programme at Trinity College, Dublin. He is co-author of a textbook on Psychiatry and the Law and the co-author and co-editor of other texts and several articles on aspects of medical law and tort law. He is co-editor, with William Binchy of the *Quarterly Review of Tort Law.*

Negligence – and more particularly professional negligence – litigation provides the basis for the analysis.

WHY HEALTH CARE RECORDS? ADMISSIBILITY, PROOF, CONFLICT AND NECESSITY

General

It might reasonably be considered that a lot of treatment can be given quite effectively without the keeping of any records whatsoever. Practical experience suggests that, even today, some clinicians – albeit a minority – nevertheless operating very effectively as sole practitioners, maintain few if any records without obvious or actionable detriment to their patients. If the sole purpose of keeping records is to assist litigants in subsequent actions, and the clinician has a very good memory, why keep any records at all? The view of the professional defence bodies has, traditionally, been "no notes – no defence!" and the reasons for such advice are not difficult to articulate.

It is not surprising that evidentiary disputes of greater or lesser importance emerge during the course of any litigation process. In medical negligence actions, these may be particularly acute, for a variety of reasons: patients' recollections may be faulty, or clouded by drugs, disease and the passage of time, clinicians may have not any active recollection whatsoever of a patient or of what was done many years after the event, and clinical notes may be incomplete, illegible, ambiguous or destroyed. When faced with faulty or absent recollection, such clinical notes as there are may be the only "independent" or corroborative evidence that is available to a trial court.

That advice, useful though it may be, and departed from at peril insofar as a professional negligence action is concerned, does not, however, address all the practical realities that arise. Firstly, it might usefully be noted that clinical records, when produced in the context of litigation, constitute hearsay evidence and do not prove themselves. Secondly, the existence of records does not dispose of real conflicts that may inevitably arise between a patient's certainty as to what happened and what the clinical writing discloses. Thirdly, the absence of records is not always fatal.

Admissibility

In *Conley v. Strain*,[1] Lynch J., having considered the nature of medical records made available on discovery,[2] stated:

> "The status of the medical records should be clearly understood …The fact that copies …were furnished [on discovery] to all parties enabled them to examine and cross-examine witness[es] by reference to those records. The fact that copies of the records were furnished to me at the trial makes them evidence in the sense that I can study them and take them into account but it does not elevate them into the status of irrefutable evidence and where their accuracy or interpretations is challenged they are obviously capable of being outweighed by other evidence."[3]

Later, in *Hughes v. Staunton*,[4] he observed:

> "Merely because a book of documents has been discovered on affidavit by a party does not prove that the contents of such documents are accurate or reliable …strictly speaking many of these documents are pure hearsay."[5]

In that case, Lynch J. essentially accepted concessions as to the veracity of certain entries and effectively overcame the limitations imposed by the rule against hearsay, and although many of the entries in the clinical and nursing notes submitted to him were not formally proved, he adopted a common sense approach and placed great reliance on professional integrity. He was of the view that to call witnesses (in this case, nurses)

> " …with a view to their verifying entries made by them …it is likely that at the trial …just five years later, many if not all

---

[1]   [1988] I.R. 629.
[2]   The question of the effect of an order for discovery in litigation on a request for access under freedom of information legislation is considered at pp.33-37, *infra*.
[3]   [1988] I.R. 629 at 637.
[4]   Prof. Neg. L.R. 244 (High Court (Lynch J) February 16, 1990).
[5]   *Ibid.*, p.252.

of the nurses would have no actual recollection of the events described in the notes. A nurse would verify that such and such an entry was in her handwriting and was therefore made by her and that while she had no actual recollection whatever of the event described she was sure that it happened because she would not have written it in the notes if it had not happened ...I do not need the nurses to tell me that they would not make fictitious entries in a patient's nursing notes; that goes without saying because it would be such an extraordinary event if a fictitious entry were to be made."[6]

Accordingly, he concluded, that even though they were technically hearsay:

"The notes are therefore quite reliable and probably every bit as good as if a nurse were called to verify them provided that there is no ambiguity or uncertainty in them ...".[7]

While noting his (as yet, both then and now, unfulfilled) aspiration that remedial legislation on foot of the Law Reform Commission Report on *The Rule Against Hearsay in Civil Cases*[8] would resolve such problems, Lynch J. set out the approach he considered appropriate to adopt:

"In finding the facts, I shall accept these documents as *prima facie* giving a reasonably accurate account of the events which they purport to record and of the opinions of the doctors from whom they emanate. If in any particular they are contradicted by sworn testimony I shall reject such documentary record unless it is supported by other sworn testimony which I prefer .... I do not regard such documentary evidence as infallible. I regard it as valuable evidence to be read in the light of all the sworn testimony oral and written ...".[9]

---

6   *Ibid.,* p.252.
7   *Ibid.,* p.252.
8   LRC 25–1998 (September 10, 1988).
9   Prof. Neg. L.R. 244 at 253.

Proof and conflicts of evidence

Given the nature of the records in question, this provides a useful and pragmatic touchstone and one which was followed, using an approach of strict factual evidence appraisal, by O'Donovan J. at first instance, in _Doherty v. Reynolds & anor._[10] Here, there were significant conflicts between the plaintiff's and his witnesses' sworn recollections – particularly in relation to his condition post-operatively and prior to his discharge from hospital - and the contents of the contemporaneous clinical and nursing records. Given the paucity of many of the entries in the clinical notes, and that none of the doctors or nurses who gave evidence had any personal recollection of the plaintiff (such that their evidence was limited, essentially, to what had been recorded at the time), these conflicts (with the exception of those in relation to relatively minor matters) were resolved in favour of the plaintiff. O'Donovan J. was not persuaded that all of the evidence which might have been available with regard to what happened to the plaintiff during the preoperative period was, in fact, available.[11] In addition, it seemed to him that the nursing evidence "had gaps in it which reduced it value". His conclusion, on point, however, is apposite:

> "...nurses and doctors, who remember nothing, can prove nothing except what should happen in an ideal hospital situation and it does not necessarily follow that because a nurse or a doctor, who remembers nothing, has not recorded an untoward event that such an event has not occurred.... [I]n the circumstance that no one was in a position to state positively that those systems and procedures had, in fact, been implemented in the case of [the plaintiff], I cannot

---

[10] [2004] I.E.S.C. 42 _rev'g_ [2004] I.E.H.C. 25 (O'Donovan J.).

[11] In the Supreme Court, Keane C.J., on this point, stated: "I am . . . satisfied that the trial judge was in error in attaching the weight that he did to the fact that some members of the staff who were present at various stages did not give evidence. If the evidence of the anaesthetist, the surgeon and the members of the nursing staff was credible evidence from which the trial judge was entitled to infer that there had been no want of care on the part of the hospital which could have resulted in the traction injury, it was not open to the trial judge to have no regard to that evidence because not all the members of the staff who had been in the relevant area at any particular time had given evidence."

exclude the possibility that an incident did occur, as a result
of which the plaintiff suffered the injury of which he
complains."

In a number of instances, O'Donovan J. was invited by the defendants to
infer that certain complaints alleged to have been made by the plaintiff
and his witnesses had not, in fact, been made, from the absence of any
references to them in the clinical and nursing notes (or, in one case, from
the absence of any note of a ward round). In an approach entirely consistent
with *Hughes*, O'Donovan J. was "... not persuaded that the evidence of
the plaintiff can or should be displaced by the fact that there are no clinical
records to support them."

Although neither *Hughes* nor *Conley* were referred to in *Doherty*,
either at first instance or on appeal, this might hardly be considered
surprising as many of those who cared for the plaintiff, and made notes
in relation to him, in fact, gave evidence. O'Donovan J., however, was
happy to accept that professional persons would not record events that
had not in fact happened and he resolved conflicts in relation to such
events in favour of the doctors and nurses involved (although such events
were of minimal relevance to the matters with which he was concerned).
In addition, his conclusions (primarily on causation) were, to an extent,
ultimately premised on omissions from the records (which, naturally, must
also raise an issue as to their completeness and, accordingly, the
reasonableness of the care afforded to the plaintiff, assuming them
otherwise to represent a picture of the care *actually* given). Insofar as his
conclusions were premised on positive assertions in the records, he did
not – in line with *Hughes* and *Conley* – accept those assertions, given the
other evidence available. O'Donovan J.:

> "...was not satisfied that the defendants' records...were
> complete or, indeed, as reliable as they might have been
> ....There were a number of...inconsistencies ....It is
> sufficient to say that, while I was invited to accept that the
> records which did exist were, as it were "gospel" I regret to
> say that I was not persuaded that that was so."

Invariable practice no defence?

This conclusion, at first blush, is a vigorous endorsement of the professional defence bodies' advice in relation to absence of records. Before addressing the wholly different approach to apparently incomplete records in *Doherty* in the Supreme Court, on appeal, it might be noted that the view taken by O'Donovan J., at first instance, in relation to the resolution of conflicts of evidence between patients and doctors is in stark contrast to that taken in non-disclosure cases where the issue arose, and in particular, in *Farrell v. Varian*,[12] *Bolton v. Blackrock Clinic*,[13] and, to a lesser extent, *Walsh v. Family Planning Services & ors*[14] and *Reid v. Beaumont Hospital & anor*.[15] Applying the mechanism of analysis adopted in *Doherty* and paying more particular and strict attention to the balancing of an alleged documentary omission with sworn evidence to the contrary might have yielded different results in such cases. (In *Geoghegan v. Harris*,[16] the most prominent of the more recent non-disclosure cases of the past 15 years, there was no such issue.) Although such situations are clearly not within the ambit of the maxim *omnia praesumuntur* such analysis might well be considered to yield similar outcomes.

The Supreme Court reverses – Invariable practice may aid defence

Notwithstanding the appeal of O'Donovan J.'s approach, the risk of injustice is obvious. Not everything might be recorded in clinical and other notes, because an invariable practice may be adopted in relation to a significant number of matters. Such was the plea of the hospital staff in *Doherty* (and of the defendant, successfully, in *Farrell v. Varian*).[17] And, there was no reason for any of them to suggest or consider that that practice would not have been followed on the occasion in question. Absent personal recollection, that is all that such defendants may be able to call

---

12 Unreported, High Court, O'Hanlon J., September 19, 1994.
13 Unreported, Supreme Court, January 23, 1997 *aff'g* unreported, High Court, Geoghegan J., December 20, 1994.
14 [1992] I.R. 563.
15 Unreported, High Court, Johnson J., July 18, 1997.
16 [2000] 3 I.R. 536.
17 Unreported, High Court, O'Hanlon J., September 19, 1994.

upon. Are they, accordingly, to be disadvantaged in any defence merely because, by virtue of the number of patients treated and the effluxion of time between the occurrence of an incident complained of and the subsequent litigation, no active memory can be called upon in aid? The Supreme Court, on the hospital's appeal, in *Doherty* considered that no such disadvantage should accrue. Keane C.J. did not have "the slightest doubt" that the trial judge was entitled to prefer the evidence of the plaintiff and his witnesses as to the plaintiff's complaints in the aftermath of his operation. He continued:

> "The absence of any records of these complaints by any of the hospital staff is certainly remarkable and reflects, at best from their point of view, a singularly inadequate system of record keeping. It is clear that the plaintiff, who had gone into hospital for an operation intended to deal with a condition of heartburn and acid reflux but was otherwise in normal health, came out suffering from a painful and disabling condition in his right shoulder and arm which did not respond to any treatment until some six years later: so much, at least, is not in dispute in this difficult case."[18]

That said, no specific liability issue arose, in relation to any defects in the system of record keeping. Keane C.J. was also of the view that the fact that the clinicians and nurses caring for the plaintiff in *Doherty* were unable to recall, at trial, any specific details of what had transpired:

> " ...did not have, as its necessary consequence, as the trial judge appeared to assume, that they could not discharge the burden of proof resting on them of establishing that there was no negligence on their part. In my view, that would be to impose a burden of proof on defendants in a case such as this which is unfair and unreasonable. The fact that the staff of the hospital cannot, at a particular remove of time, give honest evidence that they recall how a particular patient was dealt with is, of course, a fact to which the court must have

---

[18] [2004] I.E.S.C. 42 rev'g [2004] I.E.H.C. 25 (O'Donovan J.).

regard. But it must also give the appropriate weight to evidence, such as was adduced in this case, as to the procedures which would normally be applied, the inferences that can properly be drawn from the hospital records and the evidence, if it exists, as it did in this case, of those concerned that, while they did not recall the specific operation, they had no recollection in any operation of the procedures being departed from with the consequences alleged to have resulted in this case. As Stuart-Smith L.J. put it in *Delaney v. Southmead Health Authority*:[19]

> 'The criticism which (counsel) makes of (the doctor) is that, not having realised any criticism was being made of him for a considerable time, all he was able to do was to say, 'I would have done this; I would have done that; that is my usual practice'. But in the case of a doctor or anaesthetist who adopts a regular practice, very often that is all he can say unless there is some reason why he should adopt a different process in a particular case and, as I have already indicated, no such suggestion was made in this instance.'

> The conclusion to be reached after an assessment of such evidence is inevitably a matter for the court of trial and it will not normally be disturbed by this court where it rests on an assessment by the trial judge of the credibility of the evidence in question and inferences which were properly drawn by the trial judge from the evidence, but, for the reasons I have given, I am satisfied that in this case the approach adopted by the trial judge imposed an unreasonably high burden of proof on the hospital."[20]

The essence of the Supreme Court's conclusion is that an assertion that if clinicians cannot give evidence of what actually occurred, as distinct from the form of evidence adduced, they must be found negligent unless

---

[19] [1995] 6 Med. L.R. 355.
[20] [2004] I.E.S.C 42 rev'g; [2004] I.E.H.C. 25 (O'Donovan J.).

they can explain how the plaintiff's injury occurred was not reconcilable with authority. Absence of documentary evidence – or, indeed, personal recollection - is not always fatal.[21]

Necessity – The general principle

Having said that, are defensive reasons sufficient justification for keeping notes? In *Christie v. Somerset Health Authority*[22] the trial judge considered that advice given in evidence that failure to record that a particular piece of equipment had been used during the course of a dental extraction would render it very difficult to defend any ensuing legal action should nerve damage occur was "a very sad piece of defensive medicine".[23]

In addition, can a failure to keep clinical notes be a ground for imposing liability? In *Hughes v. Staunton & ors*[24] one of the allegations made against the two defendant general practitioners was that they failed to keep any clinical notes in respect of certain of the plaintiff's treatments. Lynch J. addressed the matter as follows:

> "The primary duty of a doctor is to treat the patient. Included in that will be the keeping of such records as are necessary for the continued treatment of the patient on a properly informed basis. It is not a duty to the plaintiff but a counsel of wisdom in his own interests that the doctor should also keep sufficient notes of his dealings with his patients to enable him to refresh his memory therefrom and thus be in a position to state positively and precisely if required in the future what he did. [The first general practitioner] kept sufficient records for the purposes of the plaintiff's treatment but none to enable him to be positive about various aspects of this case which he might otherwise have been able to deal with but in fact has no actual memory of at all.
> [The second general practitioner] kept no records

---

21 See, however, *Healy v. North-Western Health Board*, unreported, High Court, Flood J., January 31, 1996.
22 [1992] 3 Med. L.R. 75.
23 *Ibid.,* p.78.
24 Prof. Neg. L.R. 244.

whatsoever relating to the plaintiff. He did however telephone [the first general practitioner] ...within three days of seeing the plaintiff and reported adequately on the plaintiff ...including the fact that he ...had prescribed Largactil having first contacted [the defendant consultant] on the telephone and been advised by him so to do. The inadequacy of the two general practitioners' records in this case is certainly open to criticism but that inadequacy did not in fact affect the treatment of the plaintiff in this case at all and is therefore wholly irrelevant to the issue of liability."[25]

The first part of Lynch J.'s conclusion is probably as clear an exposition of the necessity on the part of clinicians to keep clinical records as is necessary. A similar statement is found in the judgment of Evans L.J. in *R v. Mid-Glamorgan Family Health Services Authority ex p Martin.*[26] There, he stated:

"The [medical] record is made for two purposes ...first, to provide part of the medical history of the patient, for the benefit of the same doctor or his successors in the future; and secondly, to provide a record of diagnosis and treatment in case of future inquiry or dispute."[27]

Reprise

Assuming that these two dicta encapsulate the essence of the requirement to keep health care records, the next question to be addressed is who owns the records and when, if at all, can a patient access them – or, more specifically, the information contained in them?

ACCESS AT COMMON LAW

General

Before considering the position at common law, some discussion on the

---

[25] *Ibid.,* p.275.
[26] [1995] 1 All E.R. 356.
[27] *Ibid.,* p.365.

role of discovery in the context of litigation, and its inter-relationship with a request under the Act of 1997, and the requirement for disclosure of information in assessments pursuant to the provisions of the Personal Injuries Assessment Board Act 2003, is apposite.

Discovery in personal injury litigation and disclosure in PIAB assessments[28]

During the course of personal injuries litigation (to which the Personal Injuries Assessment Board Act 2003 does not apply or pursuant to which an authorisation has been granted) – or, indeed, during the course of the conduct of a Tribunal of Inquiry pursuant to the provisions of the Tribunal of Inquiries (Evidence) Acts 1921 and 2004 - discovery of a person's health care records may be sought, often as a matter of course.[29] Where a litigant refuses to disclose his/her health care records, which the other party or parties claim to be relevant to the determination of the proceedings, an order for discovery may be made. The documents sought must be relevant and necessary[30] for disposing fairly of the cause or matter or for saving costs. A similar order may be sought and obtained against an institution or other individual, e.g. general practitioner, where necessary.

In a medical negligence action, the relevance of, and necessity for, sight of all clinical records might reasonably be considered self-evident. What about other cases, however? The starting point for discussion of this question is *McGrory v. ESB*,[31] a decision which concerns both a refusal to undergo an examination to be carried out on behalf of the defendant and the question as to the appropriate level of disclosure of

---

[28] See, also, in relation to this topic, Craven C, The Personal Injuries Assessment Board Act 2003: Medico-Legal Aspects in: *The Personal Injuries Assessment Board Act 2003: Implications for Legal Practice* Quigley P. and Binchy W. (eds)(2004, First Law, Dublin), 43-47.

[29] In the High Court, the relevant rule is RSC, O.31, r.12, in particular, that inserted by the Rules of the Superior Courts (No. 2) (Discovery), 1999 (S.I. No. 233 of 1999). This does not extend to criminal proceedings; see *People (DPP) v. Sweeney* [2001] 4 I.R. 102.

[30] As to necessity, see *Cooper-Flynn v. RTÉ* [2000] 3 I.R. 344 and *Taylor v. Healthcare Ltd* [2004] 1 I.R. 169.

[31] [2003] 3 I.R. 407.

clinical records. On the first issue, which also necessarily involves the disclosure of confidential information, it was, at least impliedly, accepted that an injured plaintiff could refuse to submit to an examination by a defendant's medical advisers. Given the nature of the constitutionally protected rights involved – bodily integrity and privacy (arising from which is the requirement to obtain consent to any medical touching, including, it must be considered, a medical examination, assessment or investigation),[32] this is hardly surprising. The effective sanction, however, both in that case and pursuant to the provisions of the Personal Injuries Assessment Board Act 2003[33] does, in reality, deprive an injured party of any real or meaningful right to refuse to undergo the examination requested, and, at such an examination, to withhold confidential information, other than at significant peril to the progressing or assessment of his or her claim. In *McGrory*, for example, Keane C.J.:

> "ha[d] no doubt that the courts enjoy an inherent jurisdiction to stay proceedings where justice so requires and that it should be exercised in cases where the plaintiff refuses to submit to a medical examination or <u>to disclose his medical records to the defendant or to permit the defendant to interview his treating doctors</u>."[34] (<u>emphasis</u> added)

The plaintiff's proceedings were, accordingly, stayed until the plaintiff consented to the defendants' medical adviser consulting with his medical advisers, involving – necessarily – the disclosure of confidential information that may not otherwise be justifiable as coming within the terms of an acceptable private interest exception to the rule against the non-consensual disclosure of such information. Pursuant to the provisions of the Personal Injuries Assessment Board Act 2003, a refusal to comply with the Board's request for a claimant to undergo a medical examination results in the making of an assessment on the basis that the contention of the respondent concerning the opinion furnished by the claimant was correct (in other words, the contention will be presumed against the

---

[32] See, in particular, the decision of the Supreme Court in *In the matter of a Ward of Court (No. 2)* [1996] 2 I.R. 100 at 156, *per* Denham J.

[33] Personal Injuries Assessment Board Act 2003, s. 25(1)(c) and (d).

[34] [2003] 3 I.R. 407 at 415.

claimant, unless the assessors see good reason for not doing so).[35] In other circumstances the assessors will proceed to make the assessment "as best they may in the absence of the information" that would otherwise have been provided.[36] In relation to the first category, however, this is really no more than an application of the evidentiary maxim *omnia praesumunter contra spoliatorem*.[37] Keane CJ noted that that maxim:

" ...is intended to ensure that no party to litigation, be they plaintiff or defendant, is subjected to a disadvantage in the presentation of his or her case because his or her opponent had acted wrongly by destroying or suppressing evidence."[38]

However, the approach in *McGrory* and under the Personal Injuries Assessment Board Act 2003 also reduces a person relying on his constitutional right to privacy and bodily integrity and who refuses voluntary disclosure of wide-reaching confidential information to *spoliator* – or wrongdoer – which is essential for the proper application of the maxim.[39]

In *McGrory* the Supreme Court made it abundantly clear that where a person sues for personal injuries, (s)he puts his or her health in issue in the proceedings. Having reviewed the authorities, and, in particular, the Canadian case of *Hay v. University of Alberta*[40] where Picard J. had found that:

---

[35] Personal Injuries Assessment Board Act 2003 s. 25(1)(c).

[36] *Ibid.*, 25(1)(d). Similar provisions under s. 25 apply in relation to other failures to comply with requests for documents or information from a claimant under s.23 of the Act of 2003.

[37] See, in particular, *O'Mahony v. Tyndale* [2002] 4 I.R. 101, *Williamson v. Rover Cycle Company* [1901] 2 I.R. 615, and *The Ophelia* [1916] 2 A.C. 206.

[38] *O'Mahony v. Tyndale* [2002] 4 I.R. 101 at 107.

[39] See, *O'Mahony v. Tyndale & anor* [2002] 4 I.R. 101 citing *Armory v. Delamirie* (1772) 1 Stra. 505, *Williamson v. Rover Cycle Company* [1901] 2 I.R. 615 and *The Ophelia* [1916] 2 A.C. 206. However, note that in *Dobson & anor v. North Tyneside Health Authority & anor* [1997] 8 Med L.R. 357, a case not referred to in *O'Mahony*, the Court of Appeal rejected the application of the maxim in circumstances where the plaintiff could not establish that the second defendant, also a health authority, was a wrongdoer responsible for the destruction of the brain which had been removed from a deceased at post-mortem examination. Absence of proof of *wrongdoing* was fatal to the application of the maxim.

[40] [1991] 2 Med. L.R. 204.

" ...the right of the patient to confidentiality ceases when he puts his health in issue by claiming damages in a lawsuit; the raison d'etre for confidentiality is gone. The right to confidentiality is then eclipsed by the right of those who face the action to know the basis of the claim being advanced ...".

which was cited with approval in *AB & ors v. John Wyeth & Brothers.*[41] Keane C.J. was satisfied that those principles which had been adopted by courts in other common law jurisdictions, should also be adopted here. He continued:

"The plaintiff who sues for damages for personal injuries by implication necessarily waives the right of privacy which he would otherwise enjoy in relation to his medical condition. The law must be in a position to ensure that he does not unfairly and unreasonably impede the defendant in the preparation of his defence by refusing to consent to a medical examination."[42]

Also arising in those circumstances, and the injured party's health being in issue, discovery of the person's medical records should ordinarily lie because of relevance. Keane C.J. continued further:

"Similarly, the court must be able to ensure that the defendant has access to any relevant medical records and to obtain from the treating doctors any information they may have relevant to the plaintiff's medical condition, although the plaintiff cannot be required to disclose medical reports in respect of which he is entitled to claim legal professional privilege."[43]

But, that is not the end of the issue. It must also be established that their discovery is necessary for a fair disposal of the proceedings or for saving on costs. However, in *Taylor v. Clonmel Healthcare Ltd*[44] Geoghegan J.

---

[41] [1996] 7 Med. L.R. 300.
[42] [2003] 3 I.R. 407 at 414.
[43] *Ibid.*
[44] [2004] 1 I.R. 169.

considered that "if a party is entitled to a document on ground of relevance to assist him in his case on the ordinary discovery principles, it will usually be 'necessary'."[45] It is always open to a person against whom discovery is sought to challenge the discovery on the grounds that it is not necessary. As Geoghegan J. stated:

> "The opposing party of course may decide to raise the issue of necessity and put forward reasons why it is not necessary and that issue can then be disposed of in due course."[46]

On one reading of *McGrory*, full disclosure, irrespective of relevance, would appear to be justified.

Discovery and Tribunals of Inquiry

Rarely, the records of a person who is not a party to the litigation may be discovered. The Tribunal of Inquiry into the Blood Transfusion Service Board[47] ordered discovery of the clinical and laboratory records of certain patients who had been treated with the Board's products, where those records were considered to be central to the issues the Tribunal had to determine. Similar orders were made in the High Court in related litigation. In such circumstances, a masking order – such that the identity of the person to whom the records relate cannot be identified – seems appropriate; given that it is the information contained in the records rather than the identity of the person to whom it relates, generally, that is relevant, this, on principle, is unremarkable. Considering the nature of the public interest justification for such a breach of confidentiality, however, it might be considered not merely unremarkable but mandatory.

In *Haughey v. Moriarty*[48] the Supreme Court was satisfied that the making of orders for discovery (in relation to confidential financial records) against third parties, who, in that case, were not the subject of a Tribunal of Inquiry:

> " ...*per se* did not unjustifiably encroach upon the

---

[45] *Ibid.,* p.182.
[46] *Ibid.*
[47] The "Finlay Inquiry", March 1997.
[48] [1999] 3 I.R. 1.

constitutional rights of the plaintiffs ...The encroachment
on such rights is justified in this particular case by the
exigencies of the common good."[49]

That "common good' or public interest also suffices, it appears, in relation
to the disclosure of confidential health care records in similar
circumstances. However, the Supreme Court continued:

> "Fair procedures require that before making such orders,
> particularly orders of the nature of the orders made in this
> case [against non-parties], the person or persons likely to be
> affected thereby should be given notice ...of [the] intention
> to make such order, and should have been afforded the
> opportunity prior to the making of such order, of making
> representations with regard thereto. Such representations
> could conceivably involve the submission ...that the ...orders
> were not necessary for the purpose ...that they were too wide
> and extensive having regard to the terms of reference ...and
> any other relevant matters."[50]

The making of orders for discovery otherwise was characterised by the
court as a "contravention of the requirements of constitutional justice".[51]

Fair procedures aside, the approach is not entirely reconcilable with
McGrory which suggests that full disclosure of health care information,
irrespective of the breadth of the disclosure sought or its immediate
(proximate) relevance does not require to be factored in.

It might reasonably be concluded that the justification for the making
of orders for discovery of confidential personal health care information
lies in the public interest in the proper and expeditious prosecution of
litigation (and conclusion of inquiries) and, for that purpose, in having
all appropriate matters before the court or tribunal. Insofar as this lends
itself to advancing the proper administration of justice or the proper
carrying out of a judicial inquiry into matters of public concern the public
interest or the exigencies of the common good seem relatively clear. That

---

[49] *Ibid.*, p.75.
[50] *Ibid.*, pp.75-76.
[51] *Ibid.*, p.76.

they should always outweigh the private interest of an individual in insisting on maintaining confidentiality in respect of his/her medical history or, indeed, the public interest in also maintaining the confidential nature of such communications is less obvious. Although only that which is necessary and relevant, in theory at least, should be discoverable, and the redacting of certain information may be in aid, recent judicial and legislative developments suggest otherwise and they prompt examination of whether or not the balance has been appropriately struck – at least insofar as civil litigation and personal injuries claims are concerned. In *O'Connor v. The Queen*[52] a majority of the Supreme Court of Canada,[53] considering a similar theme, albeit in the criminal context, noted:

> "They [i.e. victims] are entitled not to be deprived of their reasonable expectation of privacy except in accordance with the principles of fundamental justice. In cases such as the present one [i.e. a criminal trial], any interference with the individual's right to privacy comes about as a result of another person's assertion that this interference is necessary in order to make full answer and defence. As important as the right to full answer and defence may be, it must co-exist with other constitutional rights, rather than trample them ...Privacy and equality must not be sacrificed willy-nilly on the altar of trial fairness"[54] (Citation omitted)[55]

Freedom of information request in the context of a prior order for discovery

On the making of an Affidavit of Discovery, there is an implied undertaking as to confidentiality and that the documents will not be used for any purpose other than in the proceedings in which they were

---

[52] 130 D.L.R. (4th) 235.
[53] L'Heureux-Dube, La Forest and Gonthier JJ., Lamer C.J.C. and Sopinka J. dissenting.
[54] 130 D.L.R. (4th) 235 at para. 130.
[55] It might be noted that the exclusion of the discovery process from criminal proceedings in *People (DPP) v. Sweeney* [2001] 4 I.R. 102 is justified on a wholly different (and procedural) basis.

discovered. Lord Scarman (Lord Simon of Glaisdale concurring in the dissent), in *Harman v. Home Office*[56] stated:

> "The law imposes the obligation ...for the protection of the party compelled to make discovery of documents in legal proceedings. It does so by implying an undertaking by the party to whom discovery is made and his solicitor not to use them for any purpose other than that of the action. Disregard of the undertaking is enforceable by the party for whose benefit it is exacted in committal proceedings for contempt of court."[57]

Later, he stated:

> "No doubt, the value of the undertaking is that it comes into existence, as soon as discovery is made, by implication of law and without the necessity of a court order. ...The contempt aspect of the obligation is not to do with the extent or substance of the duty imposed but is a feature of its enforceability. Being imposed by the court, it is, if disregarded, enforceable by committal. But ...it is a contempt which the party for whose benefit the obligation was imposed may waive or accept."[58]

He continued:

> "If the undertaking is to the court (as it is common ground it is) the other party cannot arrogate the power to release (and yet it is conceded that such other party may waive what would be a "civil" contempt)."[59]

---

[56] [1983] A.C. 280.
[57] *Ibid.*, p.312.
[58] *Ibid.*, p.313.
[59] *Ibid.*, p.319.

The undertaking, in Lord Roskill's opinion, comes into existence

> " ...when the documents are first disclosed in an affidavit or list of documents. It is then that their existence and broad description will become known to the other side, often for the first time. Their contents, however, will not usually become known to the other side until production takes place. It should be remembered that the obligation to produce that which has already been disclosed is subject to a number of well-established exceptions."[60]

In *EH v. Information Commissioner*,[61] O'Neill J. stated:

> "Breach of the implied undertaking given in respect of discovered documents is a contempt of court. Notwithstanding that the undertaking benefits solely the party making discovery, the undertaking is given to the court and like all undertakings given to a court, breach of it is a contempt of the court. Indeed, this is abundantly clear from *Home Office v. Harman* ..."[62]

However, he continued:

> "True, in the case of the usual implied undertaking the party for whose benefit it is given, i.e. the party making disclosure can waive the undertaking but in the absence of such waiver ...the undertaking continues as an undertaking to the court with all of the attending consequences of a breach of an undertaking to the court ...Undertakings given to a court can only be discharged either in the case of the usual undertaking in relation to discovery by waiver of the party making discovery or otherwise by the express permission of the court itself. Having regard to the very important public policy

---

60 *Ibid.,* p.321.
61 [2001] 2 I.R. 463.
62 *Ibid.,* p.485.

served by these undertakings the courts are slow to vary or discharge these undertakings."[63]

Whereas it seems to be suggested in this passage that the party making discovery may waive the implied undertaking as to confidentiality on discovery, that is not quite what *Harman* says. What may be waived, strictly speaking, is the right to seek attachment and committal for the breach of the undertaking. In *EH*, the applicant had obtained certain documents on discovery on foot not just of the usual implied undertaking as to confidentiality but an express undertaking to that effect. He subsequently sought the same documents under the Freedom of Information Act 1997 and that request was refused; the refusal was upheld on internal appeal and subsequently by the Commissioner. On the question of whether or not the Commissioner was correct to refuse to allow access to documents which had previously been discovered in civil proceedings, O'Neill J. held:

> "...the purpose of s. 22(1)(b)[64] is to prevent the Act of 1997 operating in such a way as to permit interference in the administration of justice a function which is reserved by the Constitution solely to the courts established by or under the Constitution. If it were the case that one could under the provisions of the Act of 1997 obtain documents disclosure of which was prohibited by the ruling of a court or by a[n] undertaking given to a court, I have no doubt that this would amount to a gross and constitutionally impermissible interference in the administration of justice ....
>
> I have come to the conclusion that notwithstanding the entirely laudable and separate philosophy of disclosure which underpins the Act of 1997, that the Act construed in a manner consistent with the Constitution could not be used, so that access to documents under the Act would have the result of robbing an order of a court or an undertaking given to a court of the force and effect which the court in question intended

---

[63] *Ibid.,* p.486.
[64] S.22(1)(b) of the Act of 1997 prohibits the granting of access to a record if its disclosure would constitute contempt of court.

these to have. In my view s. 22(1)(b) is there to ensure that this does not happen, and it must operate accordingly."[65]

The court did not share the view expressed on behalf of the applicant that impracticalities or disadvantages would arise

" ...that by the mere fact that documents were listed in an affidavit of discovery; as if by some forensic magic they would be excluded from disclosure under the Act of 1997."[66]

It is less a case of "forensic magic" than adherence to principle.

COMMON LAW[67]

Britain

In Britain, the Access to Health Records Act 1990 was passed as a result of the decision of the European Court of Human Rights in *Gaskin v. United Kingdom*[68] which held that the refusal to allow access by the applicant to certain health records was in breach of his right to respect for his private and family life under Article 8 of the European Convention for the Protection of Human Rights and Fundamental Freedoms 1950.[69] However, access was restricted to those records that came into existence after November 1, 1991.[70]

In *R v. Mid Glamorgan Family Health Services*[71] the applicant sought access to his records for the period between 1966 and 1970 when he

---

[65] [2001] 2 I.R. 463 at 485.

[66] *Ibid.,* p.486.

[67] For a thorough discussion of this topic, see, Kennedy & Grubb *Medical Law* (3rd ed.) (2000, Butterworths, London), chap.7.

[68] (1989) 12 E.H.R.R. 36.

[69] This assumes particular relevance, in this jurisdiction, given the commencement of the European Convention on Human Rights Act 2003 – essentially incorporating the Convention into domestic law - on December 31, 2003.

[70] In this regard, it merits noting that the Freedom of Information Act 1997 applies retrospectively in respect of personal information, a matter considered in more detail at p.50, *infra*.

[71] [1995] 1 All E.R. 356.

suffered from psychiatric problems for which he received treatment in hospital. After correspondence between the health authority and the applicant's solicitors, the health authority agreed to make the records available to the applicant's medical adviser who would be in a better position to decide whether and to what extent disclosure would be made to the applicant without causing harm. As he had not been under the health authority's care for many years, they were not in a position to make such a judgment. Thus, disclosure was not being refused – rather disclosure in a supportive environment was proposed. This was in line with the provisions of the access legislation then in force, although not applicable to the applicant's case. The applicant did not accept the offer and, at first instance, his application for judicial review was refused.

Popplewell J.[72] was of the view that there had been no breach of Article 8 because of the offer that the health authority had made. He also reached "the clearest possible conclusion"[73] that at common law there was no right of access by the applicant to records pre-existing the Access to Health Records Act. Although the claim was framed in public law, Nourse L.J., in the Court of Appeal was of the view that

> " ...a public body, as the owner of medical records, can be in a position no different from that of a private doctor whose relationship with his patient is governed by contract. In other words, a public body, in fulfilment of its duty to administer its property in accordance with its public purposes, is bound to deal with medical records in the same way as a private doctor."[74]

Nourse L.J. (with whom the other members of the Court of Appeal agreed) then referred to the speech of Lord Templeman in *Sidaway v. Governors of Bethlehem Royal Hospital*[75] where he stated:

> "I do not subscribe to the theory that the patient is entitled to know everything nor to the theory that the doctor is entitled

---

[72] [1994] 5 Med. L.R. 383.
[73] *Ibid.,* p.392.
[74] [1995] 1 All E.R. 356 at 363.
[75] [1985] 1 All E.R. 643; [1985] A.C. 871.

to decide everything. The relationship between doctor and patient is contractual in origin, the doctor performing services in consideration for fees payable by the patient. The doctor, obedient to the high standards set by the medical profession impliedly contracts to act at all times in the best interests of the patient. No doctor in his senses would impliedly contract at the same time to give to the patient all the information available to the doctor as a result of the doctor's training and experience and as a result of the doctor's diagnosis of the patient. An obligation to give a patient all the information available to the doctor would often be inconsistent with the doctor's contractual obligation to have regard to the patient's best interests. Some information might confuse, other information might alarm a particular patient. Whenever the occasion arises for the doctor to tell the patient the results of the doctor's diagnosis, the possible methods of treatment and the advantages and disadvantages of the recommended treatment, the doctor must decide in the light of his training and experience and in the light of his knowledge of the patient what should be said and how it should be said."[76]

He observed that that passage provided "a sensible basis for holding that a doctor, likewise a health authority, as the owner of a patient's medical records, may deny the patient access to them if it is in his best interests to do so, for example if their disclosure would be detrimental to his health".[77] He continued:

"It is inherent in the views above expressed that I do not accept that a health authority, any more than a private doctor, has an absolute right to deal with medical records in any way that it chooses. As Lord Templeman makes clear, the doctor's general duty, likewise the health authority's, is to act at all times in the best interests of the patient. Those interests would usually require that a patient's medical records should not be disclosed to third parties; conversely,

---

[76] [1985] 1 All E.R. 643 at 665-666; [1985] A.C. 871 at 904.
[77] [1995] 1 All E.R. 356 at 363.

that they should usually, for example, be handed on by one doctor to the next or made available to the patient's legal advisers if they are reasonably required for the purposes of legal proceedings in which he is involved. The respondent's position seems to be that no practical difficulty could arise in such circumstances, but that they would act voluntarily and not because they were under a legal duty to do so. If it ever became necessary for the legal position to be tested, it is inconceivable that this extreme position would be vindicated."[78]

Although the applicant's appeal was dismissed, given the offer made by the health authority, it is clear that the Court of Appeal was of the view that a refusal to provide a patient with any access to records outside of litigation was untenable.

Canada

In *McInerney v. MacDonald,*[79] the appellant doctor, while delivering copies of all notes, memoranda and reports on the patient that she had compiled, refused to produce copies of consultants' reports and records she had received from other physicians who had previously been involved in the respondent's care stating that they were the property of those physicians and that it would be unethical for her to release them. She suggested that the respondent contact the other doctors for release of their records. She had been treated by various doctors over a period of years and, when she came under the care of the appellant she was advised to, and did, stop taking thyroid pills that had been prescribed for her previously. It was in the context of having become concerned about her previous medical care that she then sought a copy of the contents of her complete medical file. The Supreme Court of Canada was faced with two simple questions:

1. Are a patient's medical records prepared by a doctor the property of that doctor or of the patient?

---

[78] *Ibid.,* p.363-364
[79] (1992) 93 D.L.R. (4th) 415.

2. If the property of the doctor who prepares them, does a patient nevertheless have the right to examine and obtain copies of all documents in the medical records, including those that the doctor may have received which were prepared by others?

It held that a doctor owed a fiduciary duty to his or her patient to allow access to medical records, subject to certain conditions. La Forest J., who delivered the judgment of the Court, was prepared to accept that "the physician, institution or clinic compiling the medical records owns the physical records". The question, then, reduced to one of a question of access. After holding that the doctor owes a duty to his or her patient "to act with utmost good faith and loyalty"[80] He stated:

> "The fiduciary duty to provide access to medical records is ultimately grounded in the nature of the patient's interest in his or her records. …(I)nformation about oneself revealed to a doctor acting in a professional capacity remains, in a fundamental sense, one's own. The doctor's position is one of trust and confidence. The information conveyed is held in a fashion somewhat akin to a trust. While the doctor is the owner of the actual record, the information is to be used by the physician for the benefit of the patient. The confiding of the information to the physician for medical purposes gives rise to an expectation that the patient's interest in and control of the information will continue."[81]

He continued:

> "The trust-like 'beneficial interest' of the patient in the information indicates that, as a general rule, he or she should have a right of access to the information and that the physician should have a corresponding obligation to provide it. The patient's interest being in the information, it follows that the

---

[80] (1992) 93 D.L.R. (4th) 415 at 423.
[81] *Ibid.*, p.424.

interest continues when that information is conveyed to another doctor who then becomes subject to the duty to afford the patient access to that information."[82]

Although referred to at first instance in *Mid Glamorgan*, *McInerney* was not relied on in the Court of Appeal. Nevertheless, the conclusion is essentially the same: a complete refusal of disclosure is untenable although access may be restricted for good reason. The absence of statutory regulation does not prevent disclosure. In this regard, the Supreme Court of Canada concluded, in *McInerney*:

> "In the absence of regulatory legislation, the patient is entitled, upon request, to inspect and copy all information in the patient's medical file which the physician considered in administering advice or treatment. Considering the equitable base of the patient's entitlement, this general rule of access is subject to the superintending jurisdiction of the court. The onus is on the physician to justify a denial of access. …In this case, there is no evidence that access to the records would cause harm to the patient or a third party; nor does the appellant offer other compelling reasons for non-disclosure. Accordingly …the lower courts quite properly held that the respondent was entitled to copies of the documentation in her medical chart."[83]

Australian dissent

That said, however, not all common law jurisdictions are *ad idem* on this issue. Any common law right of access to medical records was robustly rejected by the High Court of Australia in *Breen v. WilliaMs*[84] Here, in 1977 the appellant had a bilateral augmentation mammoplasty which involved the insertion of a silicone implant in each of her breasts. Thereafter she developed bilateral breast capsules. In 1978, she consulted

---

[82] *Ibid.,* p.425.
[83] *Ibid.,* p.430-431.
[84] (1996) 70 A.L.J.R. 772.

the respondent plastic surgeon, but not the plastic surgeon who performed the implant. The respondent advised the appellant that the capsules should be compressed and he performed that operation. She experienced severe pain and, after two further consultations with her, the respondent operated and performed a bilateral capsulotomy. The appellant did not consult the respondent thereafter.

In 1984, another doctor diagnosed a lump in the appellant's left breast as silicone gel which had leaked from the breast implant. As a result, he performed a partial mastectomy upon the appellant. After that she had further corrective surgery on her left breast and had the right silicone breast implant replaced. Having become interested in litigation in the United States by way of a class action against the manufacturer of the breast implants claiming that they were defective, in that litigation she was given the opportunity to "opt in" to a settlement which had been given conditional approval by a United States court. It seems to have been a condition of opting in that the appellant did so before December 1, 1994 and that she file with the United States court copies of medical records in support of any claim which she wished to make. She sought to have access to the medical records kept by the respondent in her case and maintained that she did so both to secure advice whether she should opt in to the United States settlement and to comply with the condition imposed should she decide to do so. She also maintained that she had a right of access to the medical records to ensure that she had all information relating to her health at her disposal which would, in turn, ensure that she was able to make decisions regarding her future treatment.

She could have secured access to the medical records by compulsory court process. An order for discovery of the records was within the equitable jurisdiction of the Supreme Court of New South Wales. Another procedure was by way of letters rogatory. These were obtained from the United States court by several litigants in her position and orders were made by the Supreme Court of New South Wales compelling the production of medical records to the Court in aid of the United States proceedings. The appellant did not avail herself of this procedure because, she said, the time available was too short. Instead, she commenced an action in the Supreme Court of New South Wales claiming a declaration that she was entitled to access to the medical records kept by the respondent in relation to herself. The appellant also sought an order that the respondent allow her access to her medical records to examine them and obtain copies of the information contained in them.

As the claim that a patient has a right of access to his or her medical records was "a question of great social importance" it was considered at some length. But absent a contractual term, the High Court found, "such a claim has no foundation in the law of Australia."[85]

Five principal arguments were made by the appellant. First, the common law gave her a "proprietary right and interest" in the actual information contained in the records. Second, the common law implied a term in the contract between her and the doctor to the effect that she had a right of access to the documents in her medical file. Third, there was an innominate common law right of access to medical records. Fourth, the common law recognised a patient's "right to know" all necessary information concerning his or her medical treatment including, where requested, access to records containing that information. Fifth, the law imposed on the doctor a fiduciary duty, enforceable in a court of equity, to give her access to her medical records. The court dismissed each argument in turn.

Insofar as the question of a proprietary right was concerned, it was not submitted that the patient owned the actual documents which comprised the medical file. She did not, she said, "seek to divest the doctor of the pieces of paper" comprising the records and this concession "was plainly correct". Gaudron and McHugh JJ. stated:

> "Professional persons are not ordinarily agents of their clients even though they often have express, implied or ostensible authority to enter into contracts on their clients' behalf. Documents prepared by an agent are ordinarily the property of the principal. But documents prepared by a professional person to assist him or her to do work for a client are the property of the professional person, not the lay client. ....
> The doctor-patient relationship ...is not one of agent and principal. [The doctor's] notes were prepared to assist him to fulfil his professional duties. The property in the medical records relating to [the patient] which he prepared belongs to him; [she] has no proprietary right in respect of those

---

[85] Judgment of Gaudron and McHugh JJ., para.5.

records. The right of ownership of [the doctor] is, statute or contract apart, good against the world and entitles [him] to prevent any person from having access to those records."[86]

Insofar as there was an implied contractual term that access would be granted, the court was equally dismissive. Although the doctor-patient relationship is considered contractual in origin, given the informal nature of the relationship, however, a contract between a doctor and a patient rarely contains many express terMs The patient argued, relying on *Sidaway*, that, by implication of law, a doctor always contracts with a patient to act in the patient's "best interests". It was further argued, that as an incident of the "best interests" term, the doctor must make available medical records concerning a patient when the patient seeks access to them. The court refused to imply a "best interests" term, as a matter of law, into all doctor-patient contracts because, essentially, the creation of such a legal duty "would be inconsistent with the existing contractual and tortious duty to exercise reasonable care and skill in the provision of professional services.

The argument that there was an "innominate" common law right of access to clinical records, in reliance on *Mid-Glamaorgan*, was dismissed in near-peremptory fashion. The Court of Appeal's view, in that case, of the dictum of Lord Templeman in *Sidaway* was rejected by the High Court of Australia in *Breen*. Insofar as a fiduciary duty might be owed by the doctor to the patient, the court in *Breen* was simply not prepared to extend the category of those relationships in which a fiduciary duty might arise to those between doctors and patients. What La Forest J. had to say in *McInerney* did "not help analysis of the legal issues in the present class of case to say that the information 'is held in a fashion somewhat akin to a trust' or that there is an expectation that the patient's 'control of the information will continue'".[87] The information, in the view of Gaudron and McHugh JJ was not property. They continued:

"Moreover, the only control that a patient has over the information that he or she has given to the doctor is to restrain

---

[86] *Ibid.*, para.7.
[87] *Ibid.*, para.37.

its improper use. Nor is there any trust of it. Equity does not require the doctor to record, account for or even remember the information. Nor can equity at the suit of the patient prevent the doctor from destroying the records that contain the information. The records are the property of the doctor. He or she may be restrained from using the information in them to make an unauthorised profit or from disclosing that information to unauthorised persons. But otherwise the records are his or hers to save or destroy. The idea that a doctor who shreds the records of treatment of living patients is necessarily in breach of fiduciary duties owed to those patients is untenable."[88]

That said, what is set out above in relation to *spoliatores* is apposite in this regard.

    La Forest J. was subject to some further criticism by the High Court. His judgment:

" …[does] not deal with the fact that the medical records of a patient will often, perhaps usually, contain much more than the information that the patient has given to the doctor. In addition to any observations concerning the patient's condition and notes recording treatment and research, the records may contain comments by the doctor about the personality and conduct of the patient. They may also contain information concerning the patient that the doctor has obtained from other sources. The patient has no rights in relation to or control over any information that has not come from him or her. We can think of no legal principle that would give the patient even a faintly arguable case for access to information in the records that is additional to what the patient has given. If the relationship of doctor and patient was a status-based fiduciary relationship in which the doctor was under a general fiduciary duty in relation to all dealings concerning the patient, the patient might be entitled to access

---

to all the information in his or her medical records. But there is no general fiduciary duty."[89]

To an extent, however, this view misses the point. Most of the information contained in a patient's chart if not obtained from the patient is obtained as a result of information the patient has given. Third party collateral histories represent an obvious exception. But the rules on confidentiality should be sufficient to deal with this aspect of the matter.

With palpable hostility to accepting any imposition of a fiduciary duty in this context, Gaudron and McHugh JJ noted:

" ...the tendency [of the Canadian cases] to view fiduciary obligations as both proscriptive and prescriptive. ...With great respect to the Canadian courts, however, many cases in that jurisdiction pay insufficient regard to the effect that the imposition of fiduciary duties on particular relationships has on the law of negligence, contract, agency, trusts and companies in their application to those relationships."[90]

They concluded:

"If there was a general fiduciary duty to act in the best interests of the patient, it would necessarily follow that a doctor has a duty to inform the patient that he or she has breached their contract or has been guilty of negligence in dealings with the patient. That is not the law of this country."[91]

That such a robust statement would be accepted here must be considered questionable notwithstanding *Daniels v. Heskin*[92] and *Mordaunt v. Gallagher.*[93]

Finally, the court was not persuaded that the patient had "the right to

---

[89] *Ibid.,* para.38.
[90] *Ibid.,* para.40.
[91] *Ibid.,* para.41.
[92] [1954] I.R. 73.
[93] Unreported, High Court, Laffoy J., July 11, 1997.

know". Acknowledging that recent decisions of Australian courts rejected the attempt to treat the doctor-patient relationship as basically paternalistic, it held "it would require a quantum leap in legal doctrine to justify the relief for which [the patient] contends."[94]

Ireland?

The High Court of Australia – in contrast with the Court of Appeal in England and the Supreme Court of Canada - was simply not prepared to proceed other than by way of incremental reasoning. Although this approach reflects that of our Supreme Court (at least insofar as the tort of negligence is concerned) in *Glencar Exploration plc & anor v. Mayo County Council*[95] – an approach re-stated more recently in *Wildgust v. Bank of Ireland & anor*[96] – it must be considered unlikely, in light of the implementation, express language and policy of the Freedom of Information Act 1997, that, should the matter arise for decision in this jurisdiction, the restrictive Australian approach would be favoured over that of the Supreme Court of Canada or the Court of Appeal in *Mid-Glamorgan*. In addition, at this stage, the effect of Article 8 of the European Convention on Human Rights cannot be disregarded. The considerations here are far from theoretical: many institutions and health care providers, given how our health service is structured, are not amenable to the Act of 1997.

At its simplest, the message should be clear: even absent a request for access to medical records, under statute (to which the discussion now turns), there can hardly be considered to be a good reason for refusal of such access, at common law, at least insofar as one's own records are concerned. The exceptions referred to in the Freedom of Information *Act 1997* (and the Data Protection *Act 19*88) might reasonably, and on principle, apply. In summary, although the institution or the health care professional may have a proprietary interest in the actual record – be it in hard copy or digitally stored – the information contained in it, as a general rule, should be regarded as "belonging" to the patient.

---

[94]   (1996) 70 A.L.J.R. 772.
[95]   [2002] 1 I.R. 112, [2002] 1 I.L.R.M. 481.
[96]   [2006] I.E.S.C. 19.

STATUTORY ACCESS[97]

General

Personal information, including that contained in health care records, may be the subject of a request under the Freedom of Information Act 1997. The records covered by the provisions of the Act include digital and written and printed records, and, in the case of medical records, extend to diagnostic images howsoever stored.[98] "Personal information" – for the purposes of the Act – means information about an identifiable individual that (a) would, in the ordinary course of events, be known only to the individual or members of the family, or friends, of the individual, or (b) is held by a public body on the understanding that it would be treated by it as confidential, and, without prejudice to the generality of that definition, includes, *inter alia,* information relating[99] to the educational, medical, psychiatric or psychological history of the individual.[100] Although the definition is fairly generic, the discussion in this part of the Chapter will be confined to health care records, as ordinarily understood.

The Act, as originally enacted,[101] did not apply to health care providers. However, it was extended to the then health boards[102] on October 21, 1998 and to publicly funded voluntary hospitals with effect from October 21, 1999. From that date, the Act was also extended to voluntary organisations which provide substantial public mental health services or services to persons with an intellectual disability in respect of those services.[103] Thus, it extends to what were previously referred to as health board hospitals (now under the aegis of the Health Service Executive),

---

[97] The discussion that follows refers in general terms only to the provisions of the Data Protection Acts 1998 and 2003.

[98] See Freedom of Information Act 1997, s.2.

[99] As to what "relating to" means, in this and other contexts, see *EH v. Information Commissioner* [2001] I.E.H.C. 182; [2002]3 I.R. 600.

[100] Freedom of Information Act 1997, s. 2.

[101] Date of commencement of the Act was April 21, 1998 (with the exception of its application to local authorities and (the then) health boards).

[102] Freedom of Information Act 1997 (Local Authority and Health Board) (Commencement) Order 1998 (S.I. No. 397 of 1998).

[103] Freedom of Information Act 1997 (Prescribed Bodies) Regulations 1999 (S.I. No. 329 of 1999).

general practitioners in the general medical service in respect of eligible patients and public voluntary hospitals receiving a subvention out of public funds. Although access to records is limited generally to those that came into existence after the coming into force of the Act, or to other specified documents, with limitation as to time or subject-matter,[104] insofar as health care records are concerned, no such limitation applies where access is sought by the person whose records they are.[105] Where a request for medical records is otherwise made, e.g. by the parents or guardians of minors, or the administrators of the estate of a deceased, records created before the commencement of the Act may also be disclosed.[106]

Access to health care records

Although the Act confers a broad right of access to records held by health care providers to whom the Act applies,[107] and the offering of access, on request, represents the default position, a request for personal information (including personal information relating to a deceased individual) must be refused[108] by the head except where:

(a) the information concerned relates to the requester concerned,

(b) any individual to whom the information relates consents to disclosure to the requester,

(c) information of the same kind as that contained in the record in respect of individuals generally is available to the general public,

(d) the information was given to the public body concerned by the individual to whom it relates and the individual was informed on behalf of the body, before its being so

---

[104] Freedom of Information Act 1997 s.6(4).

[105] *Ibid.,* s.6(5).

[106] *Ibid.,* ss.1(2), (3), 6(4). S.6(4) was modified by the Freedom of Information Act 1997 (Section 6(4)(b)) Regulations 1999 so as to make available without limit as to time the records of minors and deceased persons under regulations made pursuant to the provisions to s. 28(6). These Regulations are discussed further at p.63 *infra*.

[107] Freedom of Information Act 1997 s. 6(1).

[108] *Ibid.,* s. 28(1).

given, that the information belongs to a class of information that would or might be made available to the general public, or

(e) disclosure of the information is necessary in order to avoid a serious and imminent danger to the life or health of an individual.[109]

In addition, if access to the record concerned would, in addition to involving disclosure of personal information relating to the requester, also involve disclosure of personal information relating to an individual or individuals other than the requester, subject to the other provisions of the Act, it must be refused.[110]

Considering these provisions in light of the general canons in relation to patient confidentiality,[111] it is readily apparent that (a) and (b) merely reflect the general prohibition – at common law and ethically and, probably, constitutionally – on the non-consensual disclosure *simpliciter* (i.e. in the absence of a countervailing public interest favouring disclosure) of confidential information.

The provisions in (c) and (d) manifestly take the information outwith the definition of confidential information in, for example *X v. Y*.[112] Paragraph (e) reflects a public interest exception that is well described in *Tarasoff v. Regents of the University of California*[113] and *W v. Egdell*.[114]

Therefore, in general terms, notwithstanding the default right of access conferred by the Act, a request for personal information must be refused unless one of the exceptions applies. Where granting the request is permissible under either paragraph (a) or (b), there is an obvious requirement that the head, before granting the request, is satisfied as to the identity of the requester, or individual.[115]

---

[109] *Ibid.,* s. 28(2).

[110] Freedom of Information Act 1997 (Section 28(1)) (Amendment) Regulations 1998 (S.I. No. 521 of 1998).

[111] See, Casey P & Craven C, *Psychiatry and the Law* (1999, Oak Tree Press), chap. 20.

[112] [1988] 2 All E.R. 648.

[113] (1976) 131 Cal. Rptr 14 (Supreme Court of California).

[114] [1990] 1 All E.R. 835 (CA).

[115] Special procedural provisions apply to requests for personal information that would otherwise fall to be refused where, in the opinion of the head concerned,

Specifically, where the request in respect of personal information relates to a record of a medical or psychiatric nature[116] relating to the requester and, the head is of the opinion that disclosure of the information concerned to the requester might "be prejudicial to his or her physical or mental health, well-being or emotional condition",[117] (s)he may decide to refuse to grant the request.[118] However, a blanket refusal of any disclosure is not permitted. Thus, where a request that would otherwise have been granted is refused on this ground, there must be included in the notice of refusal from the head a statement to the effect that, if the requester so requests, access will be provided to the records concerned to "such health professional having expertise in relation to the subject-matter of the record as the requester may specify".[119] A "health professional," in this context, means a registered medical practitioner or dentist, or a member of any other prescribed class of health worker[120] or social worker.[121]

Access under the Freedom of Information Act 1997 in action

Apart from the decision of the Supreme Court in *NMcK v. Information*

---

on balance (a) the public interest that the request should be granted outweighs the public interest that the right to privacy of the individual to whom the information relates should be upheld, or (b) the grant of the request would benefit the individual. See, Freedom of Information Act 1997, s.29. These are beyond the remit of the present discussion.

[116] Identical provisions apply to requests for records kept for the purposes of, or obtained in the course of the carrying out of, social work in relation to the requester.

[117] This phrase is virtually identical to that used in the Mental Health Act 2001, s. 10(2) justifying non-disclosure of the purpose of an examination carried out with a view to recommending a patient's involuntary detention in a psychiatric facility.

[118] Freedom of Information Act 1997 s. 28(3).

[119] *Ibid.,* s. 28(4).

[120] Clinical psychologists and social workers were prescribed by the Freedom of Information Act 1997 (Classes of Health Professionals) Regulations 2001 (S.I. No. 368 of 2001).

[121] Freedom of Information Act 1997 s. 28(7). In this regard, it should be noted that the base definition is considerably more restrictive than that contained in the Data Protection (Access Modification) (Health) Regulations 1989 dealing with the same practical problem, although slightly differently expressed.

Commissioner[122] – which is the subject of separate discussion later in this chapter[123] – there has been no express judicial consideration of the statutory provisions in relation to access to personal information. However, the published decisions of the Information Commissioner, a number of which are now considered on a thematic basis, are instructive as to how health care providers should approach requests for health care records – and indicative of how some such requests are dealt with.

Records to which the Act applies – records of private medical attendance in a public hospital

As already set out, the Act of 1997 does not apply to all health care providers and those providing private health care do not ordinarily fall within its ambit. In *Commissioner's Case 99125,* the requester had been seen privately by a consultant while he was being treated in a public (day) hospital. He applied to the then Mid Western Health Board for access to all of his medical records relating to his hospital treatment. The Board released 47 records but refused access to other records on the basis, *inter alia*, that records held by the private consultant were not held by or under the control of the Board.[124] The Commissioner found that there was no evidence to justify a finding other than that the consultant held the records of the requester's treatment as a private patient. Therefore, release under the Act of 1997 could not be directed since the records were not under the control of a public body. It was not considered relevant that the consultant also provided services to public patients in the Health Board area since her contract with the Board allowed her to have a private practice.

It merits noting, however, given how hospital records are compiled,

---

[122] [2006] I.E.S.C. 2 *aff'g* High Court (Quirke J) reported at [2004] 1 I.R. 12.

[123] See, pp.63-68, *infra*.

[124] The other ground of refusal was that the records of the requester's attendance at the day hospital had been destroyed with his agreement in 1997; the Commissioner found that it was reasonable to conclude that the paper file of the patient's day hospital attendance had been destroyed in the circumstances described by the Board and he accepted the hospital's assertion that any computer records of the requester's attendance had been deleted since the hospital's computer system was modified.

this conclusion should not be considered of general applicability. The situation presented by this case is not, after all, unusual or exceptional. By virtue of the structure of our health services, it is not unusual for a person to be treated in a public hospital – to which the Act of 1997 applies – yet under the private care of a consultant otherwise employed there in a public capacity with a contractual right to private practice. It is surely artificial to characterise the consultant's records, in such circumstances, as "private" and outwith the application of the Act. At the very least, in part, they must almost invariably form part of the records under the actual, physical control of the public hospital; they will self-evidently relate to the requester. In any event, having regard to the discussion in the previous section of this Chapter, there seems no good reason in logic or principle why, notwithstanding the apparent limiting of the provisions of the Act of 1997 to public bodies, access to "private" records held by a hospital should not be granted, in any event, as a matter of routine, subject to a risk of harm exception; even then, this would hardly justify a blanket refusal.

Adverse consequences of granting access?

A strange example of access to records having been refused – on a ground that hardly seems credible, having regard to the principles just elaborated – is found in *Commissioner's Case 000453*. Here the requester sought access to his medical records, which were in the possession of his former GMS general practitioner. The then area health board initially had difficulty retrieving the records from the general practitioner but finally obtained possession and granted partial access claiming that full release would undermine the working relationship between GMS general practitioners and the health board. In addition, it was claimed that where a GMS doctor has objections to release of a patient's records, release under FOI could jeopardise working relationships and lead to less information being recorded in future. This, it was claimed, would have a deleterious effect on the delivery by the health board of its services. Having regard to what has already been set out in relation to the duty to keep records and what the common law position, in this jurisdiction, probably is and the penumbra of the European Convention on Human Rights, this seems an extraordinary position for a statutory body to have adopted.

In *McInerney v. MacDonald*[125] LaForest J. dealt with such a scenario in robust terMs He stated:

> "The concern that disclosure will lead to a decrease in the completeness, candour and frankness of medical records, can be answered by reference to the obligation of a physician to keep accurate records. A failure to do so may expose the physician to liability for professional misconduct or negligence. It is also easy to exaggerate the importance of this argument, certainly physicians may become more cautious in what they record, but it cannot be assumed as a natural consequence that this will detrimentally affect the standard of care given to the patient. Generally, I doubt that the quality of medical records will be measurably affected by a general rule allowing access to the patient."[126]

The Commissioner noted that, although the general practitioner had concerns over the release of his records, at least two other medical practitioners had not objected to the release of their records and neither the general practitioner in question nor the then health board furnished any concrete evidence to suggest their concerns were well founded. Accepting that the possible future modification by doctors of their recording of information would constitute an adverse effect, no evidence was presented to support the likelihood of such an outcome and the Commissioner found that section 21(1)(b) did not apply to the records.

He also found that the evidence supplied to him, in support of the view that the information in the records should not be directly released to the requester, fell short of supporting the view that direct access to the records might result in a "real and tangible" possibility of prejudice to the physical or mental health, well being or emotional condition of the requester.[127] He found that section 28(3) did not apply and directed the release of the records.

---

[125] (1992) 93 D.L.R. (4th) 415.
[126] *Ibid.,* p.429.
[127] This aspect is considered further, at p.58, *infra.*

Third party information

In *Commissioner's Case 99001*, the requester, who, as a minor, had been in the care of a health board, sought access to all files relating to her. Access to a large number of the records was granted but, pursuant to section 26 of the Act, access was refused to certain records containing information supplied by her parents. On the Commissioner's review, the requester's parents were notified and they objected to the release of the information. The Commissioner found that the records contained personal information about members of the requester's family (other than her) or joint personal information relating to them. In order to meet the test of the exception set out in section 28(2)(e) of the Act, it was considered that there must be serious and imminent risk to life or health and the danger must be grave and impending or close at hand: a clear link must be established showing that disclosure of the information is necessary to avoid the harm.

Having regard to the various public interests involved, (in the provision of measures which protect and promote the health and psychological welfare of the public, in individuals who had been in the care of the State having access to information relevant to the decisions made concerning them, in members of the public knowing how public bodies perform their functions and in individuals ensuring that personal information held by public bodies about them is accurate) he found that there was a public interest in protecting the right to privacy (insofar as public bodies had to be able to continue to perform their functions in cases of this nature) and that the protection of personal privacy afforded by section 28 was intended to be strong.

The substance of the information relating to the requester, her family and the performance of the health board had been released and the Commissioner decided that the public interest that the request be granted did not outweigh the public interest that the right to privacy should be upheld. Insofar as the records of meetings attended by the requester were concerned, it was found that the invasion of privacy was minimised as the requester, having attended the meetings, ought to have been aware of the information and there was a public interest in a participant at a meeting with a public body knowing that the public body accurately recorded the meeting.

The underlying approach of the Commissioner must surely be

considered correct on principle and equally applicable to cases of third party and collateral histories, frequently – if not invariably – obtained in the mental health services. This is reflected in the next Commissioner decision to be described *Commissioner's Case 99077*. Here, the requester, through his solicitor, sought access from the then South Eastern Health Board to records relating to his admission to, and treatment in, a psychiatric hospital. He was given access to a number of records but three were withheld: (i) of a conversation between a staff member and a member of the requester's family, regarding his behaviour and condition, (ii) of a doctor's own views in relation to the applicant's mental health status and (iii) the current address of the requester's wife.

The Commissioner decided that section 26(1)(b) could only apply to a record prepared by a health board official, where disclosure of the information in question would constitute a breach of a duty of confidence. He accepted that there was an equitable duty of confidence owed by the board to the member of the requester's family and that whereas section 26(1)(b) is not subject to the public interest test set out at section 26(3), there can be circumstances in which a duty of confidence may be breached in the public interest. He considered that there was a strong public interest in a patient being able to gain access to his clinical records which describe aspects of his medical history, and which might have had a bearing on diagnosis or treatment and, also in maintaining the confidential nature of the relationship between a doctor and other members of a patient's family. Such confidentiality might be set aside in the public interest in cases where, for example, the information imparted formed the sole basis for subsequent treatment the consequence of which proved traumatic; or where the information appeared not to have been given in good faith.

In this case, it was noted that the information contained in the record was already substantially known to the requester. The Commissioner found that, if he had to consider section 26(3) in this case, he would not have found that the public interest was, on balance, better served by the release of this record to the requester. That said, he also found that section 26(1)(b) did not apply to the record containing the views of the doctor about the requester's mental health status. Rather, it related to personal information about the requester. No argument had been made that release of that information might be prejudicial to the requester's physical or mental health, well-being or emotional condition, and its release was directed. He also considered that the record, showing the current address of the requester's wife, was information held by the health board on the understanding that it would be treated by it as confidential. He found that the record's contents amounted to personal information about her and was exempt from release to the requester under section 28(1). The public interest did not warrant the release of that record.

In terms of setting out basic common law principles, this must be considered to represent the correct approach.

Access to records prejudicial to physical or mental health

Where the head considers that the granting of direct access to medical or psychiatric records to a requester might be prejudicial to his physical or mental health, well-being or emotional condition (s)he can, of course, refuse the request but must, in such circumstances, release them to a health professional nominated by the requester. Such was the case in *Commissioner's Case 99189* where the requester's request for access to his medical records was refused by the health board which held the records on the grounds that section 28(3) of the Act of 1997 applied to all of the records; pursuant to section 28(4), however, the board offered to make the records available to a health professional nominated by the requester. This offer was rejected and the matter proceeded for the determination of the Commissioner.

The Commissioner considered that the records in this case should be considered as a single composite record, in view of the fact that all the records at issue were medical records and were necessarily interlinked. He was of the view that the test, in deciding whether section 28(3) had been correctly invoked by the board, was whether the release of the records in question "might" be considered to be prejudicial to the requester's "physical or mental health, well-being or emotional condition." The Commissioner also considered that there should be evidence of a real and tangible possibility of harm being caused to the general health, welfare and good of the requester as a result of direct access to the records in question. He noted that the board had the explicit advice of four separate psychiatrists that release of the records to the requester might well be prejudicial to his health and welfare; he considered that it would be fair to say that the views expressed by the psychiatrists went well beyond the standard of proof implicit in the use of the word "might". The Commissioner concluded that the board was justified in deciding to refuse the requester direct access to the records in question.[128]

Although the conclusion is both eminently sensible and practical, and amenable to objective examination as to its reasonableness, it could be argued that the bar was set relatively high: "might" can reasonably be interpreted as denoting nothing more than a mere possibility of harm, rather than the "real and tangible" possibility of harm identified as necessary by the Commissioner. The language of "real and tangible" suggests a higher threshold. In this regard it might be noted that insofar as data protection legislation is concerned, a probability of harm is required to justify a refusal of disclosure.[129] In addition, in terms of the extent of the harm, as distinct from its likelihood, mere "prejudice" is all that is necessary. Thus a risk of harm is sufficient, serious harm is unnecessary.[130] Finally, the prejudicial effect must be on the person's health, well-being or emotional condition. These are expressed in the alternative, and not cumulatively, thus lowering the statutory threshold, on a strict interpretation, for withholding records even further.

Form and extent of access

An example of issues that may arise in requests is found in *Commissioner's Case 99265*. Here, the requester made a request to the former Eastern Health Board for records relating to his late sister who died in the Central Mental Hospital in the 1970s.[131] A copy of her hospital medical file, and copies of correspondence between the requester and the hospital since

---

[128] In support of his case for direct access to the records, the requester claimed that a number of the exceptions to s.28, i.e. ss 28(2)(a), 28(2)(c), 28(2)(e), 28(5)(a) and 28(5)(b), were applicable to the records but the Commissioner did not accept those arguments.

[129] See Data Protection (Access Modification) (Health) Regulations 1989, reg.4 and the Data Protection (Access Modification) (Social Work) Regulations 1989, reg. f. (S.I. Nos. 82 and 83 of 1989), where the corresponding phrase is "would be likely".

[130] See also, Data Protection (Access Modification) (Health) Regulations 1989 reg.4 and the Data Protection (Access Modification) (Social Work) Regulations 1989, reg. f (S.I. Nos. 82 and 83 of 1989), where the corresponding phrase is "serious harm".

[131] The issue of access to the records of a deceased person is considered more fully at p.68, *infra*.

1987 were furnished and the hospital offered to let the requester inspect the daily record books held at the hospital rather than copy them because of the size of the books, their physical layout and the fact that the books also contained entries relating to other patients. It said no other records existed in relation to the requester's sister. It also refused to release records which might reveal whether the staff, who attended his late sister on the night of her death, were still alive.

The Commissioner found that although there was evidence of the existence of other documents, the searches conducted by the hospital had been reasonable and he upheld its decision to refuse to release such further records on the grounds of section 10(1)(a) (all reasonable steps had been taken). In respect of section 12(2)(a) of the Act (which allows for a public body to provide access to records in a form, other than that requested, where to provide an alternative form of access "would be significantly more efficient"), he found that, although the Act does not expressly identify to which of the parties (requester or public body) the test of "significantly more efficient" is meant to apply, regard should be had to the requirements of *both* parties. The Commissioner also found information concerning whether the staff of the hospital, who attended the requester's late sister on the night of her death, were still alive, to be personal information about those staff. This conclusion must be considered unexceptional.

Amendment of health care records

Section 17 of the Act of 1997 provides for the amendment of a record containing personal information held by a public body where the record is incomplete, incorrect or misleading. Similar provision is made in respect of the records of minors, those under a disability and deceased persons.[132] Having regard to the definition of "personal information", this clearly includes health care records too. It is, of course, essential, that such records are complete, correct and not misleading in any respect. That requirement naturally arises from the nature of such records, and the purposes for which they are kept, the broad basis of which has already been discussed

---

[132] Freedom of Information Act 1997 (Section 17(6)) Regulations 2003 (S.I. No. 265 of 2003).

in this chapter.[133]

But, health care records do not simply come into existence in an instant: they are compiled over time, by many people and the information is, initially, almost inevitably incomplete, the conclusions, at the beginning, only tentative and – if read in isolation – potentially misleading and incorrect. They record the best considered views of those who compile them, at the point in time when they are made and the conclusions evolve as more information becomes available. In general terms, they must be considered, when ethically compiled, to represent honestly what the clinicians and others believe to be the situation at the time. If it subsequently transpires that the conclusions reached are incorrect, this is usually recorded. Insofar as clinical matters are concerned, this is generally self-evident if not expressed to be so.

An issue arises, however, in respect of other, what might be best considered to be, historical or social information obtained as part of the taking of an ordinary clinical history. Thus, for example, the manner in which an injury was caused is highly relevant for a whole variety of reasons – both for immediate and long-term management. Also, whether or not a person is (or might be) an intravenous drug user is also highly relevant for clinical purposes. And, it is not as if anyone really believes that all patients are wholly honest with their medical attendants all the time. That is counter-intuitive.[134] In the circumstances, therefore, medical records often contain speculative – but relevant entries – usually prefixed by one or more question-marks. If such a tentative conclusion subsequently turns out to have been incorrect, should the record be liable to amendment by deletion of any reference to it?

Such an issue arose in *Commissioner's Case 020220*. In 1994 the applicant was treated at the accident and emergency department of Cork University Hospital for a wound in his thigh. The hospital records of the treatment contained references to the wound having been ". . .? self inflicted . . ." or "self inflicted". In July 2001 the applicant applied to the then Southern Health Board pursuant to the provisions of section 17 of the Act of 1997 to have the references in the hospital records as to the

---

[133] P.25, *supra*.

[134] See, for example, *Caffrey v. North Eastern Health Board*, unreported, High Court, February 10, 1995, Johnson J.

source of his stab wound amended; the references clearly conveyed that the wound was, or may have been, self-inflicted whereas the applicant contended that the wound was inflicted by a third party.

The initial decision of the board, given in October 2001, was that it was prepared to add an amendment to the hospital file the effect of which was to delete the term "self" from the reference "self-inflicted". The board subsequently clarified that this amendment would be by way of addition to the record and would not involve the deletion of any part of the original record. This decision was upheld on internal review. On review of this decision the Commissioner found, in the case of one of the records in question, that it should be amended by the deletion of the words "self inflicted" from that record. In the case of a second record he found that, while no deletion or alteration of the text of the record was necessary, a statement should be attached, the effect of which would be to delete the term "self".

Apart from the obvious difficulty of how the words should actually be deleted (by *Tipex*, striking-through?) surely a dated and signed interlineation would be more appropriate, less confusing and more honest and consistent with the purpose and objective of clinical records? Records that have been altered, without annotation or dating give rise to their own probleMs In *Philip v. Ryan*[135] an admitted alteration of clinical records, which only emerged during the course of the trial of a medical negligence action, notwithstanding that the defendant urologist's legal advisers had been informed of the fact some weeks beforehand, was held to warrant an award of aggravated damages. McCracken J. had " ...no doubt that this is a classic example of a case where such damages can and should be awarded."[136]

Access to records of minors, disabled and deceased persons

General

One area that can give rise to practical difficulties in the implementation of the Freedom of Information Act 1997 relates to the granting of access to the health care records of minors and those under a disability to parents

---

[135] [2004] 4 I.R. 241 *rev'g*, in part, Peart J. [2004] I.E.H.C. 77.
[136] *Ibid.*, p.257.

or guardians, and those of a dead person to certain others. The matter is dealt with by the Freedom of Information *Act 1997* (Section 28(6)) Regulations 1999[137] which provides for access, subject to certain conditions, in each category, which are now considered in turn.

Minors and the mentally incapacitated

The section 28(6) Regulations provide for the grant of a request for personal information where a parent or guardian requests the records of a person who is a minor or who, having attained full age, has a mental condition or mental incapacity or severe physical disability, the incidence and nature of which is certified by a registered medical practitioner and who, on that account, is incapable of exercising his or her rights under the Act[138] where access to records would, in the opinion of the head and having regard to all the circumstances, be in their best interests. In this area, regard must also be had to any guidelines drawn up and published by the Minister.[139]

The wording of the regulations is clear and the use of the apparently permissive "may" in section 28(6) does not confer some kind of unfettered discretion on the head to grant or refuse to grant the request. The regulations must be read in the context of the clear language of sub-sections (1) and (6) of section 28 of the Act of 1997 and the purpose of the Act as a whole.

In *NMcK v. Information Commissioner*,[140] a case which involved the refusal of the granting of access to the applicant to his daughter's health care records, Quirke J., at first instance, stated, in relation to the section 28(6) Regulations:

---

[137] S.I. No. 47 of 1999. Identical provisions are found in respect of ss. 17 and 18 of the Act of 1997: Freedom of Information Act 1997 (Section 17(6)) Regulations 2003 (S.I. No. 265 of 2003) (amendment of records relating to personal information) and Freedom of Information Act 1997 (Section 18(5A)) Regulations 2003 (S.I. No. 266 of 2003) (right of person to information regarding acts of public bodies affecting the person).

[138] Freedom of Information Act 1997 (Section 28(6)) Regulations 1999, reg3(1)(a).

[139] The Guidelines, approved by the FOI Interdepartmental Working Group in March 1999, are stated to have been prepared under s. 28(6) of the Act of 1997.

[140] [2006] I.E.S.C. 2 *aff'g* Quirke J. [2004] 1 I.R. 12; [2004] I.E.H.C. 45.

> "*Prima facie* the terms of Article 3 (1) of the 1999 Regulations are imperative and positive requiring that access to appropriate records *shall* be granted where the requester is a parent or guardian and where the record relates to a minor (as in this case)."[141]

Insofar as the section 28 Guidelines approved by the FOI Interdepartmental Working Group in March 1999 are concerned, these do not form part of the legislative framework. Insofar as decision makers are advised by those Guidelines to put themselves in the place of the person to whom the records relate when examining requests by parents or guardians for access, it should be noted that the section 28(6) Regulations are quite clear and that substituted judgment is not mandated and is value-laden. The Guidelines in relation to the granting of access to the records of minors that are held in the minor's own right, e.g. in relation to certain health care records merit being approached with caution given the provisions, in particular, of the Non-Fatal Offences Against the Person Act 1997, section 23, and recent dicta of the Supreme Court on the rights of parents in respect of making decisions for their minor children.[142]

In *Commissioner's Case 000078*, the requester sought access to a number of records concerning appointments between his son and a clinician in the Brothers of Charity (who had been providing services to his son). The requester had been present at some but not all of these appointments. Access was refused under section 28(1) on the grounds that release of the information would disclose personal information about a person other than the requester. The records contained information about:

(i) The son alone,
(ii) the son closely intertwined with personal information about his mother, and
(iii) the requester intertwined with personal information about his son.

---

[141] [2004] 1 I.R. 12 at 18.

[142] See, in particular, *North Western Health Board v. HW* [2001] 3 I.R. 622: " . . . a presumption exists that the welfare of the child is to be found in the family exercising its authority as such." (*per* Hardiman J. at 755) and *AO & DL v. Minister for Justice* [2003] 1 I.R. 1 "A decision about a child's medical treatment is, *prima facie*, within the authority of his family." (*per* Hardiman J. at 159).

Having considered the public interest factors, the Commissioner concluded that no right of access arose under section 28(5)(a) (i.e. the public interest that the request should be granted did not outweigh the public interest that the right to privacy of the individual to whom the information related should be upheld). Insofar as the section 28(6) Regulations were concerned, the Commissioner commented that they do not provide a basis for releasing records, or parts of records, which contain personal information relating both to a minor and a third party (joint personal information) except where the third party is the requester. This must be considered correct. Although the requester was the father and joint guardian of his son and that, accordingly, the first requirement of the regulations was met, the Commissioner then indicated that it would be necessary for him to be satisfied that access to records in categories (i) and (iii) would serve his son's best interests.

The Brothers of Charity contended that release of the records would have a detrimental effect on the trusting relationship between the clinician and the son, especially in relation to those records relating to meetings at which the requester was not present. They were concerned that release would undermine the confidential relationship which they believed must exist, if their professional involvement with the son was to be successful. The requester made the point that he doubted if a child of ten years may have spoken in confidence to the clinician. However, the Commissioner accepted that the son did speak to the clinician in confidence and that it was important that the confidential nature of that relationship be protected. In addition, the Commissioner noted that the minor's mother had said she would not continue to provide to the Brothers of Charity any information concerning herself or her son, in the event that access to the records was granted, and that this would not be in the son's best interests.

The Commissioner expressed the view that where there is conflict between the parents of a minor as to how the minor's best interests are to be served, strong supporting evidence before departing from the position adopted by any professionals involved in the welfare of that minor was required. This was not to say that the professionals have a monopoly of wisdom in the matter and that their position cannot be rejected but that he accepted that the position adopted by the professionals, acting in good faith, should not be disturbed except in the light of strong supporting evidence. No such evidence having been put before him, he found that access to the records in question was not authorised by reference to section 28(6).

Assuming the father to be the joint guardian of the minor, this decision of the Commissioner must be read in the context of what Quirke J. said (later) in *NMcK*. There, of course, there was no parental conflict as such – the mother had died and the child was living with a maternal uncle and his wife. All three were joint guardians of the child and the relationship between them seems to have been strained. Quirke J. stated:

> "... the appellant, as a parent, joint guardian and joint custodian of the child concerned enjoys the parental primacy identified by Hardiman J. in *North Western Health Board v. HW* and the presumption that he has the welfare of his child at heart in the absence of evidence to the contrary. (citation omitted)
>
> The presumption is of course rebuttable, but there is no suggestion of rebuttal in this case.
>
> Reluctance by another family member to agree to access does not, in the absence of any supporting evidence, amount to rebuttal sufficient to displace the said presumption."[143]

Quirke J., accordingly, was satisfied that the Commissioner had misconstrued the provisions of section 28(6) and regulation 3(1) of the section 28(6) Regulations "by failing to recognise that the decisions of the parents of minors are presumed to be in the best interests of that minor in the absence of evidence to the contrary."[144] The essence of the court's conclusion is that the onus is not on the parent, in such circumstances, to prove that (s)he has the minor's best interests at heart. Rather, the onus is on others to displace it. To what standard, however, is less than clear.

Affirming the decision of the High Court, Denham J. (for a unanimous Supreme Court) stated:

> "As a matter of Constitutional and family law a parent has

---

[143] [2004] 1 I.R. 12 at 21.
[144] *Ibid.*

rights and duties. In general a parent would expect to be given and would be given medical information about his or her child. It would only be in exceptional circumstances that medical information about a child would not be given to a parent/guardian ....

The Commissioner erred in determining that release of the medical information would only be directed where there is tangible evidence that such release would actually serve the best interests of the minor.

The Act of 1997 and the Regulations fall to be interpreted in accordance with the Constitution. A parent, the requester, has rights and duties in relation to a child. It is presumed that his or her actions are in accordance with the best interests of the child. This presumption while not absolute is fundamental. The Commissioner took an incorrect approach in requiring tangible evidence of the parent rather than applying the presumption that a parent was acting in the child's interests. The "tangible evidence" test of the Commissioner reversed the onus of proof."

She continued:

"A parent's rights and duties include the care of a child who is ill. As a consequence a parent is entitled to information about the medical care a child is receiving so that he or she may make appropriate decisions for the child, as his or her guardian. The presumption is that a parent is entitled to access such information. That position is not absolute. The circumstances may be such that the presumption may be rebutted. But the primary position is that the presumption exists. Consequently, the approach of the Commissioner was in error when he required "tangible evidence" that the release of such information would serve the best interests of the minor. The obverse is the correct approach. The presumption is that the release of such medical information would best serve the interests of the minor. However, evidence may be produced that it would not serve her interests, and, in considering the circumstances, her welfare is paramount. That issue did not arise in this case because of the erroneous approach of the Commissioner."

Insofar as the correct approach was concerned, Denham J. stated:

"The Commissioner should have approached the request by acknowledging that a parent is presumed to be entitled to access the information. However, the Commissioner may then proceed to consider any evidence which exists addressing the issue that it would not be in the minor's best interests that the parent should be furnished with such information."

In the circumstances, however, so much time had elapsed that the minor was, by the time of the Supreme Court decision, approaching her eighteenth birthday, and her views were "now …very relevant". Denham J. considered that "the effects of the delay cannot be ignored in view of the necessity to balance the changed circumstances, including the attitude of [the minor]". The matter was, accordingly, remitted to the Commissioner to enable it to be reconsidered in accordance with the correct test and the circumstances of the case.

Should the same considerations also apply in the case of those who are caring for mentally incapacitated adults? The regulations are identical although the constitutional position is considerably less clear. Whatever practical view one might take of the societally beneficent approach of family and other carers, the fact remains that their position as lawful proxy consent givers, in our current legislative regime, is fraught with difficulty. The presumptions that exist in relation to parents and their minor children, irrespective of one's world view, hardly extend to their adult, yet incapacitated, children.

Deceased persons

The section 28(6) Regulations also provide that access to the personal records of a deceased person may be granted to (a) the deceased's personal representative acting in due course of administration of the estate or any person so acting with his or her consent, (b) a person on whom a function is conferred by law in relation to the deceased or his or her estate acting in the course of performing that function, (e.g. a trustee or administrator) or (c) the spouse or next of kin of the deceased or such other person as the head considers appropriate, having regard to all the circumstances and any relevant ministerial guidelines.[145] Here, a "spouse" includes a divorced spouse and cohabitees.[146]

The language of the regulations is clear and the ministerial Guidelines are not part of the statutory framework. In particular, the provision in the guidelines there that "[t]here is no automatic access 'as of right' for spouses, partners, next of kin or other persons" arguably overstates the true statutory position quite significantly. This assertion can only be considered, as a matter of simple statutory construction, and correct syntax, to apply to "other persons".

Provisions affecting confidentiality of a deceased person's records other than section 28

Although it is proper, and required, that the head should have regard to the other provisions of the Act of 1997 when considering requests for access to the records of a deceased person, to invoke section 26 (information obtained in confidence), in the context of the definition of "personal information" is otiose, except, perhaps, in the circumstances of a third party or collateral history. Even that, however, should not result in non-disclosure of records *simpliciter*, but rather in limited non-disclosure. In any event, such a situation is also capable of being addressed even outwith the provisions of sub-section 3 of that section and by section 28(2)(b) and section 28(5).

The invoking of section 22 (danger of prejudice to an ongoing investigation or to a law enforcement matter) in the context of a deceased person where a coroner's inquest is pending seems hardly defensible. In fact, the non-disclosure of the clinical records of a deceased person to the next of kin who are entitled, as of right, to attend and be heard at an inquest – far from giving rise to a danger of prejudice to the coronial investigation – may well significantly hinder the conduct of the inquest.[147]

---

[145] Freedom of Information Act 1997 (Section 28(6)) Regulations 1999, reg.3(1)(b).
[146] *Ibid.*, reg.3(2).
[147] The provisions of the European Convention on Human Rights, art.2 should not be discounted here.

Such consideration should not be regarded as relevant to the head's decision making.

Having regard to the provisions of section 28 and the section 28(6) Regulations, it is clear that the approach that was previously adopted generically in relation to a deceased's records has been significantly circumscribed – at least to an extent. However, the practical differences are more apparent than real. Balancing the so-called "privacy rights" of a deceased person with the statutory rights of certain identified requesters to personal information in relation to a deceased does not, in the circumstances and on the plain face of the regulations, arise, despite the proposition to the contrary contained in the Guidelines. A question as to maintaining the confidential nature of the deceased's records may legitimately arise where the requester is not an administrator, executor, spouse or next of kin of a deceased. But, then again, it probably always did.

In this regard, it merits noting that in *Murray v. Commission to Inquire into Child Abuse*,[148] Abbott J., addressing the question of whether a deceased person had a right to his or her good name or reputation, having reviewed such authority as there was, stated that he could find:

> " ...no authority in the history of the common law asserting a right of the deceased to a good name or to any property rights. Indeed in the area of property rights, the common law from ancient times is noteworthy for the extremes to which the courts went to free up land from the rule of the grave as in the cases of the evolution of the fiction laden fines and recoveries procedures which evolved for the purpose of barring the entail, and the development of the rule against perpetuities. A similar approach was adopted with the onset of legislative intervention ...".[149]

He continued:

> " ...I find much force in the arguments ...that the provisions of the Constitution providing for rights of citizens should be

---

[148] [2004] I.E.H.C. 225, [2004] 2 I.R. 222.
[149] [2004] 2 I.R. 222 at 286.

interpreted literally. While a literal interpretation of the Constitution does not always find favour with the courts, I find that when such interpretation is tested schematically by testing it against other rights in the Constitution, such as the right to equality before the law, the right to bodily integrity, the right to inviolability of the dwelling and other rights of the living, I find that there is no place in the Constitution from where the rights of the deceased may be rationally inferred. I consider that it is necessary, for the purpose of disposal of the issues in this case, to decide on the issue notwithstanding that the plaintiffs do not directly represent the deceased ...".[150]

That said, the question of a deceased's "privacy" is an issue that may vex Freedom of Information officers who are charged with making decisions on requests for access to these records. *Commissioner's Case 000077* demonstrates how easily the thinking can become unnecessarily fuzzy in the area. In this case, the requester had sought access to the medical records of his late uncle and was informed by the hospital (St. Vincent's University Hospital, Dublin) that access to the records of a deceased person should be made either by the deceased's personal representative or by a person appointed by the courts or statute. The requester was unable to make the request in either capacity and the hospital refused to release the records on the grounds that it would breach the right to privacy of the requester's late uncle. Having applied to the Commissioner for review of the decision, he furnished the hospital with a letter from the sole surviving sister of his late uncle, authorising the release of the records to him.

The Commissioner noted that the hospital purported to rely on the ministerial Guidelines in telling the requester that the records of a deceased person could only be released to a person belonging to either of the first two categories of requester provided for in the section 28(6) Regulations and that the requester had not been informed that there was a third category which might cover the circumstances of his application. The hospital was, accordingly, invited to say whether or not it considered the requester an appropriate person to whom the records could be released and if not,

---

[150] *Ibid.*

to give its reasons.

The hospital stated that the requester had been unable to meet any of the conditions set out by it, and that he had indicated he was making his request in his capacity as a member of the public. However, it did not outline whether or not it considered him to be an appropriate person to whom the records might be released under the regulations.

The Commissioner, noting that the requester's uncle had died in 1992, and that he appeared to have the consent of the remaining surviving sibling and bearing in mind that it had not been argued against the requester that he was not an "appropriate" person, concluded that he was an appropriate person to whom the records may be released and he annulled the hospital's decision to refuse access.

The decision, both on the facts and on a proper construction of the Act and the regulations must be considered quite correct. But, even in such cases, as this demonstrates, a failure to formulate reasons on FOI grounds, in a specific instance, may well result in the annulling of a decision to refuse access to a deceased's records.

This is further illustrated in *Commissioner's Case 020561* which merits setting out in some detail. Here, the requester had sought access to the medical records of her late brother held by Cork University Hospital. He was unmarried and the requester and her two sisters were his nearest next of kin. The hospital refused the records on the grounds that release would involve the disclosure of the deceased's personal information and that section 28(1) applied. The decision was upheld on internal review: at no stage was section 28(6) adverted to.

In the course of the review, the requester provided the written consent of her two sisters to the release of the deceased's records. Having been informed of this development, and notwithstanding that one of the consenting sisters was named as the deceased's personal carer on hospital records, access was still refused.

Having regard to the section 28(6) Regulations, the Commissioner considered whether a right of access arose under the third category there, i.e. whether or not the requester was a person to whom it was considered "appropriate" to release the records. The Commissioner referred to the ministerial Guidelines and their suggestions as to factors that a public body should consider in deciding whether release of such records is appropriate in the circumstances. For example, the Commissioner's Decision states, "a balance must be struck between protecting the rights to privacy of the deceased and the right of the requester to gain access to the records. The nature of the records should be considered, as well as the wishes of the deceased, if known, in relation to the release of his or her records."

The simple reality is, however, that few people make dying wills, i.e. as to the disposal of their property on their death. Fewer still, it might reasonably be speculated, make testamentary – or, indeed, other - arrangements in relation to their personal medical records. It could hardly be considered to be high on the list of priorities of a solicitor taking instructions for a will. One can only wonder at the inclusion of such a matter in the Guidelines. Even in circumstances where a will purports to determine access to the records of a deceased, compliance with any such direction must, self-evidently, be problematic. Those considerations must apply *a fortiori* in relation to any "wishes" expressed in that regard.

In any event, the hospital, in this case, contended that the only circumstances in which it was appropriate to release the medical records of a deceased person was where there was an issue of serious risk to the health of another individual, or if there was a question as to the quality of the care a deceased person had received. It also suggested that the proper way for the records to be accessed was on foot of an order for discovery.

The Commissioner disagreed: she found that section 28(2)(e) already provides for the release of personal records in a broadly equivalent situation, where it was necessary in relation to a "serious risk to the health of another individual" and commented that it had to be assumed that the provisions of section 28(2)(e) and 28(6)(b) were different in nature. She also found that in the absence of a test requiring a prior arguable case for concluding that there may have been problems with the quality of care given to a deceased person - and sustaining such an argument would itself require access to records - the second ground identified by the hospital was unworkable.

In relation to the contention that access should only be by way of discovery, the Commissioner found that, while the existence of a likely alternative may have some bearing in relation to public interest arguments under section 28(5)(a), such an alternative was not in any way definitive in relation to the provision under consideration in this case (section 28(6)(b)).

These conclusions are, not alone, correct on principle, but eminently sensible too. In conclusion, having identified and having regard to a number of circumstances which she believed were reasonable to take into account the Commissioner found that the requester should be regarded as a next of kin to whom it was appropriate, "having regard to all the circumstances and to any relevant guidelines drawn up and published by the Minister" to release the medical records of the deceased. The Commissioner also commented, however, that there may be cases where, having regard to the prevailing circumstances, a requester who is a close next of kin may not be regarded as an "appropriate" person. Having regard to the clear language of the section 28(6) Regulations, that must be considered a highly arguable proposition.

Similar reasoning was applied, and a similar conclusion reached, by the Commissioner in *Commissioner's Case 031001*. The requester in this case was attempting to gather information about her deceased father (born 1906) and his family. The father had spent much of his childhood in an institution and little was known about his background. The daughter applied to the National Maternity Hospital, Holles Street, where her father was born, for information on whether her father had siblings and in relation to the age of her grandmother when he was born. The hospital refused her any information on the grounds of privacy (section 28) and confidentiality (section 26) and this decision was upheld following internal review. At no stage were the specific provisions governing the release of records relating to deceased persons adverted to nor did the hospital deal with the public interest provisions in sections 26 and section 28 (which must be considered where section 26(1)(a) or section 28(1) are invoked as the basis for refusal of access).

Although the hospital's attention was drawn to the public interest provisions of sections 26 and 28 and the specific provisions of section 28(6) and it made a submission in general terms, it did not address them specifically. The hospital also contended that the record was exempt from release on the basis of the provisions of section 21 and refused to release the record (only one relevant record existed).

The Commissioner did not agree with the hospital's contentions and found that the requester should be regarded as a next of kin to whom it was "appropriate" to release her late father's records.

CONCLUSION

Although a great deal has been written about freedom of information in the health care context, and health care institutions have properly implemented the Act of 1997 and designated Freedom of Information Officers for that purpose, having regard to the European Convention on Human Rights, and the decisions of the superior courts in other parts of the common law world, on one level, the Act does no more than codify what is the probable position at common law in this jurisdiction insofar as access to health care records is concerned; in doing no more than codifying the principles underlying the pre-existing ethical and legal rules, it breaks no new ground – except, perhaps, in the case of deceased persons. That it otherwise reduces doubt on the general issue, however, is one of its commendable features. That the statutory regime has potentially dented to a significant extent the pre-existing ethical obligation of confidence to deceased persons – without debate – is remarkable. That, however, is a matter for policy-makers. That, in practice, the new regime has not always accorded with what was previously done is regrettable and this, in spite of one useful assertion that the Guidelines do make, is unfortunate:

> "In general, members of the public will use the FOI Act to access information only when that information is not readily available through existing sources. Where access to records is currently routinely available to parents and guardians, or where the records of deceased persons are similarly available, these practices should continue. The provisions of section 28(6) will only be used when access is required to the specific range of records covered by that subsection where such routine access is not available."

That the section 28 Guidelines then, on one level, seek to resile from what the section 28(6) Regulations provide merely underscores a failure to apply principles elaborated over two and half millennia. How the courts will ultimately address the question of access to the records of deceased persons, and the apparent underlying policy shift expressed (perhaps unwittingly, depending on one's approach to statutory interpretation) in the section 28(6) Regulations and what definitive interpretation will apply to those regulations must await another day.

What might confidently be predicted, however, is that the Commissioner's reasoning in cases like *Commissioner's Case 000078* will not pass future.muster, having regard to the decision of the High Court in *NMcK* and its unanimous endorsement by the Supreme Court. How that decision will impact on requests for access to the records of mentally incapacitated adults remains to be seen. As noted, the constitutional considerations in such circumstances are manifestly different. Whether or not presumptions of a similar kind will be applied in the context of requests for access to the records of deceased persons will also have to await future determination. All that might reasonably be said is that we are only one case away from the answer and/or range of answers! But, decisions really don't have to be that difficult.

CHAPTER 3

Role of the Freedom of Information Liaison Officer

SINEAD BYRNE*[1]

INTRODUCTION

The objective of this chapter is to show the "human" side of Freedom of Information. It describes how the system is used and applied on a daily basis in the South Eastern Health Board (SEHB).[2]

To set the scene, the SEHB provides health, welfare, personal and social services to the people of Carlow, Kilkenny, Wexford, Waterford and Tipperary South Riding. Our population is approximately 424,000 which is a major undertaking. The FOI Acts set out clear responsibilities with regard to responding to FOI requests. In order for us to meet our obligations, we put in place a structure to ensure SEHB compliance.

SEHB FOI STRUCTURES

Initial request

When a FOI request is received it is assigned to a Research Officer. This person is the first point of contact for the requester. They consult with the requester as necessary,[3] gather files, schedule the documents, consult

---

* FOI Liaison Officer, South Eastern Health Board.
[1] This chapter is based on a presentation at the TCD School of Law Third Annual Conference on Freedom of Information 2004.
[2] Since January 1, 2005 the Health Service Executive (HSE) has been responsible for providing health and personal social services for everyone living in the Republic of Ireland thus amalgamating the ten former health boards under one executive.
[3] S.7(7) requires the head of a public body to help a requester if appropriate.

with health professionals and draft a preliminary decision. This is then presented to the Decision Maker who reviews the request, decision and exemptions used and then signs off the decision. Decision Makers are usually at Service Manager level.

Internal review

When a request for an internal review[4] is received, it is part of my role to review all aspects of the original decision including, for example, scope, exemptions used. I then prepare a draft internal review decision and present this to the Internal Reviewer. Internal Reviewers are generally at Regional Service Manager level.

Review by Information Commissioner

Naturally, we hope that the requester will understand the reasons for our decision. Inevitably, however, even where our decision clearly complies with the Freedom of Information Act, there will be occasions when a requester wants to appeal our decision further to the Information Commissioner.[5] As FOI Liaison Officer I am responsible for ensuring that all dealings with the Office of the Information Commissioner (OIC) are dealt with promptly and effectively.

FOI LIAISON OFFICER'S ROLE

In addition to ensuring effective procedures and compliance with the FOI policies, my role as FOI Liaison Officer also includes:-

Liaison with OIC (Office of the Information Commissioner)

Responding to request for records, drafting internal review decisions, making submissions on appeals and generally keeping our CEO out of prison by avoiding censure under section 37! This is one section of the

---

[4] S.14.
[5] S.34.

FOI Acts which confers powers on the Information Commissioner including:

- Requiring a person to furnish records.
- Requiring a person to attend before him or her.
- Authority to examine and take copies of records.
- Enter premises and examine records.

Non-compliance with such a request from the Information Commissioner under section 37 could result in a summary conviction to a fine not exceeding €1,500 or imprisonment for a term not exceeding 6 months. As you can appreciate, that is why requests by the Information Commissioner are my top priority.

Centre of expertise

We have built up a centre of expertise on FOI and related issues and provide advice and assistance to all staff in the SEHB. For instance, on the one hand we might get a request from the CEO seeking advice on the release of a report, and, on the other, a Clinical Nurse Manager may be enquiring about the release of documents from a patient's chart.

Training

We are responsible for training and induction of new staff and ongoing training of Research Officers, Decision Makers, and Internal Reviewers. Training includes not just FOI but Data Protection Principles and Administrative Access procedures, and best practice in areas such as record keeping and record management. Generally the focus of our training is to ensure that FOI does not have a negative impact on our record keeping.

National FOI Liaison Group

I am a member of the National FOI Liaison Group. The function of the Group is to share expertise, provide support and advice on complex cases, publish standard documents, standardise FOI procedures and strive for consistent application of FOI where possible and practical. We meet regularly to share expertise, provide support and advice on complex cases and we strive for consistent application of FOI where possible and practical.

Publications

I am also responsible for certain publications including those under sections 15 and 16.[6] In conjunction with the National Group, we have published a number of documents including a staff handbook on the principles of FOI, DP and Administrative Access, a public information leaflet on how to access personal information and we are preparing to publish a manual for staff on the handling of personal health information.

LEVELS OF ACTIVITY

The following statistics give an historical picture of the levels of activity in Freedom of Information:-

Year	Personal	Non-Personal	Total
2002	221	58	279
2003	432	96	528*
01.01.2004 to 30.06.2004	174	16**	190
2004	376	25	401
2005	462	33	495

* Increase of 89% overall
** Decrease of 75% in level of non-personal request on same period in 2003

---

[6] S.15 requires a public body to publish a reference book containing *inter alia* descriptions of its structure, organisation, functions, powers and duties and the classes of records held and how these may be accessed. A s.16 publication includes *inter alia* information regarding rules, procedures and interpretations used by the public body on any schemes it administers which apply to members of the public.

Media focus on the decline in usage of FOI requests is not reflected in the SEHB or in the health sector generally; all areas are showing an increase in the numbers of requests for personal information. The figures do, however, show a surge in requests prior to the coming into force of the 2003 Amendment Act.

The serial requester

We had what we referred to as a "serial requester". Some may have only heard of the phenomenon and others may have had experience of it. Certainly, most practitioners are familiar with it. In the first six months of 2003, 71 requests for non-personal information were received as compared to 25 for the last six months. 28 of the 71 requests were from one requester accounting for 40% of the non-personal requests for that period.

Post Amendment Act

Change in recording requests

The statistics for the first six months of 2004 do show some decline in levels of requests and this may be a levelling off of the numbers of requests generally. However, it is important to note that as a result of the FOI Amendment Act 2003, non-personal requests are being recorded differently. An example shows:-

• Pre-Amendment – a requester sends in one letter with five different requests for access to separate, unrelated documents; this is recorded as five requests.

• Post-Amendment – a requesters sends in one letter with €15 fee attached for five different requests as above; this is now recorded as one request.

Impact of health reform

The "National Request"

Another anomaly which will arise with the formation of the new Health Service Executive (HSE) is the concept of a "national request". The HSE is the new body under which all former Health Boards are governed: ten health areas are covered by the HSE as one organisation. This means that one request will cover the whole country. The following example shows the significant difference:-

- Pre-HSE – a requester seeking access to capital funding allocation on a countrywide basis. The requester must write to each individual health board area, of which there were 10. This is recorded as one non-personal request in each area (1 x 10) and a €15 fee was payable to each Health Board (€15 x 10).

- Post-HSE – same requester seeking access to the same records now need only apply once to the HSE with one €15 fee. The request is counted only once as a corporate non-personal request.

The anomaly is that the same amount of work is required in order to process the request as the HSE will not have centralised records. This will result in a significant decrease in the number of requests submitted to get the same information, i.e. from 10 down to one.

It is therefore my contention that the statistics may not be a true reflection of the volume of non-personal requests.

Factors That May Influence Levels of Requests

Any number of factors may influence the levels of requests, both personal and non-personal. Examples include:-

Increased publicity of FOI as a result of the Amendment Act

The increased media attention and high profile debate on the FOI Act and the Amendment Act has led to an overall increase in awareness of the FOI Act and its implications.

Media focus on child abuse issues and Residential Institution Redress Board

All Health Boards have dealt with a significant number of requests for access to records of applicants to the Redress Board.

Media focus on organ retention issues and the establishment of the Dunne Inquiry

This Inquiry resulted in a number of FOI requests for access to post mortem records and related files.

Ad hoc incidents

These may also influence the levels of non-personal requests. A significant example is the RTE Radio 1 *Live Line* programme on Nursing Homes. This resulted in a number of requests being received by all Health Boards for access to Nursing Home Inspection Reports.

TYPES OF RECORDS HELD BY SEHB

The types of records held by the SEHB will also be an influencing factor and, as an organisation providing approximately 2 million patient contacts per year, we hold a very large and diverse range of records:-

• Personal – hospital, General Practitioner, social work, psychiatric, risk management, community, etc.

• Corporate – service plans, policies, procedures, minutes of meetings, etc.

• Personnel – employee files, recruitment, industrial relations, etc.

• Financial – payroll, creditors, expenses paid to staff, payments to GPs and pharmacies, etc.

Requests for personal information

It follows that as the majority of our records are personal in nature, the most common type of request we deal with is for personal information; this is reflected in the statistics recording 80% of our requests in 2003 for access to personal information. These requests can, however, differ greatly in complexity for example, responding to a request for access to a discharge summary versus a request for access to all records of contacts held by SEHB. As a consequence, the volume of work involved in dealing with them also differs greatly. This is especially true in relation to the area of community care. In such cases potentially there can be large volume files considering the number of different services with which a single child may be in contact e.g., Speech & Language Therapy, Public Health Nurse, Psychology, Immunisation. Each Allied Health Professional holds a separate record and this can lead to a considerable amount of time and effort in gathering all relevant files.

DEALING WITH AN FOI REQUEST FOR PERSONAL INFORMATION

Step by Step Guide

There are a number of steps we take when a request is received; some are mandated by the FOI Acts and others have been developed as part of our FOI procedures and good practice.

Step 1:   Date stamp all requests received; assign to Research Officer; acknowledge receipt of request, advise requester of appeal rights and response date for request (20 working days from receipt) and also name and contact details of Research Officer.

Step 2:   Research Officer then gathers all original files that fall within the scope of the request. If necessary, they will contact the requester to seek more information or clarify exactly what is required.

Step 3:   Once the files are gathered, each page of the file is numbered and scheduled. This schedule gives details of the contents of each numbered page in the file. The file is then copied. Two copies are made; one is the FOI office file which will be retained once request is complete and the other is the requester copy.

Step 4:   The Research Officer reads the file, highlighting sections that may fall to be exempted and documents that will require further consultation.

Step 5:   The Research Officer will then contact the health professional currently or most recently involved in provision of care to the requester and also any other third parties who have contributed significant records. The opinion of these health professionals will form the basis of the decision on release of the documents.

Step 6: Once consultation is complete, the Research Officer will then draft the decision letter, detailing the specific exemptions used to withhold the relevant documents or parts of documents based on the health professional's advice. All these details are entered on the schedule of documents providing specifics on what is being released on each page.

Step 7: This decision is then presented to the Decision Maker. The Research Officer will spend some time detailing all steps taken, advices from relevant health professionals and any other factors that have influenced the decision. The Decision Maker can accept or amend the decision at this stage as the ultimate decision on release rests with them. Once the Decision Maker is satisfied that a well-founded and widely consulted decision has been reached, they will then sign off decision for release.

The most important point to note in this whole process is that consultation is of the essence.

THIRD PARTY REQUESTS

We also receive a considerable number of third party requests, from parents seeking access to children's records, to requests for access to deceased person's records.

Records of minor child/incapacitated adult

Requests from parents or guardians for access to records of a child or an incapacitated child/adult can vary greatly in complexity, for example:-

- Parents request details of hearing test of 13 year-old son;

- 15 year-old girl attends A&E for the morning after pill and mother requests access to the records;

- 11 year old boy in long term foster care, father seeks access to social work records.

Factors considered

There are a number of factors we must consider when making our decision including:-

- Seeking consent of the child;

- The child's capacity to understand the implications of the request and release;

- The nature of the record, e.g. hearing test versus psychological assessment report;

- The nature of the consultation with the child; is it by letter, face to face, etc;

- Guardianship & custody issues, i.e. who has access, is it limited by the Courts, etc;

- Advice from health professionals familiar with the case.[7]

Having regard to all the circumstances and taking notice of decisions published by the Information Commissioner and any relevant court judgments[8] we must then consider:-

- Is release in the best interests of the child?

- How to balance the rights of the parents v right of privacy of the child;

- Is there an alternative to releasing the records?

---

[7] S.28(3) and (4) refer to requests for personal information of records of a medical, psychiatric or social work nature where direct disclosure to the requester may be detremental to the requester's physical or mental well-being.

[8] For instance, *NMcK v Information Commissioner* [2006] I.E.S.C. 2; [2004] I.E.H.C. 4 is directly relevant.

For example would it satisfy the request of the parents if they were involved in care planning?

Viewing rather than releasing records?

Is there an alternative source of the information e.g. other family members?

Other exemptions may also apply to the records. In particular Social Work files may be protected under the Child Care Acts, information given in confidence may be included as part of the Child Sexual Abuse Notification, etc.

Records of deceased persons[9]

The Central Policy Unit (CPU) guidelines set out procedures for dealing with requests for access to deceased persons' records. They detail the categories of requester who may be granted access to such records and these are:-

• Personal representative;

• Person appointed by the courts or by statute;

• Spouses/former spouses, partners/former partners, next of kin;

• Other persons as may be considered appropriate.

As with parents requesting access to minor's records, there are considerations for the Decision Makers:-

• Did the deceased make any provision in their will or is it recorded in their file who can or cannot have access?

• The nature of the records will be a significant factor in the decision;

• Is there an alternative source where they can get the information to obviate the necessity to release the records e.g. other family members, treating Consultant?

---

9   S.28(6) and S.I. No. 47 of 1999 Freedom of Information Act 1997 (Section 28(6)) Regulations 1997.

No two requests are the same; each case must be judged on its own individual merits. We must try to balance the known wishes of the deceased against the right of the requester to access the records.

RECORD RETENTION IN SEHB

It is obvious that we deal with various levels of complexity in our requests. There are also other issues that need to be addressed. It has been mentioned that the SEHB provides approximately 2 million patient contacts per year; this generates a considerable volume of records. At the moment, the SEHB is retaining all its hospital files in paper form[10] and this is creating a significant "paper mountain". Capacity is a serious issue which needs to be addressed in the near future. In doing so, we must balance what is of value and what we need to keep versus storage capacity and availability of resources.

In order to address the issue of record retention, it is vital that we look at alternative methods of storage, e.g. microfiche or microfilm. In the interim, the National FOI Liaison Group produced a document entitled "Policy for Health Boards on Record Retention Periods" in 1999.[11] This provides guidelines on record retention periods for various types and categories of records, taking into account other legislative and legal requirements. We hope to commence work on updating this policy in the near future.

ADVANCES IN TECHNOLOGY

The anticipated move to the electronic patient record through the Hospital Information Systems Project (HISP) and an automated personnel system with PPARS (Personnel, Payroll & Related Systems) was expected to address some of our paper dependence in the coming years.

---

[10] A new policy is currently being developed with regard to Acute Hospital personal records and it is proposed to microfilm records of five years and older.
[11] http://www.mwhb.ie/Documents/PoliciesandProcedures/CorporateServices/ CustomerService/Policy-HealthBoardsOnRecordRetentionPeriod/ Document,16310,en.pdf

Hospital Information Systems Project (HISP)

Hopefully, the HISP project will provide the SEHB with a good foundation for the electronic patient record. It will provide one integrated system for use across acute hospitals in the area including modules such as Medical Records & Chart Tracking, Accident & Emergency, Admissions/Transfers/Discharges, Waiting Lists, etc. Once the basic modules are implemented and bedded down, they can be built upon with new modules, for example clinical notes. This will advance the use of the technology in our acute hospitals and will potentially lead to a fully electronic patient record, eliminating our reliance on paper records. It is hoped to roll this system out across the country and this will enhance the availability of statistics if all areas are working from a common technology platform.

PPARS (Personnel, Payroll & Related Systems)

PPARS is a new human resources and payroll system which was intended to be introduced in all the Health Service Areas and major Dublin hospitals. The vision had been for one linked personnel and payroll system and standardised best practice policies and processes throughout the Irish Health Services. The system was to cover the full spectrum to HR management incorporating recruitment, personnel administration, organisational management, personnel development including training and events and employee qualifications/professional registration, staff time management, travel expenses, payroll and a pension service repository. Now that the PPARS project has been shelved we are awaiting other possible answers to provide electronic databases.

CHANGING STRUCTURES IN HEALTH

Currently, and in the coming years, we see major reforms in the health sector. The Health Boards have become one public body under the Health Service Executive (HSE). As yet, no decisions have been made with regard to the FOI structures in the new HSE, is it to be a "shared service" or will we stay as we are currently? We'll have to wait and see.[12]

---

[12] In the move to the new structure under the HSE, the FOI function is now included under the Office of the CEO.

FOI now integral

While there are questions to be answered about future structures, it remains that FOI has become an integral part of the way we operate. We are constantly striving to make as much information available as possible through Administrative Access and we will continue to promote best practice in the areas of record keeping and record retention. We will also continue to work in conjunction with other initiatives and opportunities to improve our practices in all areas and, in particular, with the Accreditation process currently underway in our acute hospitals.

CONCLUSION

In conclusion, a quote from a speech by the Information Commissioner to the Public Affairs Ireland Group in October 2003–

> "FOI legislation on its own will not change the attitudes and the culture within those public bodies which have not already adopted work practices which support and enhance transparency and accountability."

To borrow a phrase from our politicians, "we've a lot done and a lot more to do."

CHAPTER 4

Freedom of Information: A Litigation Tool?

NIALL MICHEL*

INTRODUCTION

By way of introduction, I am an administrative and public lawyer and much of my daily work comprises of advising and assisting the Information Commissioner in carrying out her functions under the Freedom of Information Acts, 1997 and 2003 (to which I will also refer variously in this chapter as "the FOI Acts" and "the Acts"). I am at pains to point out, however, that the contents of this chapter should not be taken as representing the position of the Commissioner on any given point. I have also advised other persons, including public bodies coming under the Acts, as well as requesters, in relation to freedom of information matters.

I have been involved in all appeals to the High Court on points of law from decisions of the Commissioner since 1998 and was involved in various appeals to the Supreme Court from certain decisions of the High Court on such matters. I have acted as a solicitor-advocate in the High Court in some of these cases.

I should also say, to get the preliminaries out of the way, that, whilst I have tried to address my topic and carefully to construct an analysis of freedom of information as a litigation tool, this chapter does not purport to be a complete exposition of the topic, nor does it purport to amount to legal advice and should not be relied upon on either count.

I hope that these materials are nevertheless illuminating.

---

* Partner in Mason Hayes & Curran. This chapter is based on a paper which was delivered at Trinity College, Dublin, School of Law, Fourth Annual Freedom of Information Conference, Saturday, October 15, 2005.

In order to litigate, it is necessary to identify whether the law has a remedy for the grievance of the person considering litigation. In "lawyerspeak", this is known as identifying whether there is an established "cause of action". The law can only be applied to a set of facts – otherwise, there is nothing for it to be applied to. Establishing all the facts and, subsequently, analysing them carefully with a view to ascertaining whether there is a cause of action (and, if so, how strong the action might be), is therefore of critical importance. Any tool that assists in gathering information is, accordingly, going to be of utility to a litigant or, as the case may be, a person contemplating litigation.

Prior to the enactment of the Freedom of Information Act 1997 ("the FOI Act"),[1] in effect, the only enforceable information-gathering tool available to a litigant[2] was the pre-trial discovery-of-documents process.[3] However, following the introduction of a freedom of information ("FOI") regime in Ireland, a new facility came on stream, whereby, amongst other things:

(a)   recorded information held by public bodies could be obtained on foot of a statutory right to request access to the same;[4]

(b)   formally published documents were to be made available by public bodies, giving information about themselves, their remits and the classes of records held by them, together with information designed to facilitate the exercise of the right of access.[5]

---

[1]   The FOI Act was amended in 2003 by the Freedom of Information (Amendment) Act 2003. References in this chapter to the "FOI Act" include references to that Act as amended by the 2003 Act where the context so admits or requires.

[2]   Save, perhaps, the Data Protection Act 1988, the (then) Access to Information on the Environment Regulations 1996 (S.I. No.185 of 1996) and the National Archives Act 1986.

[3]   In the case of the Superior Courts, see O.31 of the Rules of the Superior Courts 1986 (as amended).

[4]   FOI Act, s.7.

[5]   *Ibid.*, s.15.

These could be helpful generally in any litigation involving public bodies, whether from the point of view of garnering an understanding of the bodies concerned, or what they say about themselves, or from the point of view of finding out how to seek access to records and how likely it is that the records one might be seeking will be held by the bodies concerned;

(c) formally published documents were to be made available by public bodies, setting out the rules, procedures, practices, guidelines and interpretations used by them, and an index of any precedents kept by them for the purposes of decisions, determinations or recommendations, under or for the purposes of any enactment or scheme administered by them with respect to rights, privileges, benefits, obligations, penalties or other sanctions to which members of the public are or may be entitled or subject under the enactment or scheme. These are to be complemented by appropriate information in relation to the manner or intended manner of administration of any such enactment or scheme.[6]

This is, perhaps, the more interesting of the "section 15 and 16 manuals" and, again, could be useful in litigation with a public body for a variety of reasons which it is not necessary to spell out here. Suffice it to say that a person seeking to litigate against a public body with regard to some act or ommission will doubtlessly find it of assistance to have available a document soberly prepared by the body concerned, setting out all of the above-mentioned matters 'on the record', as it were;

(d) incomplete, inaccurate or misleading information in records held by public bodies could be amended upon application.[7]

It might be interesting to use this to change the factual matrix of any litigation or contemplated litigation with a

---

[6] *Ibid.*, s.16.
[7] *Ibid.*, s.17.

public body (or, perhaps, another, or others), in that the successful amendment of a record pursuant to this facility could, for example, entirely change the import of a record which it might be considered relevant to adduce in the litigation, whether for, or against, the litigant concerned; and

(e) written statements of reasons and material fact-finding underpinning decision-making on the part of public bodies could be obtained upon application.[8]

This is potentially a highly valuable litigation tool that might be used in contemplated or actual litigation with a public body. Unusually, when compared with the primary statutory right provided for in the FOI Act (the right of access to records), section 18 provides for the creation by a public body of something new in response to the application made by an applicant under the Act, viz., —the written statement concerned. Its nature may become clearer when one realises that it mirrors, for example, a section[9] in Australian legislation known as the Administrative Decisions (Judicial Review) Act 1977. This Australian equivalent of section 18 of our FOI Act is found in a piece of legislation governing judicial review procedure, and entitles any person who is entitled to make an application to the Federal Court or the Federal Magistrates Court of Australia for judicial review of administrative decisions, to furnish a written statement analogous to the one available under our section 18.

CONSIDERATIONS

The true utility of the new facility requires some analysis, however. The following points bear consideration:

(a) It is important to note that, apart from the right conferred

---

8 *Ibid.*, s.18.
9 S.13.

by section 18 of the FOI Act, the Acts do not confer a right to elicit information that is not already recorded – the general right of access provided for being to "records" and not "information" *per se*.

(b) Subject to certain exceptions,[10] the right of access does not extend to so-called "pre-commencement" records[11] (that is to say, those created before April 21, 1998).

(c) Only records "held" by "public bodies"[12] are amenable to access under the FOI Act. (Note that records "held" by a public body include those under its control.[13])

(d) Note also that records in the possession of persons who are or were providing services for a public body under a contract for services are deemed, for the purposes of the Acts to be held by the body concerned - if and in so far as they relate to the services.[14]

---

[10] One of which, in s.6(5)(b), provides that, if the pre-commencement records concerned relate to personal information about the person seeking access, the temporal limitation is removed. Depending on the type of litigation contemplated or in train, of course, this may prove very useful to litigants, as the records they seek will often be ones either containing their personal information or relating to the same. In this regard, the expression "relate[s] to personal information" has been given a reasonably wide interpretation by the High Court in *E.H. v. Information Commissioner (No.2)* [2002] 3 I.R. 600, such that, in effect, records containing personal information of a requester, records naming the requester and records having a sufficiently substantial link to something in which the requester has a personal interest, will qualify.

[11] FOI Act, s. 6(4).

[12] *Ibid.*, ss.7 and 2(1) and sch.1.

[13] *Ibid.*, s.2(5)(a). See now *Minister for Enterprise, Trade and Employment v Information Commissioner* [2006] I.E.H.C. 39, for an example of a case in which the records at issue were held not to have been "under the control" of the relevant public body – in that case, the appellant Minister, for the reasons set out in the judgment.

[14] *Ibid.*, s.6(9). Note also, pursuant to that section, that "there shall be deemed to be included in the contract a provision that the person shall, if so requested by the body for the purposes of this Act, give the record to the body for retention by it for such period as is reasonable in the particular circumstances."

(e) A public body has four weeks from receipt of a request for access within which to deal with the request.[15]

(f) In the case of a request for access to records, the public body can extend the period within which it deals with the request by a further four weeks in certain circumstances.[16] A person may apply to the Information Commissioner for a review of the decision to extend,[17] but this will take time also.

(g) There are numerous exemptions which may be applied by the body to refuse to grant access[18]. There is also a number of so-called "administrative grounds" for refusing to grant a request for access under the FOI Act.[19]

---

[15] FOI Act, s.8. The time prescribed by the Acts for dealing with applications to amend records (s.17) and for written statements of reasons and material fact-finding underpinning decisions (s.18) is also four weeks from the date of receipt of the associated application.

[16] *Ibid.*, s.9.

[17] *Ibid.*, s.34(1)(d).

[18] *Ibid.*, Pt III and s.46. See also the definition of "exempt record" in s.2(1).

[19] *Ibid.,* s.10. S.10 provides for the refusal to grant access on the grounds that

　　(a)　the record concerned does not exist or cannot be found after all reasonable steps to ascertain its whereabouts have been taken;

　　(*b*)　the request does not comply with the minimal formalities specified in *section 7(1)(b)* of the FOI Act;

　　(*c*)　granting the request would, by reason of the number or nature of the records concerned, or the nature of the information concerned, require the retrieval and examination of such *number* of records, or an examination of such *kind* of the records concerned, as to cause a substantial and unreasonable interference with, or disruption of, work of the public body concerned;

　　(*d*)　publication of the record concerned is required by law and is intended to be effected not later than 12 weeks after the receipt of the request by the head;

　　(*e*)　the request is frivolous or vexatious, or forms part of a pattern of manifestly unreasonable requests from the same requester, or from different requesters who appear to have made the requests acting in concert; or

　　(*f*)　a fee or deposit payable under *section 47* in respect of the request concerned, or in respect of a previous request by the same requester, has not been paid.

(h) The FOI Act provides for the charging of fees for the making of requests, and applications for internal, and external, review, as well as for search and retrieval and copying of records.[20]

(i) Whilst there exist rights of review, both internally within a public body,[21] and externally before the Information Commissioner,[22] these take time. In addition, in the event that a person is dissatisfied in point of law with a decision of the Commissioner, a right exists to appeal her decision to the High Court, but that, again, takes time. Furthermore, since the passing of the 2003 Amendment Act, the bar on an appeal to the Supreme Court contained in the Principal Act has been removed, and there accordingly exists the further possibility that the matter will be appealed to that Court, with further delay ensuing.

In summary, therefore, whilst the advent of FOI as an information-gathering tool in contemplated or actual litigation is welcome, it is as well to be realistic about what, and when, it might deliver, and from whom.

FOI VERSUS DISCOVERY

As I have already mentioned, prior to the introduction of FOI, the only real means a litigant had of gaining access to potentially relevant records or documents not already possessed by him was to seek the production of documents by way of discovery. Clearly, this is still an avenue open to litigants, which continues to be used.

However, whatever about the relationship between FOI and discovery – which is the subject of the next following section – it might be useful to set out some of the points of difference between obtaining the production of documents on discovery and being granted access to records under FOI:

---

[20] *Ibid.*, s.27.

[21] *Ibid.*, s.14.

[22] *Ibid.*, s.34.

(a) Access to records may be sought under FOI at any time and not merely once litigation has commenced. Normally, pre-action (as opposed to pre-trial) discovery is not available (although there are exceptions).

(b) An entitlement to discovery (by reference to established criteria) needs to be demonstrated by the person seeking it.

   No criteria need to be satisfied in order to demonstrate an entitlement to exercise the right of access provided for in the FOI Act. Indeed, section 8(5) provides that, in most cases, any reason that a requester gives for a request, and any belief or opinion on the part of the public body as to what are the reasons of the requester for the request, are to be disregarded.

(c) Discovery is made by way of sworn affidavit. Access to records is not granted with an accompanying sworn document.

(d) Where legal professional, or other, privilege is claimed, the documents containing the communications over which privilege is claimed nevertheless require to be listed in a schedule to the affidavit of discovery.

   Leaving aside the other listing of records being released or not being released under FOI, as regards a record considered by a public body to be exempt under section 22(1)(a) (legal professional privilege), section 22(2) provides that the request should be refused and, where disclosure of the existence or non-existence of the record concerned would be contrary to the public interest, the existence or non-existence of the record should not be disclosed to the requester.

(e) Failure to make discovery, whether having voluntarily agreed to do so, or having been ordered to do so by way of actual court order, renders the person in default susceptible to being "attached" and, in addition, to having his claim dismissed or his defence struck out, as the case may be.

   Failure to grant a request for access, on the other hand, has no particular consequences. Indeed, section 41 of the FOI Act contemplates a public body not making any decision within the statutory timeframe at 'first instance' and then again on 'internal review', on both of which occasions the legislation, in effect, deems a decision refusing to grant access to have been made.

(f) Discovery brings with it the facility to inspect the documents produced on discovery, as well as that of taking copies of documents.

Various forms of access (including inspection and copying) are provided for in the FOI Act[23] and a requester is entitled to specify his or her preferred form. However, a public body may decide, in certain circumstances, to give access in a form or manner other than that sought.[24]

(g) Subject to some exceptions, FOI requests are attended by 'up-front' fees, fees for search and retrieval and copying fees, but these are extremely modest when compared with the costs of the discovery.

(h) Finally, and importantly, under FOI, no restriction can be placed by a public body on the use or uses to which a record might be put by a requester once access has been granted to it.[25]

In discovery, however, the documents disclosed are subject to an implied undertaking, given to the Court and to the other party by the party to whom the documents are produced, that the documents disclosed, or information obtained or derived from them, shall not be used otherwise than within and for the purposes of, the action in which they were disclosed.

---

[23] *Ibid.*, s.12.

[24] *Ibid.*, s.12(2).

[25] In *E.H. v Information Commissioner (No.1)*, O'Neill J. accepted that " neither the head of a public body nor the Commissioner has any jurisdiction under the Act of 1997 to impose any conditions on the type or extent of disclosure or the use of the documents after disclosure and hence, in permitting disclosure, a head of a public body and the Commissioner must assume that the disclosure of the record will be to the world at large".

FOI or Discovery – or Both?

As we have just seen, a person who obtains documents by way of discovery gives an implied (and sometimes an express) undertaking to the court and to the person producing the documents to him, that he will not make ulterior use of the documents concerned. As we have also just seen, no such strictures attend a grant of access to records under the FOI Act.

This might lead one to think it a good idea, if having obtained documents by way of discovery, to obtain the same documents under FOI so that the ones obtained under FOI could be used as one saw fit, not being subject to the implied undertaking given as the *quid pro quo* for discovery.

This is precisely what Mr H. thought. However, his quest resulted, eventually, in High Court proceedings involving him called *E.H. v. Information Commissioner (No.1)*,[26] in which the High Court held, so far as is relevant here, that he was not entitled to a grant of access to the records concerned on the ground that the records were such that their disclosure would constitute contempt of court (i.e., on the ground that the mandatory exemption contained in section 22(1)(b) of the FOI Act applied).

Having interpreted the word "disclosure" as meaning disclosure in its widest sense, or "any disclosure", O'Neill J. went on to say that:

> "the Act construed in a manner consistent with the Constitution could not be used so that access to documents under the Act would have the result of robbing an ... undertaking given to a court of the force and effect which the court in question intended th[is] to have" and that "notwithstanding that the undertaking benefits solely the party making discovery, the undertaking is given to the court and like all undertakings given to a court, breach of it is a contempt of the court."[27]

---

[26] [2001] 2 I.R. 463.
[27] *Ibid.*, p.485.

So the lesson is that, if one might want to make ulterior use of documents which might be produced on discovery and which might also be available by way of FOI, a request ought first to be made under the FOI Act and discovery sought subsequently. If that is the order chosen, and assuming fruitful FOI access and discovery processes, both FOI and discovery might be available.

Evidential Matters

I will finish by mentioning briefly that copies of records obtained under FOI will not themselves prove a case. They may point in interesting directions and appear to indicate the facts of a situation. However, it is important to realise that, to the extent that a litigant might try to adduce the documents as evidence of the truth of their contents, this will, strictly speaking, fall foul of the rule against hearsay and the records will be found to be inadmissible as evidence in this regard.

Now, it is often the case that parties will agree to relax the hearsay rule, but, to the extent that this does not happen (and it often only happens late in the day as a hearing approaches), it will be necessary to think about assembling those witnesses who will have to give first hand oral evidence of the information contained in the records obtained or, in paper-based proceedings such as judicial review, to assemble those who will have to swear affidavits, deposing to the facts concerned, and exhibiting documents to those affidavits. In terms of witnesses, some may be unwilling and may have to be ordered by subpoena or witness summons, for example, to attend to give evidence.

Conclusion

The FOI Act contains an interesting mix of provisions of potential interest to intending, or actual, litigants. These are likely to be of utility to those involved in proceedings with public bodies, although public bodies hold a variety of records, some of which may well be useful in proceedings between a person and another person who is not the public body holding the records.

The time involved in obtaining material under FOI may be a

disadvantage, but the unencumbered nature of the process may be an advantage.

The timing of FOI requests and discovery applications will have to be carefully considered. Even if one were to make an FOI request first in point of time, that request may take some time to be dealt with and go to internal review or a review before the Commissioner, at any point of which, for whatever reason, discovery needs to be applied for. If the discovery timing outstrips that in the FOI process, the FOI request may end up having to be refused.

Obtaining records that seem to support one's case does not mean that one will be able to use them, without more, to prove one's case. Whilst the rule against hearsay may be relaxed by agreement between the parties, this is not necessarily going to be the case.

CHAPTER 5

The Freedom of Information Act and the Courts*

It is undeniable that there are certain legal instruments which can only thrive with litigation. The emergence within our legal lifetime of a vast corpus of case-law has given the Constitution a status and importance in Irish society which it might otherwise never have acquired. This explosion in constitutional jurisprudence is but the most striking domestic example of this phenomenon, but at an international level the same can be said of roughly parallel developments with the EC Treaty and the European Convention of Human Rights.

Perhaps one does not find quite as many examples of the same phenomenon at the level of statute law. Nevertheless, there seems little doubt but that certain very special statutes have a generality and adaptability comparable to that found to be desirable in the provisions of the Constitution itself. The Freedom of Information Act 1997 is, of course, one such statute, as in its own way it is designed to be a sort of mini-charter of information rights. There seems little doubt but that a statute with such a high level of generality requires litigation for sustenance and life in much the same way as a plant needs water. Litigation helps to bring the Act alive and assists the organic evolution of the legislation.

In the eight years since the Act has come into force, 16[1] substantive

---

* Gerard Hogan, Law School, Trinity College, Dublin.
[1]   There have been 14 appeals to date and two of these appeals went to the Supreme Court: *Sheedy v. Information Commissioner* [2005] 2 I.R. 272 and *NMcK v. Information Commissioner* [2006] 1 I.L.R.M. 504.

The other 12 appeals are *Minister for Agriculture and Food v. Information Commissioner* [2000] 1 I.R. 309; *Minister for Education and Science v. Information Commissioner* [2001] I.E.H.C. 116; *Deely v. Information Commissioner* [2001] 3 I.R. 439; *EH v. Information Commissioner (No.1)* [2001] 4 I.R. 463; *Minister for Justice, Equality and Law Reform v. Information Commissioner* [2002] 1 I.L.R.M. 1; *EH v. Information Commissioner (No.2)*

decisions have proceeded to full hearing before the High Court by way of appeal from the Information Commissioner. The Supreme Court has in turn heard and decided two appeals from these decisions. The purpose of this chapter is to consider these decisions with a view to seeing whether any general conclusions may be drawn regarding the interpretation and application of the 1997 Act to date.

THE APPEALS SYSTEM

Before doing so, however, it is necessary first briefly to sketch out the nature of the appellate system created by the 1997 Act and subsequently amended by the Freedom of Information (Amendment) Act 2003. The right of appeal from any decision of the Information Commissioner to the High Court is contained in section 42 of the 1997 Act. As we shall presently see, this section raises yet again the perennial theme of the scope of such an appeal and the extent to which it is broader and differs from the traditional remedy of judicial review.

As amended, this section now provides:

"(1) A party to a review under section 34 or any person affected by a decision of the Commissioner following such a review may appeal to the High Court on a point of law from the decision.

(2) The requester concerned or any other person affected by –
(a) The issue of a certificate under section 25,
(b) A decision, pursuant to section 8, to refuse to grant a request under section 7 in relation to a record the subject of such a certificate, or
(c) A decision, pursuant to section 14, to refuse to grant, or

---

[2002] 3 I.R. 600; *Killilea v. Information Commissioner* [2003] I.E.H.C. 29; *CW Shipping Co. Ltd. v. Whelan's Limestone Quarries Ltd.* [2004] I.E.H.C. 1; *RTE v. Information Commissioner* [2004] I.E.H.C. 113; *South Western Health Board v. Information Commissioner* [2005] 2 I.R. 547; *Gannon v. Information Commissioner* [2006] I.E.H.C 17; *Minister for Enterprise, Trade and Employment v. Information Commissioner* [2006] I.E.H.C. 39. One of these appeals – *EH v. Information Commissioner* – has given rise to two separate judgments.

to uphold a decision to refuse to grant, such a request, may appeal to the High Court on a point of law from such issue or from such decision.

(3) A person may appeal to the High Court from–

(a) A decision under section 14, or

(b) A decision specified in paragraphs (a), (b), (c), (d), (e), (f) or (g) of subsection (1) of that section (other than such a decision made by a person to whom the function stood delegated under section 4 at the time of the making of the decision), made by the Commissioner in respect of a record held by the office of the Commissioner or (in a case where the same person holds the Office of Ombudsman or the Office of Commissioner) made by the Ombudsman in respect of a record held by the Office of the Ombudsman.

(4) An appeal under subsection (1), (2) or (3) shall be initiated not later than four weeks after the notice of the decision concerned was given to the person bringing the appeal.

(5) The Commissioner may refer any question of law arising in a review under section 34 to the High Court for a determination, and the Commissioner may postpone the making of a decision following the review until such time as he or she considers convenient after the determination of the High Court.

(6)(a) Where an appeal under this section by a person other than a head is dismissed by the High Court, that Court may, if it considers that the point of law concerned was of exceptional public importance, order that some or all of the costs of the person in relation to the appeal be paid by the public body concerned.

(b) The High Court may order that some or all of the costs of a person (other than a head) in relation to a reference under this section be paid by the public body concerned.

(7) A decision of the High Court following an appeal under subsection (1), (2) or (3) shall, where appropriate, specify the period within which affect shall be given to the decision."

Section 42(8) of the 1997 Act originally provided:

"(8) The decision of the High Court on an appeal or reference
under this section shall be final and conclusive."

As originally enacted, section 42(8) precluded a right of appeal to the
Supreme Court in accordance with Article 34.4.3° of the Constitution.
While this was not constitutionally objectionable, it is hard to see what
the logic behind this prohibition actually was. After all, given that there
are now some thirty judges of the High Court and that a decision of one
High Court judge does not strictly bind another High Court judge, it was
inevitable that inconsistencies would arise in the application of the Act
absent the capacity of the Supreme Court to give an authoritiative and
binding interpretation. While the provisions of the Freedom of Information
(Amendment) Act 2003 have proved controversial in other respects, the
repeal of section 42(8) of the 1997 Act by section 2 of the 2003 Act has
met with general approval.

THE PROCEDURE TO BE FOLLOWED

The procedure to be followed by any litigant wishing to appeal is set out
in Order 130 of the Rules of the Superior Courts.[2] The key provisions of
Order 130 are as follows:

"2. An appeal to the Court pursuant to section 42(1), section
42(2) or section 42(3) of the [1997 Act] as amended by the
Act of 2003[3] shall be brought by way of originating notice
of motion.
    3. The notice of motion shall be issued within eight[4]
weeks after notice of the decision concerned is given to the
person bringing the appeal. The notice of motion shall be
served upon the Commissioner and upon any other person

---

[2] Order 130 was inserted by Rules of the Superior Courts (No.3)(Freedom of
    Information Act 1997) 1998 (S.I. No. 325 of 1998) and was amended by Rules
    of the Superior Courts (Order 130)(Amendment) Rules 2004 (S.I. No. 471 of
    2004).
[3] As inserted by Rule 1 of the Rules of the Superior Courts (Order 130)
    (Amendment) Rules 2004 (the 2004 Rules).
[4] As inserted by Rule 1 of the 2004 Rules.

affected by the decision the subject matter of the appeal. Service shall be effected by ordinary pre-paid post.

4. The notice of motion shall be entitled "In the matter of the Freedom of Information Acts, 1997-2003"[5] and on the application of the appellant.

5. Every notice of motion bringing an appeal shall be grounded upon the affidavit of the appellant which shall:
(a) state the nature of the decision against which the appeal is brought;
(b) exhibit a copy of the decision, if any;
(c) state the grounds of the appeal and the point of law, where appropriate;
(d) state the nature of the direction or order sought from the Court;
(e) exhibit all relevant documentation; and
(f) specify whether the appellant is requesting that the appeal be heard otherwise than in public.[6]

6. An appeal brought pursuant to section 42(1), (2) or (3) of the [1997] Act as amended by the Act of 2003 shall be heard and determined upon affidavit unless the Court otherwise directs, and the Court may give such directions as to the giving of oral evidence as appear appropriate in the circumstances."[7]

---

[5] As inserted by Rule 1 of the 2004 Rules.

[6] This, of course, reflect s.42(9) of the 1997 Act which empowers the Court to take precautions to prevent disclosure of the document in order not to pre-empt the final decision of the Court:

"9. Any party to an appeal under section 42(1), (2) or (3) or to a reference under section 42(5) may, either by affidavit or by letter in writing or at the hearing, request that the Court take precautions to prevent disclosure to the public or, if appropriate, to a party, of information referred to at section 43(1)(a) and (b) of the said Act. The Court shall take all such reasonable precautions as it thinks fit for the purposes of section 43 of the Act whether or not any such precautions have been requested by the parties or any of them."

[7] In *CW Shipping Co. Ltd. v. Whelan's Limestone Quarries Ltd.* [2004] I.E.H.C. 1 Murphy J. rejected the argument that the Information Commissioner was *functus officio* having given his decision and that the Commissioner had no role to play in any appeal under s.42(1). Murphy J. considered that it was "implicit that the Commissioner be a respondent" to the statutory appeal.

Order 130, rules 7 and 8 deal with the procedure to be followed where the Commissioner elects to refer any question of law to the High Court and these rules provide that any such reference shall be by way of case-stated.

THE NATURE OF THE APPEAL TO THE HIGH COURT

Section 43(1) simply provides that any party to a review under section 34 or any person affected by a decision of the Commissioner following such a review "may appeal to the High Court on a point of law from the decision." In common with many other statutory regimes creating an appellate structure of this kind, the scope of this appeal is, to some degree at least, uncertain. Is the scope of this statutory appeal wider than that of judicial review? If it is not, why did section 43 go to the trouble of providing this form of statutory appeal? Is the High Court confined to reviewing the material before the Commissioner or can new evidence be received?[8]

This issue as to the scope of the appeal arose in the very first appeal, *Minister for Agriculture v. Information Commissioner.*[9] In this case a civil servant, Mr Glynn, had applied for his personnel file. Section 6(5) permits an individual to have access to personal information created before the coming into force of the Act, but section 6(6)(c) provides that this right of access is not to be construed as entitling access to such records where such records are being "used or proposed to be used in a manner or for a purpose that affects, or will or may affect, adversely the interests of the person." The Minister initially refused access to certain pre-commencement personnel files, but the Commissioner reversed that decision and granted the applicant full access to certain records specified in his decision and partial access to other records.

The records in question had been sealed by the Department and a note had been attached to the file stating that these were not to be used

---

[8]   In some instances it may be necessary for the High Court to inspect the documents itself in order to enable the appellant to conduct a meaningful appeal: see the discussion of this issue by O'Neill J. in *EH v. Information Commissioner (No.1)* [2001] 2 I.R. 466 at 488.

[9]   [2000] 1 I.R. 309.

"in any manner or form which might adversely affect Mr Glynn's interest [and] are not to be consulted in the future." It was thus argued that the very act of sealing the files to which this note had been attached demonstrated that the files could never be used in a manner likely to prejudice Mr Glynn's interests and that they thus constituted an exempt record.

O'Donovan J. accepted that the very act of sealing the file and attaching the note meant that the Commissioner was correct in concluding that the records were not being "used" for the purposes of section 6(6) as of the date of the request. But what of the future?

Here O'Donovan J. sought to interpret the Act in the light of its purpose and answer this question having regard to the traditional boundaries of the scope of an appeal:

> "In this regard, in the light of its preamble, it seems to me that there can be no doubt but that it was the intention of the legislature, when enacting the provisions of the Freedom of Information Act 1997, that it was only in exceptional cases that members of the public at large should be deprived of access to information in the possession of public bodies and this intention is exemplified by the provision of section 34(12)(b) of the Act which provides that a decision to refuse to grant access to information sought shall be presumed not to have been justified until the contrary is shown. Accordingly, it seems to me that the entire Act must be construed in that light and, in particular, the provisions of section 6(6)(c) of the Act must be construed as meaning that, if there is evidence to suggest that future use of a record to which access is sought appears to be contemplated, then that subsection cannot be used to justify a refusal to grant access to that record. In this regard, *Henry Denny and Sons (Ireland) Limited T/A Kerry Foods v. The Minister for Social Welfare*[10] ....is authority for the proposition that the High Court should not interfere with findings of a person, whose decision is being reviewed by the Court, unless those findings are

---

[10] [1998] 1 I.R. 34.

incapable of being supported by the facts or are based on an erroneous view of the law."[11]

Was there then such evidence as would justify the Commissioner's conclusions? O'Donovan J. felt it was significant that the sealing took place only after the request for access had been made. The judge also noted that:

> "This is all the more so when regard is had to the fact that the note attached to the sealed envelope is only signed by the Personnel Officer and, therefore, is unlikely to be perceived as having binding effect on a superior officer or even an officer of equal rank and, in any event, the respondent was entitled to ask himself why was the file being maintained at all, if it was not proposed to use it? Is not its continued maintenance a statement of intent to use? I would accept the validity of the submission on behalf of the appellant that, when considering the application of section 6(6)(c) of the Act to records in respect of which access is sought, one does not have to be satisfied as a matter of certainty that those records will not be used in a manner adverse to the interests of the person to whom they relate before deciding that the subsection does not apply to them. Indeed, far from requiring certainty as to the future use of those records, I would accept that the subsection does not even contemplate consideration of a remote or hypothetical possibility with regard to the use to which those records might be put at some time in the future; assuming that there are no circumstances which obtain at the time when the request for access to them is made which might suggest that the possibility of future use has been contemplated. However, if, when considering whether or not the provisions of section 6(6)(c) of the Act apply to a record

---

[11] [2000] 1 I.R. 309 at 319. It may be noted that O'Donovan J. held that the Commissioner had erred in law in taking into account the provisions of ss.22, 23 and 26 of the 1997 Act in his decision when these provisions had not been relied on by the Department in arriving at its decision. This did not, however, mean that the decision had to be set aside as it could be justified on independent grounds: see [2000] 1 I.R. 309 at 319-320.

in respect of which access is sought, there are reasonable grounds for believing that the possibility of future use has not been ruled out, then I think that it would be wrong to conclude that the provisions of the subsection apply to such a record. In this case, for the reasons that I have given, I think that there were grounds upon which the Respondent was entitled to conclude that the Department of Agriculture and Food had not ruled out the possibility of future use of the records in respect of which Mr Glynn sought access."[12]

The judge thus upheld the Commissioner's conclusion that section 6(6)(c) did not apply to these records on the basis that there was "adequate evidence" to support this conclusion.

On the wider issue of principle, O'Donovan J. held that the Commissioner was not entitled to have regard to legal grounds other than those actually advanced by the Department which refused access:

"As I have already indicated, as a matter of law, I am satisfied that, when reviewing the appellant's decision of the 24th June, 1998, the respondent was not entitled to take into account the relevance or otherwise of the provisions of sections 22, 23 or 26 of the said Act to the records in respect of which access was sought by Mr Glynn for the reason that the provisions of those sections were not relied on by the appellant when arriving at his decision of the 24th June, 1998. To that extent, in the light of the decision given in *Henry Denny and Sons (Ireland) Limited v. The Minister for Social Welfare*,[13] I think that I am obliged to conclude that, insofar as the respondent affirmed the decision of the appellant to refuse access to any portion of the records in respect of which Mr Glynn sought access on the grounds that they were records to which the provisions of sections 22, 23 or 26 of the Act applied, he was wrong in law."[14]

---

[12] [2000] 1 I.R. 309 at 318-319.
[13] [1998] 1 I.R. 34.
[14] [2000] 1 I.R. 309 at 319-320. It may be noted that a similar issue arose in *Deely*

One may query the correctness of this rather limited approach. It is one thing to say that no new evidence can be admitted or, at least, that such evidence should only be admitted on a review by the Commissioner in special circumstances. But in these circumstances the Minister – or any other administrative authority which is called upon to apply the Act – is not a lawyer, even if they presumably will have access to legal advice. If, however, the Minister refuses access on grounds A and B, but the Commissioner disagrees with this conclusion while considering that access should be refused on ground C, what it is so wrong with the Commissioner taking this approach? This type of reasoning is indeed in the nature of the appellate process: how often have we seen the Supreme Court uphold a decision of the High Court, albeit for reasons different from those given by the High Court itself.

The issue of the scope of the review was also considered by McKechnie J. in *Deely v. The Information Commissioner*,[15] although many of the expansive comments which he made concerning both the scope of review and the manner in which the Act should be interpreted were decidedly obiter. The judge thus took the opportunity to set out the circumstances in which the courts would exercise its powers of review under section 42:

> "There is no doubt but that when a court is considering only a point of law, whether by way of a restricted appeal or via a case stated, the distinction in my view being irrelevant, it is, in accordance with established principles, confined as to its remit, in the manner following:-
> (a) it cannot set aside findings of primary fact unless there is no evidence to support such findings;
> (b) it ought not to set aside inferences drawn from such facts unless such inferences were ones which no reasonable decision making body could draw;
> (c) it can however, reverse such inferences, if the same were based on the interpretation of documents and should do so if incorrect; and, finally;
> (d) if the conclusion reached by such bodies shows that they

---

v. Information Commissioner [2001] 3 I.R. 439 but McKechnie J. did not find it necessary to decide this point.

[15] [2001] 3 I.R. 439.

have taken an erroneous view of the law, then that also is a ground for setting aside the resulting decision."[16]

But, as will become presently clear, these comments were entirely obiter, simply because given the circumstances of the appeal, this issue simply did not arise for consideration. In any event, as the Supreme Court subsequently stressed in *Sheedy v. Information Commissioner*,[17] the courts should intervene where it is plain that the Commissioner has, in fact, erred in law.[18]

---

16 [2001] 3 I.R. 439 at 452. This passage has received approval in a number of other cases: see, e.g., *Ryan v. Information Commissioner*, unreported, High Court, May 20, 2003; *Gannon v. Information Commissioner* [2006] I.E.H.C. 17. In *EH v. Information Commissioner (No.1)*, O'Neill J. applied traditional judicial principles to determine whether the Commissioner had erred in law. The same judge nevertheless held in the companion case, *EH v. Information Commissioners (No.2)* that, in some circumstances, an error of fact (such as whether the documents contained personal information) could amount to an error of law.

It may be noted that in *Gannon v. Information Commissioner*, Quirke J. applied the irrationality judicial review standard in determining the appeal. Here the requester sought details of an application made by a third party for legal aid to the Legal Aid Board. The Commissioner concluded that these records came within the confidentiality exception in section 26 and Quirke J. concluded that he could only disturb this finding if was irrational in the *O'Keeffe* sense of that term. While this decision seems certainly correct on its own facts, it equally seems that Quirke J. should have applied the less onerous appeal (and not judicial review) standard.

17 [2005] 2 I.R. 272.

18 As Kearns J. put it, having quoted this passage from the judgment of McKechnie J. in *Deely* ([2005] 2 I.R. 272 at 294):

> "This is a helpful resume with which one would not disagree, but it would be obviously incorrect to apply exclusively judicial review principles to matters of statutory interpretation in the way that might be appropriate to issues of fact. A legal interpretation of a statute is either correct or incorrect, and the essence of this case is to determine whether the interpretation given first by the Commissioner and later by Gilligan J. [in the High Court] to section 53 of the Education Act 1998 was correct or otherwise."

In *Minister for Enterprise, Trade and Employment v. Information Commissioner* [2006] I.E.H.C. 39 the Commissioner held that the records of a local enterprise board were under the control of the Minister for the purposes of s.2(5)(a). Murphy J. held that while the Commissioner's conclusion was "based on stateable grounds", it was nevertheless "on balance" not factually justifiable having regard to the operating agreement between the Board and the Minister. This standard of review here seems closer to that of an appeal as distinct from judicial review.

The circumstances of this case were indeed unusual. The appellant had been driving his motor vehicle on a public road when a collision occurred between an oncoming vehicle and one immediately behind him. Though not involved either by reason of personal injury or by way of impact damage, the appellant on the instructions of the Director of Public Prosecutions was subsequently charged with an offence under section 52 (1) of the Road Traffic Act 1961. Being aggrieved at being so prosecuted and being further aggrieved at being the only driver to face any criminal charge, Mr Deely sought to invoke the provisions of the 1997 Act in order to get from the Director the reason or reasons why this prosecution was proffered against him.[19] The Director contended, however, that by virtue of section 46, the 1997 Act did not apply to these records and that, as the giving of reasons under section 18 would inevitably involve the disclosure of such exempt records,[20] this obligation did not apply in the instant case.

This view was upheld by the Commissioner who reasoned as follows:

> "Section 18 of the FOI Act provides for a right, in the case of a person affected by an act of a public body, to be given reasons for that act. However this is not an absolute right as section 18 (2)(a) qualifies it to the extent that reasons need not be given where to do so would involve the giving of information contained in an exempt record. Whatever the wording of its initial response, I am satisfied that the decision

---

[19] McKechnie J. noted that the District Court had already ordered disclosure of the witnesses statements to the appellant. This disclosure was, of course, in the context of the criminal prosecution and was governed by entirely separate considerations from that of the 1997 Act.

[20] McKechnie J. noted that the Commissioner had also found that this was the case and that this finding was not challenged on appeal. The Commissioner had found that:

> "the information required to provide the reasons requested by you is contained on a specific file created in connection with the decision on whether or not to prosecute. No case has been made by you that the records on this file are records concerning the general administration of the DPP's office and I am satisfied that the records are exempt records by virtue of section 46. Accordingly I am satisfied that the DPP's office could only have granted your request by the release of information contained in an exempt record ".

of the DPP's office rests on its view that the giving of reasons in your case would inevitably require the giving to you of information which is contained in an exempt record.

The term "Exempt Record" is defined in section 2 of the [1997] Act to include "a record in relation to which the grant of a request under section 7 would be refused pursuant to Part III or by virtue of section 46". Accordingly, section 18 does not require the giving of reasons where to do so would involve revealing information contained in a record which is exempt under section 46.

Under section 46 (1)(b), the [1997] Act "does not apply" to a record held or created by the DPP's office other than a record concerning the "general administration" of that office. In your case, the information required to provide the reasons requested by you is contained on a specific file created in connection with the decision on whether or not to prosecute. No case has been made by you that the records on this file are records concerning the general administration of the DPP's office and I am satisfied that the records are exempt records by virtue of section 46. Accordingly, I am satisfied that the DPP's office could only have granted your request by the release of information contained in an exempt record."

McKechnie J.'s careful analysis of the key provisions of the 1997 Act led him to focus on the provisions of section 46(1) and section 18. He noted first that section 46(1) provides:

"(1) This Act does not apply to
(a) ....
(b) a record held or created by the Attorney General or the Director of Public Prosecutions or the Office of the Attorney General or the Office of the Director of Prosecutions (other than a record concerning the general administration of either of those offices)."

Any such records became "exempt records" for the purposes of section 2. The judge then noted that section 18(2)(a) provided that:

"Nothing in this section shall be construed as requiring -
(a) The giving to a person of information contained in a
exempt record...".

Against this background it was scarcely surprising that McKechnie J.
found against the appellant:

"Given that the appellant is attempting to establish a right
which compels the DPP to furnish the information sought,
he must, in my view, also establish that such right is
enforceable by or under the provisions of this Act. It is quite
insufficient to say that the DPP is not prohibited by section
18 (2) from giving the information requested. That may be
the case and indeed, though I express no view on it, the DPP
may not by law be injuncted from supplying such information.
But once he decides against the request, Mr Deely must be
able to demonstrate a compulsion arising from law which
removes any discretion which the DPP might otherwise have.
Very definitely in my opinion he cannot do so in this case.
Subsection (2) qualifies the section itself. It commences with
the words quoted above. These can only mean that whatever
rights are otherwise contained in section 18, such rights do
not and cannot extend to a requirement to give information
which is contained in an exempt record as above defined.
This, I believe, is the correct interpretation of this section
and not that as suggested by Mr Deely for if it was that, as
submitted, it would render the entire section futile."[21]

The scope of review also featured in what is still probably the single
most important decision to date, *Sheedy v. Information Commissioner*,[22]
although the inter-relationship between the 1997 Act and other legislation
is probably the most important feature of this case. Here the appellant
was the principal of Scoil Choilm, a primary school situated in Crumlin
in Dublin which had been subject to an inspection report prepared by an
inspector appointed by the Department of Education. The reports were

---

[21] [2001] 3 I.R. 439 at 459.
[22] [2004] 2 I.R. 533 (HC); [2005] 2 I.R. 272 (SC).

prepared in accordance with Department Circulars numbers 31/82 and 12/83, the latter of which provides:

> "A school report containing an assessment of the organisation and work of the school as a whole is to be furnished to the Department at regular intervals of approximately four years...and will be drawn up after discussion with the Principal and staff of the school. Because the School Report deals with the work of the school as a whole, reports on the work of individual teachers will not be issued in connection with it."

As it happens, the report in this case presented a favourable view of the school. The report also contained a considerable amount of information about the school, including factual background material about the history and location of the school, school accommodation, management arrangements within the school, links with parents and the wider community, organisation of classes, preparation and planning of educational programmes, languages and mathematics, social, personal and health education, creative and aesthetic activities, pupils with special needs, a post inspection meeting and a conclusion.

The Irish Times subsequently applied to the Department of Education under the 1997 Act for access to a number of such school reports, including the report written in respect of the appellant's school. The Department refused to grant such access, having regard, *inter alia*, to section 53 of the Education Act 1998, and sections 21, 26 and 28 of the 1997 Act. Following a review, the Information Commissioner set aside the decision of the Department and directed that access be given to redacted versions of the reports for some five schools, including Scoil Choilm. All personal information (within the meaning of section 28 of the 1997 Act) was excluded from the redacted version.

The appellant then appealed the Commissioner's decision to grant access to the redacted version of the report in respect of Scoil Choilm to the High Court, pursuant to the provisions of section 42(1) of the 1997 Act.

In the High Court, Gilligan J. found that the appellant had *locus standi* to bring the proceedings, but he nonetheless found in favour of the respondent on the same grounds as those relied upon by the Commissioner.

He then stayed publication of the *Tuairisc Scoile* ("school report") dated July 30, 2001, pending the final determination of an appeal to the Supreme Court. A majority of that Court allowed the appeal.[23]

The principal grounds of appeal related to section 53 of the Education Act 1998 and section 32(1) of the 1997 Act of 1997. Section 53 of the 1998 Act provides that:-

> "Notwithstanding any other enactment the Minister may–
> (a) refuse access to any information which would enable the compilation of information (that is not otherwise available to the general public) in relation to the comparative performance of schools in respect of the academic achievement of students enrolled therein, including, without prejudice to the generality of the foregoing -
>> (i) The overall results in any year of students in a particular school in an examination, or
>> (ii) The comparative overall results in any year of students in different schools in an examination, and
> (b) Refuse access to information relating to the identity of examiners."

It was common case that the inspector's report did not disclose any individual marks or performances in any examinations, so that the case did not come within either of the specific examples contained in section 53 (a) (i) or (ii) of the 1998 Act. The first question, therefore, was whether the release of such reports would "enable the compilation of information... in relation to the comparative performance of schools in respect of the academic achievement of students" within the meaning of section 53. That in turn raised the question of whether the 1997 Act had been impliedly amended by the provisions of section 53 of the 1998 Act.

Kearns J. first noted that section 32(1)(a) provides that:

> ".... a head *"shall refuse"* a request to disclose where disclosure is *"prohibited by any enactment"*. There is no

---

[23] Denham and Kearns JJ.; Fennelly J. dissented.

discretion of any sort where this sub-section applies. It does not appear to have been considered that the non-disclosure in this case might more properly have been seen to have been one falling within section 32(1)(b) of the Act of 1997 where non-disclosure is authorised (as distinct from prohibited) by an enactment and the case is one in which the head would, pursuant to the enactment, refuse to disclose the record. Section 53 is clearly discretionary in nature."[24]

The judge then referred to the opening "notwithstanding" clause in section 53 and continued:

"The use of a *'notwithstanding'* clause is a convenient form of drafting which skirts or avoids textual amendments to existing legislation but nonetheless operates by implication to bring about amendments or repeals of such legislation. A recent example is to be found in the constitutional amendment effected pursuant to the Citizenship Referendum, 2004, whereby Article 2 of the Constitution (which provided that every person born in the island of Ireland enjoyed a constitutional right to citizenship) was effectively amended by the addition of Article 9.2.1 which now provides:-

'Notwithstanding any other provision of this Constitution, a person born in the island of Ireland....who does not have, at the time of birth of that person, at least one parent who is an Irish citizen...is not entitled to Irish citizenship or nationality, unless provided by law'
(emphasis added).

Such a clause can clearly operate to nullify or override other provisions of the same piece of legislation or inconsistent provisions contained in previous legislation.

Because of the *'notwithstanding'* clause in section 53 it seems to me impossible to construe the Acts of 1997 and 1998 together, or as forming part of a continuum. The word *'notwithstanding'* is in this instance a prepositional sentence-

---

[24] [2005] 2 I.R. 272 at 295.

starter which unequivocally means, and can only mean, *'despite'* or *'in spite of* **any** other enactment. It underlines in the clearest possible manner the free-standing nature of the provision thereafter set out in section 53."[25]

Kearns J. then continued by stressing that section 53 of the 1998 Act must thus be taken to have qualified the interpretation of the 1997 Act and not the other way around:

"The court cannot force a construction on section 53 of the Act of 1998 in some way so as to yield up an interpretation which fits the aims and policy of the Act of 1997 when there is no ambiguity whatsoever in the opening words of section 53. On the contrary, it seems quite possible, having regard to the temporal proximity of its enactment in 1998 to the Act of 1997, that s. 53 may well have been inserted in the Act of 1998 with the unspoken intention of 'batting off' the application of the Freedom of Information Act 1997, to what historically has been a highly contentious issue, namely, that of making public certain findings in relation to the comparative performance of schools.

In my view s. 53 of the Act of 1998 overrides or 'trumps' any provision of the Act of 1997, unless of course, it can be shown that the school reports in question do not come within the protection offered by section 53."[26]

Fennelly J. dissented strongly from this particular conclusion, arguing powerfully that, given the important nature of the change effected by the 1997 Act, it was improbable that the Oireachtas ever intended that this legislation could effectively be amended indirectly in this fashion.

Kearns J. nevertheless then went on to hold that disclosure would, in fact, breach the prohibitions contained in section 53:

---

[25] [2005] 2 I.R. 272 at 295-296. It may be noted that Ó Caoimh J. had previously taken a broadly similar view of the effect of s.53 of the 1998 Act in *Minister for Education and Science v. Information Commissioner* [2001] I.E.H.C. 116.
[26] [2005] 2 I.R. 272 at 296-297.

"In this regard it is common case that the information gathered does not contain examination results. However, the general words of section 53 go further than examination results and I think it obvious that the reference to 'comparative performance of schools in respect of academic achievement of students' may include a whole range of other considerations in respect of which comparisons between different schools could still nevertheless be drawn up. Academic achievements include examinations. Academic achievement can, however, be taken as meaning something more and the parties to this appeal have not argued that a purely mechanistic and functional meaning should be given to the words 'academic achievement' so as to limit the meaning of those words to examination results alone. A range of other considerations must be included, some of which will show one school to differ from another and perhaps be performing better than another across a range of subjects or activities. These might include considerations of how pupils appear to be doing in particular subjects, such as Irish or English, or in activities such as sport or drama. Even without the criteria of examination results being brought to bear, significant performance related differences may be evident from a description of the activities carried out in any school or group of schools. These are precisely the kind of matters addressed by the school report. Given that primary schools, with which we are here concerned, no longer have examinations, so that section 53 (a)(i) and(ii) can never apply to them in any event, it is not difficult to see that the general words of section 53 have a particular relevance to their situation and it is equally clear that the release of the information in the reports could lead to comparisons being drawn between different schools. Indeed there is a recognition and acknowledgement of that fact in the Commissioner's review. That recognition having been given, it does not seem to me to be open to the Commissioner to then dis-apply the section's general words by introducing the concept of subjectivity to downplay any comparison that might be drawn. The section itself does not distinguish between any subjective or objective test for comparisons which might be drawn, and the importation of this concept may be seen as effectively re-writing the section to a particular end."[27]

Having found for the appellant on the section 53 of the 1998 Act issue, Kearns J. upheld the Commissioner on the other two discrete grounds of appeal under sections 21 and 26 of the 1997 Act respectively. Section 21 provides as follows:-

> "(1) A head may refuse to grant a request under section 7 if access to the record concerned could, in the opinion of the head, reasonably be expected to -
> (a) Prejudice the effectiveness of tests, examinations, investigations, enquiries or audits conducted by or on behalf of the public body concerned or the procedures or methods employed for the conduct thereof,
> (b) Have a significant, adverse effect on the performance by the body of any of its functions relating to management (including industrial relations and management of its staff), or
> (c) Disclose positions taken, or to be taken, or plans, procedures, criteria or instructions used or followed, or to be used or followed, for the purpose of any negotiations carried on or being, or to be, carried on by or on behalf of the Government or a public body.
> (2) Subsection (1) shall not apply in relation to a case in which in the opinion of the head concerned, the public interest would, on balance, be better served by granting than by refusing to grant the request under section 7 concerned."

The argument against disclosure of the school reports was that disclosure would be likely to have had a "chilling effect" on the inter-action between the school inspectorate and teachers. The Commissioner rejected this argument and pointed to the statutory nature of the mandate for the work

---

[27] [2005] 2 I.R. 272 at 297.

of Inspectors under section 13 of the 1998 Act[28] as meeting any concerns that schools would not co-operate with the compilation of future inspection reports if disclosure were to be directed. In any event, the Commissioner noted that even if the prohibition in section 21(1) applied, section 21(2) permitted disclosure if this was in the public interest. Given "the vast expenditure of public funds on the education system, it can hardly be argued that what goes on in a school is always the business only of the board of management, teachers, parents or pupils" and, hence, the public interest required disclosure.

Kearns J. endorsed this reasoning:

"In my view the onus to produce evidence of prejudice fell on the Department and, in the absence of same the Commissioner was entitled, under section 34 of the Act of 1997, to hold against the Department. A mere assertion of an expectation of non co-operation from teaching staff could never constitute sufficient evidence in this regard, particularly in the circumstances shown to apply, namely, that as a consequence of both Circular 12/83 and section 13 of the 1998 Act, there was no choice left to schools or their staff as to whether or not to co-operate with the Department's inspectors in terms of furnishing the information sought. Nor do I believe that any exhaustive analysis conducted by reference to detailed evidence was necessary before the Commissioner could decide to apply the public interest

---

[28] S.13(a)(i) of the 1998 Act provides that the inspectors:
"Shall visit recognised schools and centres for education on the initiative of the Inspectorate, and, following consultation with the board, patron, parents of students and teachers, as appropriate, do any or all of the following:...evaluate the organisation and operation of those schools and centres and the quality and effectiveness of the education provided in those schools or centres... evaluate the education standards in such schools... assess the implementation and effectiveness of any programmes of education... and report to the Minister, or to the board, patron, parents of students and teachers, as appropriate, on these matters...an Inspector shall have all such powers as are necessary or expedient for the purpose of performing his or her functions and shall be accorded every reasonable facility and co-operation by the board and the staff of the school".

provision of section 21(2) to direct release of the reports. Once there was some evidence before him as to the circumstances in which these reports are compiled, as undoubtedly was the case here, the well established principles of *O'Keeffe v An Bord Pleanála*[29] make it clear that his decision is not to be interfered with. This assessment, which involved a balancing exercise between various competing interests, was one uniquely within his particular remit."[30]

This passage shows, however, that once the Commissioner has correctly defined the law and there is at least *some* evidence to support his or her conclusions, the courts will be reluctant to interfere. The reference to *O'Keeffe* is, however, somewhat surprising given that Kearns J. had elsewhere in his judgment warned (correctly, it is submitted) against the dangers of importing exclusively judicial review standards into a statutory appeal. *O'Keeffe* is, of course, the quintessential judicial review case. Besides, *O'Keeffe* proceeds on the even more exacting "no evidence" standard and it is re-assuring that this unsatisfactory aspect of that decision was at least not imported into appeals under the 1997 Act given that Kearns J. opted for the more accommodating "some evidence" standard.

Kearns J. finally tersely rejected the argument based on section 26. The Commissioner had taken the view that they did not contain any information that could be said to have been imparted in circumstances imposing an obligation of confidence or have the necessary quality of confidence about it. He thus did not accept that release of any part of the reports would give rise to a breach of any duty of confidence and in the circumstances found that by virtue of section 26(2), the exemptions in section 26(1) could not apply. The judge concluded that this reasoning was impeccable and was amply supported by the evidence.

THE FREEDOM OF INFORMATION ACT AND DISCOVERY

Since the coming into force of the 1997 Act, it has become common practice for litigants and prospective litigants to seek to use the legislation

---

[29] [1993] 1 I.R. 391
[30] [2005] 2 I.R. 272 at 299.

almost as a form of pre-trial discovery. This, in principle, is a perfectly legitimate use of the 1997 Act. The limits of this practice were, however, explored by O'Neill J. in *EH v. Information Commissioner (No.1)*[31].

In this case the requester sought certain documents under the 1997 Act regarding the conduct of a Health Board and a medical practitioner. The requester had previously commenced an action for damages against the Board and the doctor concerned, claiming that they had been negligent in the diagnosis of child sexual abuse. In those proceedings the requester had obtained discovery, but this had been subject to an *express* undertaking that he would not use the documents for any collateral purpose save with leave of the court. As requester he sought substantially the same documents under the 1997 Act, since in that way he would be free to use the documents as he saw fit. His avowed purpose was to be free to transmit these documents before the Fitness to Practice Committee of the Medical Council which was then currently investigating allegations of child sexual abuse against the medical practitioner concerned.

The Commissioner refused access to the documents in question on the ground that, having regard to the express undertaking given in this case, the release of those documents would amount to a breach of that undertaking and might in turn amount to a contempt of court. The Commissioner thus refused to order disclosure having regard to the provisions of section 22(1)(b) which sanction refusal if this would amount to a contempt of court.

O'Neill J. first noted that, despite the apparent similarity between discovery and disclosure under the 1997 Act, the two concepts were, in fact, quite different. In the case of disclosure under the 1997 Act, O'Neill J. accepted that:

> "...neither a head of public body or the Commissioner has any jurisdiction under the Act to impose any conditions on the type or extent of disclosure or the use of the documents after disclosure and hence in permitting disclosure a head of public body and the Commissioner must assume that the disclosure of a record will be to the world at large. Indeed this is at the heart of the scheme of the Act, which ...creates

---

[31] [2001] 4 I.R. 463.

in the circumstances in which the Act operates, an untrammelled right to information, based on a philosophy of disclosure wholly different to that which is at the root of the discovery process in Court proceedings."[32]

In the case of discovery the situation was very different. Here the courts required a party to produce otherwise private and confidential documents in aid of the court process and, thus, with a view to protecting the party making discovery, there was then an implied undertaking that the documents would be used only for the purposes of the litigation.[33]

The judge then went on to explain why, in his view, the disclosure would have amounted to a contempt:

"In my view the purpose of section 22(1)(b) is to prevent the Act operating in such a way as to permit interference in the administration of justice a function which is reserved by the constitution solely to the Courts established by or under the Constitution. If it were the case that one could under the provisions of the Act obtain documents disclosure of which was prohibited by the ruling of a Court or by a undertaking given to a Court, I have no doubt that this would amount to a gross and constitutionally impermissible interference in the administration of justice [contrary to Article 34(1) of the Constitution].

I have come to the conclusion that notwithstanding the entirely laudable and separate philosophy of disclosure which underpins the Act, that the Act construed in a manner consistent with the Constitution could not be used, so that access to documents under the Act would have the result of robbing an order of a Court or an undertaking given to a Court of the force and effect which the Court in question

---

[32] [2001] 4 I.R. 463 at 483-484.

[33] O'Neill J. cited *Home Office v. Harmon* [1983] A.C. 280 as authority for this proposition. The Commissioner had, indeed, drawn a distinction between express and implied undertakings for this purpose, but O'Neill J. did not think that such a sharp distinction could be drawn and that the distinction was, in any event, immaterial for the purposes of the appeal.

intended these to have. In my view section 22(1)(b) is there to ensure that this does not happen, and it must operate accordingly ... I have come to the conclusion that where a head of a public body or the Commissioner is aware that there is in existence an undertaking to a Court be it expressed or implied, that disclosure must be refused on the basis of section 22(1)(b)."[34]

The correctness of this analysis may be queried. Of course, the breach of the usual discovery undertaking (whether express or implied) would amount to a contempt of court. But the reason why that undertaking is imposed is because the party seeking discovery has, generally speaking, no right to have access to the documents other than for the purposes of the litigation. If, however, the party has a right, entirely separate from the litigation process, to have access to the documents then the rationale for the undertaking simply falls away. In those circumstances, to refuse access to documents on section 22(1)(b) grounds when the requester would otherwise have been entitled to access the documents under the general provisions of the 1997 Act, *simply* because the requester had previously obtained the documents in the course of the litigation process and had been subject to the implied undertaking for that purpose seems merely to conflate the two separate processes of disclosure, namely under the 1997 Act and the discovery process.[35]

---

[34] [2001] 2 I.R. 463 at 485.

[35] It may be noted that O'Neill J. would not accept ([2001] 2 I.R. 463 at 486) that the overlap between disclosure given in the discovery process and the right of access in the 1997 Act would (on this analysis) give rise to anomalies:

"[Counsel for the appellant] pointed to what he perceived as impracticalities or disadvantages arising from the conclusion I have just reached. He expressed the view, that by the mere fact that documents were listed in an affidavit of discovery; as if by some forensic magic they would be excluded from disclosure under the Act. I do not share his apprehension in this regard. I think it will undoubtedly be the case that as the public grow accustomed to the opportunities of disclosure contained in the Act, as time goes by and where litigation may be contemplated or indeed where it has even occurred they may opt to seek disclosure of documents via the Act rather than via the traditional method of discovery. Thus it is to be anticipated that a difference of practice may emerge where a defendant or plaintiff is a public body. That is not of course to say the existing policy of requiring an implied undertaking in relation to discovered

THE 1997 ACT AND THE CONSTITUTION

Two appeals - *NMcK v Information Commissioner*[36] and *South Western Area Health Board v. Information Commissioner*[37] have raised fairly significant constitutional issues. It may be co-incidental, but it is nonetheless of interest that both raise issues touching on the inter-action of constitutional and family law.

In *NMcK.* the appellant was a widower who had been separated from his late wife during her lifetime. During the course of family law proceedings in the Circuit Court in 1993 an allegation was made that the appellant sexually abused his daughter, L., (then aged three) at the end of 1991. The appellant vigorously denied this allegation and in 1994 the Garda Síochána, having investigated the allegations, concluded that there was "no evidence to warrant a prosecution" against him and so informed the relevant Health Board. Following her death in 1998, he was made joint guardian along with Mr and Ms J. (his wife's brother and his wife in turn) of the two children of the marriage.[38] The children, however, resided with their mother's family and they had limited and supervised access to their father.

The issues arising under the 1997 Act resulted from the admission of the appellant's daughter - then aged eleven - to hospital in January 2000. When the appellant went to visit his daughter he was advised that she had been admitted for an unspecified viral infection. Being unable to obtain any further information about his daughter's admission, the appellant made a written request pursuant to section 7 of the Act of 1997 seeking access to the personal medical records of his daughter. The hospital did not actually respond to the request in time, so that a refusal was deemed to have been made pursuant to section 41 of the 1997 Act.[39]

---

documents should change. The vast majority of defendants or indeed plaintiffs will not be public bodies and will be entitled to privacy in respect of their confidential documents save to the extent that they are required to be discovered under order of the Court. Therefore it is easy to foresee that there will be a rational and harmonious co-existence between the two regimes of disclosure."

[36] [2004] 1 I.R. 12 (HC); [2006] 1 I.L.R.M. 504 (SC).

[37] [2005] 2 I.R. 547.

[38] Mr. J. subsequently died in 2000.

[39] The appellant also sought a review of this decision, but since no response was received in time, this was also deemed to have been refused for the purposes of section 41 of the 1997 Act.

The appellant then appealed to the Commissioner to review the failure to disclose the records in March 2000 under section 34 of the 1997 Act, but this request was finally refused by decision of the Commissioner in August 2002.

The first issue raised concerned section 28 of the 1997 Act. Section 28(1) precludes personal information in the following terms:

> "Subject to the provisions of this section, a head shall refuse to grant a request under section 7 if, in the opinion of the head, access to the record concerned would involve the disclosure of personal information …".

Section 28(6), however, provides that:

> "Notwithstanding subsection (1), the Minister may provide by regulations for the grant of a request under section 7 where:-
> (a) The individual to whom the record concerned relates belongs to a class specified in the regulations and the requester concerned is the parent or guardian of the individual…".

As it happens, the Minister had made such Regulations: Freedom of Information Act 1997 (Section 28(6) Regulations) 1999.[40] Article 3(1) of the 1999 Regulations provides as follows:

> "Notwithstanding section 28 (1), a request under section 7 in relation to a record access to which involves the disclosure of personal information … shall, subject to other provisions of the Freedom of Information Act 1997, be granted where:
> (a) the requester is a parent or guardian of the individual to whom the record concerned relates and that individual belongs to one of the following classes of individual:
> (i) individuals who, on the date of the request, have not attained full age (within the meaning of the Age of Majority Act 1985 (No. 2 of 1985)), or

---

[40] S.I .No. 47 of 1999. See chap.1 *infra*.

...being individuals specified in clauses (i) and (ii) access to whose records would, in the opinion of the head having regard to all the circumstances and to any guidelines drawn up and published by the Minister, be in their best interests... ".

It was common case that the hospital records in question contained personal information within the meaning of these provisions. Why, then, did the Commissioner affirm the hospital's refusal? The Commissioner reasoned thus:

"...As you are the father and joint guardian of L, it is clear that you satisfy the first of the two requirements set out above. Accordingly, the question to be addressed is whether release to you of material containing personal information relating solely to L, or relating jointly to L and to yourself, would be in L's best interests.

In the ordinary course of events, and in general terms, one might accept that it is likely to be in the best interests of a minor that a parent/guardian will have access to the minor's medical records. However, in the ordinary course of events, the parents/guardians are likely to be in agreement on the matter. As you know, both in contacts with this office and with the hospital, Mr and Mrs J (joint guardians and custodians of L) have opposed the release of these records. Following the recent and regrettable death of her husband, I understand that Mrs J remains firmly opposed to these records being released to you. Furthermore, it is the view of the hospital that the records should not be released to you. In any situation in which there is disagreement between parents/ guardians regarding the release of records relating to a minor, the Commissioner has taken the view that release would only be directed where there is tangible evidence that such release would actually serve the best interests of the minor.

I note you make the case that, as the father of L and as a person holding joint guardianship and custody in relation to her, you hold certain rights in relation to decision-making regarding her health and general welfare. You maintain that release of the records to you may assist in the making of such decisions regarding L and would therefore be in her best interests. I accept that in certain instances access by parents or guardians to medical records in relation to children may offer substantial assistance to them in making decisions in relation to the seeking of medical treatment of their children or consenting to such treatment. Having regard to the contents of the records in this case, I consider that their release would not offer substantial assistance to you in relation to the making of decisions to seek medical treatment or to consent to medical treatment, for L in the future. Further I note that, where appropriate such records could be made available to medical personnel treating L in the future.

On balance, I find that you have not presented evidence that release of L's medical records to you would actually serve her best interests.

In the absence of evidence showing that disclosure would actually be in L's best interests, the requirement to protect her privacy remains strong. While it has not been proven that release of the records would be to the detriment of your daughter, neither am I satisfied that release of the information would be to her benefit or serve her best interests. I do not see any significant benefit accruing, or likely to accrue, to your daughter by granting you access to these records. I am not satisfied that the requirements of S.I. 47 of 1999 are met in this case and I find, therefore, that you do not have the right of access to these records pursuant to its provisions."[41]

Two comments may be made immediately about this reasoning. First, it seems curious that the decision fails even to mention Article 41 and Article 42 of the Constitution, given their self-evident relevance to this topic.

Second, the Commissioner's reasoning downplays the significance of these medical records and by noting that they would, in any event, be available to medical professionals, the Commissioner has by implication cut across the role of a parent in making an informed decision concerning

---

[41] This reasoning is set out in the judgment of Quirke J., [2004] 1 I.R. 12 at 16-17.

the medical welfare of their children. No parent who ever had the responsibility of dealing with a chronically ill child could possibly subscribe to this complacent reasoning. Children's hospitals are awash with instances of where, through the doggedness of dedicated parents, medical professionals have been alerted to faulty diagnoses and misguided treatments.

It is, perhaps, therefore not terribly surprising that both the High Court and the Supreme Court made short work of this reasoning. In the High Court, Quirke J., finding in favour of the appellant, observed that:

> "In the instant case I am satisfied that by enacting section 28(6) of the 1997 Act the Legislature was, *inter alia,* legislating in the interests of vindicating and defending the rights of children. Accordingly, the provisions of the Act fall to be interpreted in the light of the provisions of the Constitution generally and of Articles 41 and 42 in particular.
>
> Although a complaint has in the past been made about the appellant, it remains unsubstantiated and the appellant comes before this Court enjoying the presumption of innocence which is enjoyed by every citizen of the State. The evidence indicates that he is concerned with the welfare of both of his children and avails of his rights of access to them in a conscientious fashion.
>
> No suggestion has been made of any failure of duty on the part of the appellant of the kind contemplated by Article 42.5 of the Constitution.
>
> Accordingly the appellant, as a parent, joint guardian and joint custodian of the child concerned enjoys the parental primacy identified by Hardiman J. in *North Western Health Board v. H.W.*[42] and the presumption that he has the welfare of his child at heart in the absence of evidence to the contrary.
>
> The presumption is of course rebuttable, but there is no suggestion of rebuttal in this case. Reluctance by another family member to agree to access does not, in the absence of any supporting evidence, amount to rebuttal sufficient to displace the presumption referred to.

---

[42] [2001] 3 I.R. 622.

It follows from the foregoing that I am satisfied that in reaching the decision made in this case the [Commissioner] has misconstrued the provisions of section 28 (6) of the Act of 1997 and Article 3 (1) of the 1999 Regulations by failing to recognise that the decisions of the parent of minors are presumed to be in the best interests of that minor in the absence of evidence to the contrary. The appellant should not have been required to discharge an onus of the type identified by the [Commissioner] and the test applied by the [Commissioner] in so doing was incorrect in the circumstances."[43]

A similar view was taken by Denham J. for the Supreme Court:

"As a matter of constitutional and family law a parent has rights and duties. In general, a parent would expect to be given and would be given medical information about his or her child. It would only be in exceptional circumstances that medical information about a child would not be given to a parent/guardian.....The Act of 1997 and the Regulations fall to be interpreted in accordance with the Constitution. A parent, the requester, has rights and duties in relation to a child. It is presumed that his or her actions are in accordance with the best interests of the child. This presumption while not absolute is fundamental. The Commissioner took an incorrect approach in requiring tangible evidence of the parent rather than applying the presumption that a parent was acting in the child's interests. The 'tangible evidence' test of the Commissioner reversed the onus of proof.

The relationship between parent and child has a special status in Ireland. Under the Constitution the family is the primary and fundamental unit group in our society: Article 41.1.1°. The State has guaranteed to protect the family in its constitution and authority: Article 41.1.2°. The State encompasses the judicial branch of government which has a consequent duty to protect the family and its authority. While

---

[43] [2004] 1 I.R. 12 at 20-21.

the family unit has its rights, so too each member of the unit has rights. Thus while the parents have duties and rights in relation to a child, and a child has rights to parental care, the child also has personal rights which the State is required to vindicate if the parent fails in his or her duty.

A parent's rights and duties include the care of a child who is ill. As a consequence a parent is entitled to information about the medical care a child is receiving so that he or she may make appropriate decisions for the child, as his or her guardian. The presumption is that a parent is entitled to access such information. That position is not absolute. The circumstances may be such that the presumption may be rebutted. But the primary position is that the presumption exists. Consequently, the approach of the Commissioner was in error when he required 'tangible evidence' that the release of such information would serve the best interests of the minor. The obverse is the correct approach. The presumption is that the release of such medical information would best serve the interests of the minor. However, evidence may be produced that it would not serve her interests, and, in considering the circumstances, her welfare is paramount. That issue did not arise in this case because of the erroneous approach of the Commissioner."[44]

The Supreme Court, however, varied the High Court order in one critical respect. Whereas Quirke J. had directed that the records be released, the Supreme Court noted that some two further years had elapsed since that decision and L. was now approaching her 18th birthday. While Denham J. pointedly noted that this "most unfortunate" delay was not the fault of the appellant, nonetheless "the effects of the delay cannot be ignored in view of the necessity to balance the changed circumstances, including the attitude of L."[45] The Court accordingly directed that the matter be remitted back to the Commissioner to re-assess in the light of the proper test and the changed circumstances.

---

[44] [2006] 1 I.L.R.M. 504 at 511-512.
[45] *Ibid.*

While *NMcK* is, in many ways, a straightforward case, given that the Commissioner's reasoning so obviously flew in the face of the provisions of Article 41 and Article 42, it highlights the obvious fact that the 1997 Act must be construed in the light of the Constitution. There were, however, much more difficult questions lurking in the background. How, for example, would the principles in *NMcK* be applied where a parent sought medical records which, for example, disclose the nature of the medical advice given to an under-age teenage girl who was seeking access to contraceptives or, for that matter, an abortion.[46] Indeed, quite apart from the provisions of the 1997 Act itself, would, for example, the provisions of Article 41 and Article 42 as interpreted in *NMcK* entitle the parents of a seriously ill child to require the treating clinician to make disclosure of his own medical notes upon request? Given that there is clear authority for the proposition that Articles 41 and Article 42 can produce third party effect (i.e., can apply to litigation between purely private parties)[47], *NMcK* would appear to suggest that parents have such a prima facie constitutional entitlement even quite independently of the 1997 Act.

In *South Western Health Board* the requester was the forty year old daughter of a child who had been born out of wedlock. At the time her birth mother - who was described as coming from a poor, but good, family - felt that she no option but to hand up her daughter for adoption. In 1995 the requester began the process of seeking information about her birth mother from the Health Board. When the Board attempted to contact the birth mother they gave her an assurance on each attempted contact that all correspondence would be treated in the strictest confidence. In 1997, however, the Health Board gave the requester a letter from her birth mother. As Smyth J. poignantly explained:

> "Without disclosure of name or address it very plaintively explains that the birth mother had no choice when she was made pregnant and adoption was the only choice (she came of a poor but good family). The birth mother states why she is unable to make contact with the requester and in wishing

---

[46] Cf. the reasoning of the House of Lords in *Gillick v. West Norfolk and Wisbech Area Health Authority* [1986] A.C. 112.

[47] *Hosford v. J Murphy and Sons Ltd.* [1987] I.R. 621.

the requester well, pleads that each be permitted to get on with their own individual lives."[48]

The requester applied in November 1998 under the 1997 Act for access to these recent records which would disclose the identity of the birth mother.[49] The Health Board's decision was to refuse access to all of the records covered by the request. This position was subsequently maintained by the Health Board in its decision following the requester's application for internal review. As Smyth J. put it:

> "The requester became an adopted child, both mother and child have made new and more structured lives for each other since. The requester has spent much time and effort in seeking to establish who her birth mother is, the latter who is long since married with a family of her own has a husband and family and does not wish the structured trust and security built up over the years to be shattered by a disclosure that might be brought about by the requester contacting the birth mother.
>
> The Health Board, years ago had given the birth mother an assurance of confidentiality and feels itself honour bound

---

[48] [2005] 2 I.R. 547 at 552.

[49] It was not in dispute but that these were pre-commencement records which are normally exempt unless they come with the proviso contained in section 6(5):
"Notwithstanding subsections (1) and (4) but subject to subsection (6) where–
(a) access to records created before the commencement of this Act is necessary or expedient in order to understand records created after such commencement; or
(b) records created before such commencement relate to personal information about the person seeking access to them subsection (1) shall be construed as conferring the right of access in respect of these records."
While Smyth J. did not accept that it was necessary to have access to these records to understand post-commencement records, he did accept - applying the test enunciated by O'Neill J. in *EH v. Information Commissioner (No.2)* [2002] 3 I.R. 600 - that the records constituted "personal information" about the requester, i.e., they relate "to something in which the requester has a substantial personal interest as distinct from something in which he has an interest as a member of the general community or large-scale class of same."

to keep faith with the birth mother, to adhere to the basis of the Board's contract with the mother." [50]

In the decision under appeal the Commissioner had refused to order disclosure of material which would identify the birth mother. There was a statutory prohibition on disclosure of such information and the Commissioner concluded that this matter thus came within section 32 of the 1997 Act. But so far as the other documentation was concerned, the Commissioner concluded that this was personal information within the meaning of section 28 and that public interest favoured disclosure:

"As well as the public interest in your having information about your background and your adoption, including the limited amount of information in the records about your birth mother's health, I take the view that the public interest also favours your knowing how the Board dealt with your request in 1995 for information about your birth mother. Accordingly, it is my finding that the public interest in your having access to these records overrides the rights to privacy of your birth mother having regard to the fact that you do not have access to her name and address, that you have already been made aware of most of the information in the records through the Board's social workers and that your mother is aware of your efforts to trace her."

The Board appealed against this decision and sought a variation of the order of the Commissioner so as to provide for the release of those parts of the enumerated records as do not contain personal information or medical or health history of the requester's birth mother or record that encompass confidential exchanges between the parties. Smyth J. found for the appellant Board on four main grounds.

First, Smyth J. accepted that the Commissioner erred in placing undue emphasis on the motivation of the requester, since this was an irrelevant consideration under the 1997 Act:

"I can well understand and appreciate the importance for most

---

people of the fullest comprehension of their identity, the sense
of roots and the security of the knowledge from whence they
come is: nonetheless, motivation of the requester in the
adjudication process is an irrelevant consideration."[51]

Second, Smyth J. noted that the Commissioner formed the view that it
was not necessary to contact the birth mother because "the degree of
invasion of the birth mother's privacy occasioned by the release of the
records was minimal and justified in the public interest." The judge then
referred to section 34(6) which provides:

"As soon as may be after the receipt by the Commissioner of
an application under subsection (2), the Commissioner shall
cause a copy of the application to be given to the head
concerned, and, as may be appropriate, to the relevant person
concerned and, if the Commissioner proposes to review the
decision concerned, he or she shall cause the head and the
relevant person and any other person who, in the opinion of
the Commissioner, should be notified of the proposal to be
so notified and thereupon the head shall give to the
Commissioner particulars in writing or in such other form as
may be determined of any persons who he or she has, or, in
the case of a refusal to grant a request to which section 29
applies, would if he or she had intended to grant the request
under section 7 concerned, have notified of the request."

---

[51] [2005] 2 I.R. 547 at 554. S. 8(4) makes it clear that the motives of the requester
are irrelevant for this purpose. This point was also made by O'Neill J. in *EH v.
Information Commissioner (No.1)* [2001] 2 I.R. 463 where the requester sought
the information to assist the prosecution of charges of professional misconduct
against a medical practitioner before the Medical Council. O'Neill J. held ([2001]
2 I.R. 463 at 483) that these reasons were not relevant to the request:
   " In my view his reasons, be they to pursue his case in the Fitness to Practice
   Committee Inquiry, to generally vindicate his good name; or if it was merely
   idle curiosity are entirely immaterial and must be disregarded by the head of
   body, the Commissioner and by me on this appeal. Section 8(4) makes that
   absolutely clear."

Smyth J. was of the view that the Commissioner had plainly erred in law in arriving at these conclusions without consulting the birth mother:

> "What the papers clearly reveal is that the persistence of the inquiries had angered the birth mother's husband and caused her to seek medical advice and treatment. The concerns of the birth mother were not only for her good name and reputation, but principally for the harmony of her marriage and stability, cohesion and protection of her family. To have formed a view or opinion that "the degree of invasion of the birth mother's privacy occasioned by the release of the records was minimal and justified in the public interest" is to fail to consider relevant issues and rights such as the constitutional rights of the birth mother's family and the protection of her marriage and to make a value judgment as to the extent or degree of invasion of rights without according the birth mother directly, or indirectly through her legal advisors, to make representations in support of the rights she sought to protect.
>
> In my judgment, natural and constitutional justice and fair procedures required that the birth mother be given an opportunity to make representations prior to the decision being taken by the Commissioner. His failure to do so is procedurally unfair and the decision made as a result cannot stand.
>
> I accept the Commissioner's submission that the public interest with which the Act of 1997 is concerned is of prime importance, but when put into the balance with the various other constitutional rights to which I have referred the principle of proportionality must be applied. However, as the rights expressly referred to in this judgment do not appear to have been considered and informed the decision of the Commissioner, the purported proportionality test applied between the public interest and the right to privacy is less than adequate to sustain the decision."[52]

---

[52] [2005] 2 I.R. 547 at 556.

For good measure Smyth J. drew attention to the fact that the
Commissioner was influenced by certain proposals by the Department of
Health and Children to give adopted parents "statutory rights to
information about their adoption as well as to provide for the setting up
of a voluntary contact register for persons seeking contact with their birth
parents." The judge, however, was of the view that "decisions must be
based on the law as it stood at the date of the decision."[53]

Finally, Smyth J. was of the view that the information in question was
confidential information which came within the scope of section 26:

> "The records created by the health authority who promised
> that the frantic concealment of a distraught young mother -
> very often little more than a child herself - would not be
> disclosed should be honoured in the public interest.... In my
> judgment the disclosures made to the appellant - if to be
> transmitted even in the redacted form the subject of the
> Commissioner's decision, would as a matter of probability
> prejudice the giving to the appellant or any other health
> authority of further similar information. I accept the evidence
> and the submissions to the court that it is of importance to
> the appellant that future similar information should be given
> to it and other health authorities. It is, in my judgment, not in
> the public interest that persons such as the birth mother in
> the instant case should have their distress compounded and
> maybe put at risk the life of a baby because there is in fact no
> health authority that they can completely trust."[54]

CONCLUSIONS

What, if any, conclusions can be drawn from this somewhat motley
collection of individual appeals? Many of the (relatively limited) number
of appeals concern cases either with special facts or relatively arcane

---

[53] *Ibid.*, p.557.
[54] [2005] 2 I.R. 547 at 558.

aspects of the 1997 Act itself.[55] It is, frankly, difficult to extract any general themes from this myriad of often very special instances. Even probably the most important decision on the 1997 Act to date – *Sheedy v. Information Commissioner* – is just as likely to be remembered more as a case on aspects of statutory interpretation than for its own intrinsic importance as a leading decision on the scope of the 1997 Act.

It is clear from the nature of the decisions under appeal (as well, indeed, as the relatively limited number of appeals) that there is no doubt but that the overall quality of the Commissioner's decisions is strikingly impressive. The courts are nevertheless prepared to reverse these decisions where an error of law is disclosed. Despite the dicta of McKechnie J. in *Deely* – which suggested a high level of judicial deference – the overall picture which emerges is that the standard of review is much closer to the ordinary appellate standard. This is particularly evident in cases such as *NMcK* and the *South Western Health Board* (where the Commissioner was venturing into relatively deep constitutional waters and into an area where the courts would be traditionally reluctant to show deference to conclusions drawn by non-judicial personages) or where – as in cases such as *Sheedy* – the issue involves a pure point of statutory interpretation.[56]

If, however, any general theme emerges, it is probably that the courts have been at pains to give the 1997 Act a liberal interpretation. This sentiment was, perhaps, most strikingly expressed by McKechnie J. in *Deely* where he observed that the enactment of the 1997 Act:

"...it is no exaggeration to say, affected in a most profound

---

[55] See, e.g., *RTE v. Information Commissioner* [2004] I.E.H.C. 113 where Ó Caoimh J. held that the Commissioner had misconstrued the relevant provisions of Sch.3 of Freedom of Information Act 1997 (Prescribed Bodies) (No. 2) Regulations 2000.

[56] Another example of this type of case is *Minister for Justice, Equality and Law Reform v. Information Commissioner* [2002] 1 I.L.R.M. 1, a case which involved the construction of s.46 which excludes courts records from the scope of the 1997 Act. Here Finnegan J. was also required to have regard to O.86 of the Rules of the Superior Courts 1986 and, again, it is not surprising that in this area the High Court simply arrived at its own conclusion - which it substituted for that of the Commissioner - as to the construction of the section and its inter-action with other legal instruments, in this instance, O.86.

way, access by members of the public to records held by
public bodies and to information regarding certain acts of
such bodies which touch or concern such persons. The
purpose of its enactment was to create accountability and
transparency and this to an extent not heretofore contemplated
let alone available to the general public. Many would say
that it creates an openness which inspires a belief and trust
which can only further public confidence in the constitutional
organs of the State...

As can thus be seen, the clear intention is that, subject to
certain specific and defined exceptions, the rights so
conferred on members of the public and their exercise should
be as extensive as possible, this viewed, in the context of
and in a way to positively further the aims, principles and
policies underpinning this statute, subject and subject only
to necessary restrictions. It is, on any view, a piece of
legislation independent in existence, forceful in its aim and
liberal in outlook and philosophy."[57]

Allied to this is the belief that there is a presumption in favour of
disclosure[58] and that the ordinary principles of interpretation may not
necessarily apply to a special statute of this kind. This is reflected in the
reasoning of McKechnie J. in *Deely*[59] and also accounts for the division

---

[57] [2001] 3 I.R. 439 at 441-442.

[58] Thus, as O'Donovan J emphasised in *Minister for Agriculture and Food v.
Information Commissioner* [2000] 1 I.R. 309 at 319:
"...in the light of its preamble, it seems to me that there can be no doubt but
that it was the intention of the legislature when enacting the provisions of the
Freedom of Information Act 1997, that it was only in exceptional cases that
members of the public at large should be deprived of access to information in
the possession of public bodies and this intention is exemplified by the
provision of s. 34 (12)(b) of the Act which provides that a decision to refuse
to grant access to information sought shall be presumed not to have been
justified until the contrary is shown".

[59] Here McKechnie J. observed ([2001] 3 I.R. 439 at 451) that:
"Being a creature of the Oireachtas, of a type without direct or parallel
precedent, it is not possible to cite Acts, pari passu, upon which the Courts
have expressed a view as to the correct method of statutory interpretation.
The primacy of the test of any statute, is of course, an approach which pervades

of judicial opinion in *Sheedy*.[60] But the very fact that the courts have reacted so positively and enthusiastically to the 1997 Act is probably the best assurance there is that the objectives of this most important item of legislation will ultimately be realised.

---

the commencement of any interpretative process, which is, to ascertain the will of parliament and to identify the intention of the legislature; this from the wording of the provision or provisions in question: see *Howard v. Commission of Public Works in Ireland* [1994] 1 I.R. 101, and in particular the judgment of Blayney J, is a decision on point.

However that approach may not in all cases be a complete answer to the exercise demanded. Different statutes may require additional methods to be adopted. Certainly, one is entitled to look at the Act as a whole and if there is any doubt or ambiguity, the purpose, intention and objects of the Act, may also be considered. As may the title. See *People (DPP) v. Quilligan* [1986] I.R. 495 at 523, per Walsh J. An interpretation, which if otherwise is consistent with accepted cannons of construction, and is one which recognises the different roles of the legislature and the judiciary, can, nevertheless, be positively and actively adopted for the purposes of furthering the declared aims and intention of parliament as expressed or found in the Act in question.

I am not therefore certain that given the vision of the 1997 Act, it is altogether a complete statement to suggest, that, the provisions thereof in their entirety can adequately be interpreted, for the purpose of implementation, simply by a straightforward application of *Howard*."

60 Thus, in his dissenting judgment, Fennelly J. took a similarly expansive view of the purpose of the 1997 Act ([2005] 2 I.R. 272 at 275):

"The passing of the Freedom of Information Act constituted a legislative development of major importance. By it, the Oireachtas took a considered and deliberate step which dramatically alters the administrative assumptions and culture of centuries. It replaces the presumption of secrecy with one of openness. It is designed to open up the workings of government and administration to scrutiny. It is not designed simply to satisfy the appetite of the media for stories. It is for the benefit of every citizen. It lets light in to the offices and filing cabinets of our rulers. The principle of free access to publicly held information is part of a world-wide trend. The general assumption is that it originates in the Scandinavian countries. The Treaty of Amsterdam adopted a new Article 255 of the EC Treaty providing that every citizen of the European Union should have access to the documents of the European Parliament, Council and Commission."

CHAPTER 6

Access to Tender Related Information under FOI

MAEVE MCDONAGH*

This chapter will explore the operation of the FOI Act in the area of commercial information. The main focus of the chapter will be on the disclosure of information relating to public contracts. It will assess the way in which the Act, as applied by the Information Commissioner, balances the commercial interests of those doing business with government against the public interest in obtaining access to information relating to such contracts.

The chapter will begin by discussing the role of disclosure of information in the awarding and operation of public contracts. It will go on to describe the categories of information to which access might be sought. The relevant provisions of the Act will be outlined and this will be followed by an exploration of the application of Irish FOI law in this field.

THE ROLE OF DISCLOSURE OF INFORMATION IN THE AWARDING AND OPERATION OF PUBLIC CONTRACTS

The interest in disclosure of information relating to public contracts can be considered from three main perspectives:

- that of public authorities with which such contracts are concluded.

- that of contractors.

- that of the broader public.

---

* Associate Professor of Law, University College Cork.

Public authorities can gain from disclosure of information relating to the awarding of public contracts through achieving better value for money on future contracts. This is because the withholding of information from potential contractors restricts their ability to compete. In particular, limiting access clearly favours the incumbent, making it more difficult for newcomers to enter the market, thus restricting competition.

Contractors can benefit in terms of gaining knowledge about their competitors that will allow them to compete more strongly on future contracts. They can also gain in terms of the role which disclosure of information can play in ensuring that the awarding of the contract is conducted fairly and in a non-discriminatory fashion.

Gains to the broader public accrue not only in respect of the awarding of the contract, but also from disclosure of information that allows for the monitoring of the operation of the contract during its lifetime. In terms of the awarding of contracts, the public can gain through the achievement of better value for money and through protection against inefficiency and corruption within contracting authorities. In terms of monitoring the operation of public contracts, the disclosure of contractual performance indicators, for example, will allow the public to determine whether the successful contractor is meeting the promised standards. Such opportunities for oversight are particularly important in an era of contracting out of government services. As the Australian Administrative Review Council Report on Contracting Out of public services observed:

> "A service recipient may need information in order to provide evidence of service delivery problems or to ascertain what the contract requires of the contractor. A minimum amount of information must be available for the service recipient to know whether they are being dealt with properly by the contractor. Access to information by members of the public in general and service recipients in particular also enables a broader evaluation of the performance of contractors and of government agencies."[1]

The disadvantages of disclosure of information relating to public contracts

---

[1] Administrative Review Council Report No. 42, *The Contracting Out of Government Services,* (1998), paras 5.16 - 5.17.

are likely to accrue mainly to contractors. They may argue, for example, that information submitted by them in order to win a contract amounts to a trade secret, the disclosure of which could damage their competitiveness. From the contracting authorities' perspective, disclosure of information might be unwelcome in so far as it could reveal inefficiencies or corruption within the authority. Another more defensible argument that is sometimes advanced is that disclosure of information might deter potential contractors from competing for contracts, thus reducing the level of competition. From the perspective of the public at large, it is difficult to see what deleterious effects could accrue from disclosure of information, apart from possible effects in terms of value for money that could arise from the withdrawal of potential contractors.

The categories of information to which access may be sought can be divided into pre- and post-contractual information. Pre-contractual information includes the following:

- The names of successful/unsuccessful tenderers and candidates for pre-selection.

- Applications for selection of successful/unsuccessful candidates for pre-selection.

- Tender submissions (including prices) of successful/unsuccessful tenderers.

- Correspondence between tenderers and the public authority.

- Criteria used in selection.

- Records of evaluation process including rankings.

- Reasons for selection/rejection of candidates/tenderers.

- Justification for use of negotiated procedures.

Post-contractual information includes:

- The contract document.

- Performance reports.

THE FREEDOM OF INFORMATION ACT

The two most significant exemptions in terms of disclosure of information concerning public contracts are the confidentiality and the commercially sensitive information exemptions.[2]

Information obtained in confidence

The confidentiality exemption, the application of which is mandatory, is made up of two parts, each of which constitutes a separate ground of exemption from the right of access. They are designed to protect respectively: documents the disclosure of which would be likely to hinder the future supply of confidential information of importance to the public body (section 26(1)(a)) (referred to below as the "future supply confidentiality exemption"); and documents the disclosure of which would form the basis of an action for breach of confidence (section 26(1(b)) (the "breach of confidence exemption"). The Act places important limitations on the use of section 26 to protect records prepared internally by public bodies,[3] The application of section 26(1)(a) is also subject to a public interest test, which requires disclosure where the public interest would, on balance, be better served by granting than by refusing to grant the request. No public interest test is provided for in respect of section 26(1)(a), but the public interest defence to the action for breach of confidence has been held to be applicable to this limb of the exemption[4].

In order for section 26(1)(a) (the future supply confidentiality exemption) to apply, four cumulative conditions must be met:

- the information in question must have been given to the public body concerned in confidence and

- on the understanding that it would be treated as confidential;

- disclosure must be likely to prejudice the future supply of such information; and

---

[2] See further McDonagh, M. *Freedom of Information law in Ireland* (Thomson Round Hall, Dublin) 2006 forthcoming.
[3] S.26(2).
[4] *ABY and Department of Education and Science,* Long Form Decision No. 98169, July 6, 2000.

- it must be of importance to the body that such future supply should continue.

Section 26(1)(b) (the breach of confidence exemption) applies where disclosure of the information concerned would constitute a breach of a duty of confidence provided for by a provision of an agreement or enactment or otherwise by law. Section 26(1)(b) appears to incorporate the general law relating to the action for breach of confidence, the essential elements of which are:

- The information must be confidential i.e. have the necessary quality of confidence about it.

- The information must have been imparted in circumstances imposing an obligation of confidence.

- There must be an obligation of confidence arising either from the relationship between the parties or from the fact that the information was imparted for a limited purpose.[5]

Commercially sensitive information

The structure of this exemption is somewhat complex – it is really four exemptions in one. The first element of the exemption (section 27(1)(a)) protects trade secrets against disclosure (the "trade secrets exemption"). This is a class type exemption in that once it is shown that the requested information amounts to a trade secret, no inquiries can be made as to whether disclosure would give rise to any harm. The other three limbs of the exemption incorporate harm tests. Section 27(1)(b) protects against disclosure "financial, commercial, scientific, technical or other information", but only where its disclosure could reasonably be expected to result in material financial loss or gain to the person to whom the information relates (the "material loss exemption") or where its discloser could prejudice the competitive position of the person to whom the information relates in the conduct of his business, profession or occupation (the "competitive position exemption") . The third and fourth limbs of

---

[5]   *Coco v. A.N.Clark (Engineers) Limited* [1969] F.S.R. 415 per Megarry J. at 419-420.

the exemption, (section 27(1)(c)), protects information concerning negotiations (the "negotiation exemption"). It applies where disclosure could prejudice the conduct or outcome of contractual or other negotiations of the person to whom the information relates. The application of section 27 is subject to a public interest override that again requires disclosure where the public interest would, on balance, be better served by granting than by refusing to grant the request.

FOI DECISIONS RELATING TO PUBLIC CONTRACTS

The Commissioner has dealt with a number of cases involving requests for access to records concerning public contracts. All of the cases dealt with to date have concerned requests for access to tender related made information after the conclusion of the tender process, though the Commissioner has, in some instances, indicated his or her likely approach to information relating to ongoing tender processes. The cases have involved requests for access to the following categories of information:

1. Successful tenderers:
   a. Tender prices of successful tenderers;
   b. Tender submissions of successful tenderers;
2. Unsuccessful tenderers:
   a. Tender prices of unsuccessful tenderers;
   b. Names of unsuccessful tenderers;
   c. Tender submissions of unsuccessful tenderers;
3. Records of the evaluation process.
4. Contract documents.

Successful tenderers

Tender prices of successful tenderers

In *Henry Ford & Son Ltd v. Office of Public Works*,[6] a case which involved an application by a third party for access to total tender prices relating to the supply of army vehicles, the Commissioner considered the application of both the confidentiality and commercially sensitive information

---

[6] Long Form Decision No. 9849, March 31, 1999.

exemptions to the prices of successful tenderers. With regard to the breach of confidence exemption, the Commissioner concluded that at the time the tender was entered, it had the necessary quality of confidence about it, in the sense that the price was known only to each tenderer and each disclosed its price to the contracting authority on the understanding that it, in turn, would keep the information confidential – at least until the conclusion of the tendering process. In deciding whether the information was imparted in circumstances imposing an obligation of confidence, the Commissioner considered the relationship between the successful tenderer and the contracting authority and concluded that it was not of a kind which is generally understood to attract the badge of confidentiality. Indeed he said that it was more likely that the reverse would be true, adding that in the relationship of vendor/purchaser there is no general expectation that a purchaser will keep secret the price he pays for goods or services. The limited purpose test was also held to be inapplicable on the basis that the test has developed generally in the context of one party becoming privy to another's secret information and using that information to its own benefit, and to the possible detriment of the others, and that such circumstances are very far removed from the "disclosure" by a vendor to a purchaser of the purchase price. The Commissioner also expressed the view that disclosure on foot of a request under the FOI Act of the price paid by a public body for goods, would be unlikely to amount to "an unauthorised use" for the purposes of satisfying this requirement of the action for breach of confidence.

In applying the future supply confidentiality exemption, the Commissioner accepted that there was an understanding that the price would be treated as confidential until the end of the tender process, but he found that there was no evidence of a mutual understanding that the information would be kept confidential indefinitely. In arriving at this conclusion, the Commissioner remarked

> "One would have to question, having regard to the coming into force of the FOI Act how any public body could have an understanding that the details of its expenditure of public money would be kept confidential."

---

[7] Letter Decision No. 99183, January 21, 2003.
[8] (1996) 3 Q.A.R. 376.

The Commissioner also rejected the argument that disclosure would be likely to prejudice the giving of information in the future, saying he did not accept that it was likely that disclosure of prices would result in commercial enterprises refusing to tender. The non-application of section 26 to successful tender prices was confirmed by the Commissioner's decision in *McKeever Rowan and Department of Finance*,[7] a case concerning the awarding of a contract to advise the Minister for Finance on the sale of a state owned bank.

In applying the commercially sensitive information exemption to tender prices, the Commissioner found, in *Henry Ford,* that the tender price did not amount to a trade secret, although he indicated that tender prices might amount to a trade secret prior to the conclusion of the tender process. With regard to the application of the competitive position exemption (section 27(1)(b)) to tender prices, the Commissioner quoted with approval a passage from a decision of the Queensland Information Commissioner in *Re McPhillimy and Queensland Treasury*[8] to the effect that knowledge by future tenderers of the price quoted by an earlier successful tenderer does not automatically give them a significant advantage over the previously successful party. However, he upheld the application of section 27(1)(b) to the successful tender price in the particular circumstances of *Henry Ford*, which were that the price was a preferential one not available to the tenderer's other customers. This was because disclosure of the price charged could result in other customers of the company becoming aware that such a price differed from that quoted to them and knowledge of this discrepancy could disrupt those other business relationships and perhaps cause some customers to seek other suppliers.

In the absence of such a preferential pricing situation, it appears that total tender prices are unlikely to qualify as commercially sensitive for the purposes of section 27(1)(b) once a contract is awarded. This view is supported by the Commissioner's comments in *X v. Department of Enterprise Trade and Employment*:[9]

> "Once a competition is over, the tender price and the tender awarded become historic, pertaining as they do to a single transaction, and it seems to me that knowledge by other

---

[9] Decision No. 020295, September 9, 2002.

tenderers of the price accepted in an earlier tender does not
of itself allow those parties to deduce with any certainty the
price which will be offered in a later competition. In such
circumstances, the disclosure of the tender price could not,
in my view, damage the competitive position of [the tendering
company] in the future."

Total tender prices must, however, be distinguished from detailed
information about a company's pricing strategy, which the Commissioner
has acknowledged, could qualify as commercially sensitive for the
purposes of section 27(1)(b) after a contract has been awarded. Thus in
Henry and Office of Public Works,[10] the Commissioner said:

"I should add that I accept, as a general proposition, that
tender documents which would reveal detailed information
about a company's current pricing strategy ... could fall
within the scope of section 27(1)(a) even following the
conclusion of a tender competition.."

The issue of the commercial sensitivity of unit prices in the context of
successful tenders arose for consideration in *Collins v. Department of
Communications, Marine and Natural Resources.*[11] Here the
Commissioner found that information consisting of successful bid prices
for the sale of wind energy to the ESB for a period of 15 years, which
took the form of a unit rate for the sale of a kilowatt-hour of energy,
qualified as commercially sensitive information under section 27(1)(b).
In so doing, she took the view that disclosure of the precise bid prices
could be used by competitors to undercut successful tenderers in future
competitions. The Commissioner went on to hold that disclosure of the
information in question would not be in the public interest.

One of the cases relied upon in arriving at the decision that the bid
prices in *Collins* qualified as commercially sensitive under section
27(1)(b), was the Queensland case of *Dalrymple Shire Council and
Department of Main Roads*[12] in which it was held that unit prices in a

---

[10] Long Form Decision No. 98188, November 25, 2001.
[11] Letter Decision No. 040275, June 24, 2004.
[12] (1998) 4 Q.A.R. 474.

construction contract were commercially sensitive. That decision was, however, arrived at in the context of the total tender price already having been disclosed. It was clear in those circumstances that detailed unit prices, for example, the cost per metre of the construction of fencing, could be commercially sensitive in that their disclosure would allow competitors to assess comparative cost advantages and disadvantages between itself and the successful tenderer across a range of construction items (thus enabling it to assess in detail those areas in which it would need to find savings/efficiencies in order to be more competitive in future tenders, and those areas in which it may not need to find savings/efficiencies).

The situation in *Dalrymple Shire Council* differed sharply from the situation in *Collins* since, in the latter case, the only price that existed was the unit price. As the former Commissioner acknowledged in *Henry and Office of Public Works*,[13] it may be possible, in exceptional circumstances, for a company's pricing strategy to be deduced through price disclosure alone, for example, if individual prices for items forming part of the contractual requirements would disclose underlying costs and profit on that item. Cases of this nature will however be very much the exception rather than the rule, and it is submitted that the situation in *Collins* did not fall into such a category. Here the price at issue was not a unit price in the sense of a unit per metre of fencing, but rather it represented the overall price for a unit of electricity, taking into account a wide range of variables including cost of land, labour rates, profit etc., which happened to be quoted as a rate per unit. Knowledge of this amount, it is submitted, would do little to assist a competitor to make a more informed estimate of the unit rates likely to be submitted by the tenderers in future tenders for the supply of electricity. More importantly, withholding this amount could deprive the public of knowledge of the amount paid by a public body for the large scale supply of an important commodity at tax payers' expense.

Overall, it appears that the circumstances in which successful total tender prices would qualify as commercially sensitive would appear to be limited to situations where the price in question was a preferential one not available to the tenderer's other customers, or where it consists of a unit price which could disclose underlying costs and profit on that item.

---

[13] *Op cit.*, n.10.

On the other hand, details of pricing strategies will most likely be found to be commercially sensitive under section 27(1)(b). Nonetheless, the disclosure of price related information will often be found to be in the public interest. For example, in *Henry Ford,*[14] the Commissioner held that the public interest in disclosure of the total tender price outweighed that in withholding it.

Having acknowledged that there is legitimate public interest in persons being able to conduct commercial transactions with public bodies without fear of suffering commercially as a result, the Commissioner emphasised the importance of the public interest in ensuring the maximum openness in relation to the use of public funds. Such openness, the Commissioner said, "is a significant aid to ensuring effective oversight of public expenditure, to ensuring the public obtains value for money, to preventing fraud and corruption and to preventing the waste or misuse of public funds". The public interest will not, however, always weigh in favour of disclosure of successful tender prices. For example, in *Collins v. Department of Communications, Marine and Natural Resources*[15] the Commissioner concluded that disclosure of the requested successful bid prices was not in the public interest. The public interest arguments which weighed against the release of the requested information in *Collins* included the public interest in the protection of commercially sensitive information and the public interest in Ireland meeting its obligations to reduce greenhouse emissions through operating a successful programme for the supply of electricity produced from renewable energy sources.

The tendency on the part of the Commissioner to favour disclosure of tender prices of successful tenderers is very much in keeping with the practice in jurisdictions such as Queensland, Western Australia and Canada of publishing such prices, as described by the Commissioner in *Henry Ford & Son Ltd and Office of Public Works.*[16]

Tender submissions of successful tenderers

The Commissioner's approach in relation to successful tender submissions has been to examine each element of the submission to see which should

---

[14] *Op cit.,* n.6.

[15] *Op cit.,* n. 11.

[16] *Op cit.,* n. 6.

be withheld. Thus in *McKeever Rowan v. Department of Finance*,[17] the Commissioner expressly rejected a suggestion that a successful tender document automatically qualified for exemption as a whole.

In *Henry v. Office of Public Works*,[18] which concerned the same tender competition as that which was the subject of the decision in *Henry Ford & Son Ltd and Office of Public Works*,[19] the Commissioner accepted detailed information about otherwise unavailable product information could come within the scope of the commercially sensitive information exemption. In *McKeever Rowan*, the Commissioner accepted generally that undisclosed, detailed information about a successful tenderer's business, understanding of, and approach to, a particular project, and approach to tendering in general, remains confidential and commercially sensitive following a tender competition. Such information, the Commissioner said, should not be disclosed in the public interest unless it was necessary to explain the nature of the goods or services paid for by the public body.

Amongst the categories of information the Commissioner held to be exempt in *McKeever Rowan* was client information which was found to be exempt under both the confidentiality and commercially sensitive information exemptions. The Commissioner also held in *McKeever Rowan* that the names and positions of, and other identifying information about, individuals put forward as members of the proposed project team, but who were not named as such in the contract for services, qualified as personal information within the meaning of the Act. The Commissioner said that such information relates to the employment or employment history of the individuals and thus falls within the scope of the categories of information listed as personal information for the purposes of the Act. He went on to decide that the public interest in releasing this information did not outweigh the right to privacy of the individuals concerned.

This finding goes against the decision of the Queensland Information Commissioner in *Wanless Wastecorp Pty v. Caboolture Shire Council*,[20] where it was held that the personal information exemption did not apply

---

[17] *Op cit.*, n. 7.

[18] *Op cit.*, n. 10.

[19] *Op cit.*, n. 6.

[20] Queensland Information Commissioner, unreported, Decision No.03/2003, June 30, 2003.

to résumés of staff members included in a tender submission. The basis of this finding was that such résumés which focus only on the professional qualifications and work experience of the relevant staff members are properly characterised as information concerning the employment affairs of the relevant staff members, rather than their personal affairs. It is also at odds with other decisions of the Information Commissioner which indicate that in order to qualify as personal information for the purposes of section 28, the information in question must "derive from a private aspect of an individual recipient's life, such as family circumstances or inadequacy of means"[21] However the Commissioner did hold in *McKeever Rowan* that a reference to a Director or executive of a company or a partner in a law firm acting solely in his or her representative capacity for, and on behalf of, the company or firm in a tender for a public contract, did not qualify as personal information since such a reference is about the company or firm, not the individual.

Other information in successful tender documents that has been held to be outside of the scope of the exemptions includes marketing and promotional information[22] and information available on a tenderer's website or in other publications.[23]

The age of a requested tender submission will have a bearing on the possible application to it of either the confidentiality or commercially sensitive information exemptions. In *Company X and Department of Communications Marine and Natural Resources,* [24] for example, the Commissioner held that neither exemption was applicable to a request for access to a successful tender submission relating to the controversial floatation of Eircom. In the case of section 26, the Commissioner found that the successful tenderer could not reasonably expect that any of the information would be treated as confidential when it was five years old. She accordingly did not accept that an obligation or mutual understanding

---

[21] *ACG and Others and Department of Agriculture, Food and Rural Development* Long Form Decision Nos. 99591, 99594, 99596, 99598, and 99606, November 27, 2001. See also *X and the Western Health Board,* Letter Decision No. 000282, May 8, 2003 and *X and A Department,* Letter Decision No. 000542, February 10, 2003.

[22] *Henry and Office of Public Works,* above, n.10; *McKeever Rowan and Department of Finance,* above, n. 7.

[23] Above, n. 7.

[24] Letter Decision No. 030182, July 23, 2003.

of confidence existed with respect to the tender submission. In the case of section 27, the decision to release was based on public interest arguments. The Commissioner found that while some of the information was commercially sensitive, any harm arising from release of the tender would be minimal given the passage of time, and the fact that some of the information had already entered the public domain. This harm was outweighed by the strong public interest in openness and accountability in relation to the floatation.

Unsuccessful tenderers

Total tender prices of unsuccessful tenderers

In *Henry and Office of Public Works,*[25] the Commissioner found that the prices of unsuccessful tenders qualified as commercially sensitive information and that they also met the requirements of both limbs of the confidentiality exemption. With regard to the public interest in disclosure, the Commissioner drew a distinction between successful and unsuccessful tenders in terms of both their expectations of confidentiality and of the benefits accruing to them from tendering. He noted that it is reasonable for an unsuccessful tenderer to expect that the terms of the offer will remain confidential and that while any harm or detriment which might result from disclosure of information about a successful tender would be outweighed by the benefits of being awarded the contract, this is not true with respect to an unsuccessful tender. He went on to say that as a general rule, where the confidential or commercially sensitive information of a tenderer does not involve the expenditure or public money, the public interest lies in protecting that information from disclosure.

Names of unsuccessful tenderers

In *Henry and Office of Public Works*, the Commissioner considered the case for disclosure of the names of unsuccessful tenderers. The Commissioner found that records identifying the tenderers as unsuccessful were not exempt. He held that in order for either section 26 or section 27 to be applicable, he must be satisfied that at least some tangible form of

---

[25] *Op cit.,* n. 10.

detriment or harm would occur as a result of the disclosure. The Commissioner stated that the only argument which was put to him in that regard was that a company would be the subject of adverse publicity in cases where its tender was the lowest, but was nevertheless rejected. The Commissioner noted that the rejection of the lowest tender may simply indicate that the tender was not considered to be the most economically advantageous when all of the award criteria were taken into account. He rejected the application of either exemption to the names of the unsuccessful tenderers.

In *X and Leitrim County Council*[26] the tender prices of the three tendering companies had already been revealed, and the applicant sought access to the identities of the companies. The Commissioner characterised this request as one for access to the identity of the tenderers along with their respective tender prices, as opposed to a request solely for the identities of the tenderers. He held that disclosure of the requested information fell within the scope of section 27(1)(b) on the basis that it could prejudice the competitive position for the parties whose prices are disclosed. In considering where the public interest lay, the Commissioner decided that release of the identities of unsuccessful tenderers associated with their tender prices would not enhance the public interest in the openness and accountability of government to an extent sufficient to overcome the countervailing public interest in the protection of commercially sensitive information. The Commissioner adverted to the fact that he had considered whether the identities of the unsuccessful tenderers should be released disassociated from their tender prices, but as there were only two unsuccessful tenderers, he had decided against this course of action.

In practice, it appears that provided that the number of tenderers is sufficiently high, the disclosure of a list of the unsuccessful prices and names of unsuccessful tenders disassociated from one another is common.

Tender submissions of unsuccessful tenderers

In *Henry and Office of Public Works,*[27] the Commissioner held that

---

[26] Letter Decision No. 99557, November 29, 2001.
[27] *Op cit.,* n. 10.

product information of unsuccessful tenderers was commercially sensitive, and given the differences between successful and unsuccessful tenderers, there was no public interest in the disclosure of the unsuccessful tender submissions. Similarly, in *McKeever Rowan and Department of Finance,*[28] the Commissioner upheld the refusal of access to details regarding an unsuccessful tenderer's fee structure, as well as details regarding its business and its understanding of and approach to the project, as well as the details of its team. These decisions are in keeping with the approach of the Western Australian Information Commissioner who held in the case of *Maddock, Lonie and Chisholm and Department of State Services,*[29] that information included in the submissions of unsuccessful tenderers, such as detailed descriptions of the manner in which the total prices were calculated, details of the systems and equipment proposed and specific proposals and processes of how that equipment would be used, qualified for exemption on the grounds that its disclosure could reduce the competitiveness of the unsuccessful tenderers in any future tender process.

Records of the evaluation process

The issue of access to tender evaluations has arisen in only one Irish case. In *McKeever Rowan* the Commissioner accepted the argument that disclosure of the assessments of all but the highest placed tenderer could be expected to prejudice the competitive position of the firms concerned and was thus exempt under section 27(1)(b). This approach is in keeping with that adopted in the Queensland case of *Wastecorp Pty and Caboolture Shire Council*[30] where the Commissioner found that disclosure of the documents generated in evaluating the successful tender submission was important in order to further accountability of the Council's decision to award the contract to that tenderer, but that disclosure of evaluation documents which related to the unsuccessful tenderers would not be in the public interest. Access to evaluation scores was also refused by the Western Australian Commissioner in *Sideris and City of Joondalup*[31] on

---

[28] *Op cit.,* n. 7.
[29] [1995] WAICmr 15 (June 2, 1995).
[30] *Op cit.,* n. 20.
[31] [2001] WAICmr 37 (October 10, 2001).

the grounds that the tenderers' business, commercial or financial affairs could be adversely affected by such disclosure and that disclosure was not necessary to satisfy the public interest in accountability.

Contract documents

The issue of access to contract documents also arose in *McKeever Rowan*. The respondent Department had agreed to release certain information from the contract, such as information relating to total fees and the names of the signatories, but it sought to withhold significant amounts of information contained in the contract, such as the fee structures of the joint successful tenderers, including the fee rates payable to each of the parties as well as the terms and timetable for payment, and the fees payable in the event of termination of the project prior to its completion. The Department also sought to withhold the names and positions of the project team. All of this information was claimed to be exempt under section 27(1)(b). The information relating to the names of the project team was also claimed to be exempt under section 28 (the personal information exemption). In addition, the Department sought to rely on a confidentiality provision in the Request For Tenders document to ground a refusal of access based on section 26.

The Commissioner found that once the contract was awarded, the successful tender information lost confidentiality with respect to the fee rates and other details necessary to understand the nature of the services contracted for. The Commissioner noted that the contract was for services to advise the Minister on the sale of a valuable State asset and stated that, in the circumstances, there was significant need for openness and accountability in relation to the contract.

With regard to the fee information, the Commissioner rejected the contractors argument that since the fee information was out of date, its disclosure would give a misleading indication of the firm's charge-out rates and could reasonably be expected to result in a material financial loss to the firm. The Commissioner refused to accept that the possibility of information being misunderstood is a good reason to refuse access to information under the FOI Act, noting that, in any event, any potential client or competitor would be likely to understand that the firm's rates had changed. The Commissioner noted that neither of the contractors had claimed that the fee rates were preferential to the Government, which was the basis for his finding that section 27(1) applied to the tender prices in *Henry Ford*. He also refused to accept that the total prices or the timetable for payment or the fees payable in the event of termination prior to completion of the project, could be indicative of pricing strategy. However, he accepted that the details of the fee structures, including details about what the fees did or did not include, and the terms of payment could be of interest to competitors and, if released, could be harmful to the competitive position of the affected parties. Nevertheless, the Commissioner found that, on balance, the public interest would be better served by the release of this information in light of the significant need for openness and accountability in relation to the contract.

With regard to the claim for exemption under the personal information exemption concerning the names of the project team, the Act expressly excludes from the scope of that exemption the names of those providing a service to a public body under a contract for services. In applying the commercially sensitive information exemption to the names of the project team, the Commissioner acknowledged that such information, if confidential, could be commercially sensitive. However the Commissioner found that since the proposed teams of the tenderers were among the key determinants in the selection process, as confirmed by the very inclusion of the project team as an appendix to the contract for services, on balance, the public interest was better served by the release of the information.

The disclosure of information in the contract document is in keeping with the approach in *Wanless* where the Queensland Commissioner remarked that *inter alia* performance indicators in the contract eventually concluded with the successful tenderer is the kind of information that attracts a sufficiently strong public interest consideration favouring disclosure.

CONCLUSION

The approach of the Irish Information Commissioner to the disclosure of information relating to public contracts has taken account of the stage at which access is sought and the type of information concerned. The Commissioner has indicated that prior to the awarding of a tender, significant information relating to it will be treated as confidential and may also qualify as a trade secret. Once the tender has been awarded the tendency is to favour disclosure of the total price of the successful tender, the contract document and elements of the successful tender submission. Other more commercially sensitive elements of successful tenders such as detailed pricing strategies may become subject to disclosure with the passage of time.

In the case of unsuccessful tenderers, the Commissioner has tended to restrict access to information relating to them on the basis that the public interest does not mandate disclosure of information that does not involve the expenditure of public funds. Disclosure of the names of unsuccessful tenderers has however been required, but not of the names of such unsuccessful tenderers linked to their tender prices. The Commissioner has adopted a similarly cautious approach to records of the evaluation process, holding that while such information regarding the successful tenderer should be disclosed, it should not be revealed in the case of unsuccessful tenderers.

With regard to the various benefits and disadvantages accruing in relation to disclosure of information relating to public contracts, it is clear that the Commissioner's approach prioritises the broad public interest in the provision of access to information about public contracts. To date, the Commissioner has tended to focus on the value for money benefits to be gained from disclosure of such information rather than on the role of such information in monitoring the performance of public contracts. The Commissioner has firmly rebutted the suggestion that disclosure of contract related information might deter potential contractors from competing for contracts, thus reducing the level of competition, but has indicated a willingness to protect unsuccessful tenderers, so as not to hinder them in competing in the future. Generally, the Commissioner's approach has succeeded in balancing the interest of the public and the contracting authorities in disclosure against those of the tenderers in protecting their business interests. However, the focus on value for money to the seeming exclusion of all other matters may require reconsideration in so far as issues relating to monitoring of the ongoing performance of public contracts are not just concerned with value for money, but also touch on issues such as accountability to customers with regard to service provision.

CHAPTER 7

Access to Information on the Environment: The Challenge of Implementing Directive 2003/4/EC[1]

ÁINE RYALL*

INTRODUCTION

Timely access to information on the environment is vital if individuals and environmental non-governmental organisations (NGOs) are to be equipped to participate effectively in environmental decision-making and to fulfil their role as environmental "watchdogs" with any measure of success. Where the right of access is delayed or denied, then parties aggrieved by a public authority's decision must have recourse to a suitable review mechanism that is capable of enforcing the right of access without excessive complexity, cost or delay.

Directive 2003/4/EC on public access to environmental information[2]

---

* Faculty of Law, UCC.

[1] This chapter is an updated version of an article published in (2005) 12 *Irish Planning and Environmental Law Journal* 162. Early drafts of this material were presented at the TCD School of Law FOI conference in October 2005 and at the following events: *Freedom of Access to Information Law: Key Issues for Practitioners* organised by the Irish Centre for European Law (ICEL) at the Inn of Court of Northern Ireland, Royal Courts of Justice, Belfast, April 21, 2005; *Access to Information: the Freedom of Information Act and the Aarhus Convention* conference organised by Chambers of Robin Purchas QC, Public, Parliamentary and Planning Barristers, 2 Harcourt Buildings, London, June 6, 2005; and a workshop organised by Friends of the Irish Environment at Allihies, Co. Cork, October 28–31, 2005. I am most grateful to participants at these events for their questions, comments and observations, which I found to be of great assistance in preparing this material for publication.

[2] [2003] OJ L 41/26. For detailed analysis see: L Krämer, "Access to Environmental

repealed and replaced an earlier Directive on the freedom of access to information on the environment (Directive 90/313/EEC).[3] A detailed review of the operation of the original 1990 Directive published by the European Commission in 2000 revealed serious difficulties with the operation of that Directive in practice, including: uncertainty over the definition of the information required to be disclosed and of the public authorities required to disclose it; differences in the practical arrangements put in place for ensuring that information is made available across the Member States; uncertainty over the scope of the exceptions to the duty to provide access and the scope of the obligation to "respond" to requests for access; delays in the provision of information; lack of effective review procedures; and the scope of the Member States' discretion to levy charges under the terms of the Directive.[4] This Report was informed by national reports submitted to the Commission by the Member States pursuant to Article 8 of Directive 90/313/EEC and by feedback on the operation of the Directive received from NGOs working in the environmental field.[5] The persistent practical difficulties associated with the 1990 Directive generated a strong case for systematic revision of the basic legal framework. The main impetus behind the recent strengthening of Community rules governing access to information on the environment came via an international Convention.

In June 1998, the European Community and (the then 15) Member States signed the United Nations Economic Commission for Europe (UN ECE) *Convention on access to information, public participation in decision-making and access to justice in environmental matters* (the Aarhus Convention).[6]

Information in an Open European Society – Directive 2003/4/EC" 4 *Yearbook of European Environmental Law* (2004) 1.

[3]   [1990] OJ L 158/56.

[4]   See *Report from the Commission to the Council and the European Parliament on the experience gained in the application of Council Directive 90/313/EEC of 7 June 1990, on freedom of access to information on the environment* COM(2000) 400 final, 29.06.2000, especially at 9–12.

[5]   See, for example, the report submitted by the Irish Department of the Environment entitled *Review of the implementation of Council Directive (90/313/EEC) of 7 June 1990 on freedom of access to information on the environment: Report to the Commission of the European Union* (1997).

[6]   The text of the Convention is available at: http://www.unece.org/env/pp. For commentary see J. Wates, "The Aarhus Convention: a Driving Force for

THE AARHUS CONVENTION

The Aarhus Convention is a very significant international Treaty in the environmental field which entered into force on October 30, 2001. It is built around three core "pillars": access to information; public participation; and access to justice. Article 4 of the Convention deals with access to environmental information while article 5 governs the collection and dissemination of environmental information. Article 6 is concerned with public participation in specified environmental decision-making procedures. Articles 7 and 8 govern public participation in the context of the elaboration of programmes, plans and polices relating to the environment. The Convention places considerable emphasis on "access to justice" in environmental matters. Article 9 sets down basic requirements regarding "access to justice" with a view to ensuring that information and participation rights are "effective" and enforceable in practice. Article 15 deals with "Review of Compliance" and an innovative compliance mechanism has been put in place.[7] At the time of writing, there are 39 Parties to the Convention including the Community itself and 23 of the EU25. Though Ireland signed the Convention in June 1998, it is not, as yet, a Party to the Convention. Work towards ratification is ongoing within the Department of the Environment, Heritage and Local Government, but to date there is no firm indication as to when Ireland intends to ratify. Ireland and Germany are the only Member States who have yet to ratify the Convention.

Initial drafts of the aspects of the Aarhus Convention that deal with access to information were based on the text of Directive 90/313/EEC. In the course of negotiations on the text of the Convention, interventions from environmental NGOs stressed the weaknesses that had come to light in the practical operation of the 1990 Directive at local level. Draft

---

Environmental Democracy" [2005] *Journal of European Environmental and Planning Law* 2.

[7] See Decision I/7 on review of compliance adopted at the First Meeting of the Parties, Lucca, Italy, October 21–23, 2002, full text available at: http://www.unece.org/env/pp/documents/mop1/ece.mp.pp.2.add.8.e.pdf. For commentary see V. Koester, "Review of Compliance under the Aarhus Convention: a Rather Unique Compliance Mechanism" [2005] *Journal of European Environmental and Planning Law* 31. See further: www.unece.org/env/oo/compliance.htm.

Convention provisions were strengthened as a result of these interventions. In the Commission's view, "the final text of the Aarhus Convention represents a clear advance on the provisions of [Directive 90/313/EEC]".[8]

Specific measures have been adopted with a view to aligning Community environmental law with Aarhus requirements.[9] First, as noted earlier, Directive 2003/4/EC operates to strengthen the basic rules governing access to environmental information. Second, Directive 2003/35/EC[10] (the public participation directive) introduced important amendments to the Environmental Impact Assessment (EIA) Directive[11] and the Integrated Pollution Prevention and Control (IPPC) Directive.[12] The amendments aim to bring these Directives into line with Aarhus requirements in terms of increased provision for public participation and "effective" access to justice where it is alleged that participation rights have been breached. This Directive also makes provision for public participation in the preparation and modification of certain plans and programmes.[13] Member States were required to implement the public participation Directive by June 25, 2005. Ireland has yet to transpose this Directive in full.[14] Third, the (European) Council has adopted a common

---

[8] See COM (2000) 400 final, 29.06.2000, at 8–9.

[09] For details see: http://europa.eu.int/comm/environment/aarhus/.

[10] [2003] OJ L156/17.

[11] Directive 85/337/EEC on the assessment of the effects of certain public and private projects on the environment [1985] OJ L175/40 as amended by Council Directive 97/11/EC [1997] OJ L73/5.

[12] Directive 96/61/EC concerning integrated pollution prevention and control [1996] OJ L257/26.

[13] Directive 2003/35/EC, art.2 and Annex 1.

[14] Art.5, Planning and Development Regulations 2005 (S.I. No. 364 of 2005) amends Pts I and II of Sch.5, Planning and Development Regulations 2001 (S.I. No. 600 of 2001) to reflect the requirements of art.3(8) and (9) of Directive 2003/35/EC (concerning the lists of project categories for the purposes of the Environmental Impact Assessment (EIA) Directive). At the time of writing, the Planning and Development (Strategic Infrastructure) Bill 2006 contains provisions purporting to improve the position of certain environmental NGOs as regards access to judicial review procedures under Planning and Development Act 2000, s.50. This proposal is inspired by the Aarhus Convention and art.10a of Directive 2003/35/EC. See generally, Friends of the Irish Environment (FIE), *The Transposition into Irish Law of Directive 2003/35/EC* (June 27, 2005). Text available at: www.friendsoftheirishenvironment.net.

position on a (draft) Regulation applying Aarhus obligations to the Community institutions and bodies.[15] Fourth, a further general measure aimed at introducing basic rules governing access to justice in environmental matters at national level attracted strong opposition from the Member States and it now seems unlikely that this proposal will be pursued with any real vigour.[16]

DIRECTIVE 2003/4/EC

For present purposes, Directive 2003/4/EC on public access to environmental information, which is one element in the series of Community measures adopted in light of Aarhus obligations, is of greatest relevance. Given the practical problems with implementation of the 1990 Directive, and the pressing need to bring Community law in this field into line with Aarhus requirements, the Commission took the view that the best way forward was to replace the 1990 Directive with an entirely new Directive rather than attempting to introduce the necessary changes via an amending Directive which would have necessitated extensive and complex cross-referencing. Member States were required to implement Directive 2003/4/EC by February 14, 2005. At the time of writing, Ireland has not, as yet, taken steps to transpose the requirements of the Directive into national law.

Directive 2003/4/EC, which had a long and controversial gestation period, represents a considerable improvement on the original 1990 Directive. Many of the improvements on the text of the 1990 Directive were inspired by the requirements of the Aarhus Convention. The 2003 Directive establishes a "right" of access to environmental information

---

[15] European Council, *Common Position with a view to the adoption of a Regulation on the application of the provisions of the Aarhus Convention on Access to Information, Public Participation in Decision-making and Access to Justice in Environmental Matters to Community institutions and bodies*, 2003/0242 (COD) July 18, 2005 [2005] OJ C 264E/18.

[16] European Commission, *Proposal for a Directive on access to justice in environmental matters* COM (2003) 624 final, 24.10.2003. This proposal aims to give effect to Art.9(3) of the Aarhus Convention. See European Council, General Secretariat, *Proposal for a Directive on access to justice in environmental matters – state of play* 2003/0246 (COD) June 10, 2005.

held by or for public authorities, subject to certain specified exemptions (Article 1(a), Article 3 and Article 4). Recall that the 1990 Directive merely provided for "freedom of access" to information falling within the scope of the Directive. The 2003 Directive sets down broad definitions of the core concepts of "environmental information" (Article 2(1)) and "public authority" (Article 2(2)). Information falling within the scope of the Directive must now be made available "as soon as possible" or, at the latest, within one month of the receipt of the request by the public authority—except in the case of voluminous and complex requests (Articles 3(2) and (3)). The provisions governing exceptions to the right of access have been substantially reworked (Article 4). Specifically, the grounds on which a public authority may legitimately refuse a request for access are much tighter. The provisions governing exceptions to the right of access now fall to be interpreted in a restrictive way and are subject to a public interest test. The rules governing charges for supplying information have also been revised and clarified (Article 5). Furthermore, Member States are now required to ensure that public authorities organise the environmental information relevant to their functions and which is held by or for them "with a view to its active and systematic dissemination to the public" (Article 7). Particular emphasis is placed on electronic access.[17] Article 8 deals specifically with the quality of environmental information and requires Member States "so far as is within their power" to ensure that any information that is compiled by them or on their behalf "is up to date, accurate and comparable."

DIRECTIVE 2003/4/EC AND "EFFECTIVE" REMEDIES

One of the most interesting features of the 2003 Directive is that it contains a specific provision dealing with "access to justice" (Article 6). This provision aims to deliver the right to an "effective" remedy where the right to information is diluted or undermined by a public authority. Previously, Article 4 of the original 1990 Directive had simply provided

---

[17] See also Decision II/3 on *Electronic Information Tools and the Clearing-House Mechanism* adopted at the Second Meeting of the Parties to the Aarhus Convention, Almaty, Kazakhstan, May 25–27, 2005. Text available at: www.unece.org.env/pp.

that a person who considered that their request for information had been unreasonably refused, ignored, or inadequately answered by the public authority in question, could seek "a judicial or administrative review of the decision in accordance with the relevant national legal system". Article 6 is a detailed provision and merits careful study. It is modelled closely on the relevant provisions of Article 9 of the Aarhus Convention on which it is based (Articles 9(1) and Article 9(3) to (5)).[18]

Article 6 of Directive 2003/4/EC provides for a two-stage review process. The first stage is set out in Article 6(1) and requires the Member States to put in place an administrative review procedure in which the acts or omissions of the public authority on a request for access to information can be reconsidered by that public authority *or* by another public authority (*i.e.* a form of administrative review which takes place within the public authority itself or an external review undertaken by a different public authority) *or* administrative review by "an independent and impartial body established by law."

The three options presented here are framed as alternatives and a Member State is free to choose the option that is best suited to its domestic legal system. In practical terms, a Member State could satisfy the obligation created here by simply providing for formal internal review of a public authority's initial decision on a request for access in its implementing legislation. It is not necessary for a Member State to go so far as to establish a special body to deal with disputes over access to environmental information. So, in reality, this requirement is not very onerous on the Member States.

Article 6(1) stipulates that the administrative review procedure must be "expeditious and either free of charge or inexpensive". This formulation, which follows Article 9(4) of the Convention, does not preclude a Member State from charging a fee in order to invoke the review procedure. The importance of expedition cannot be overstated in the context of disputes over access to environmental information where the data at issue will often have a short shelf life. The express obligation to ensure that disputes are determined promptly is therefore most welcome. The second stage of the review process is found in Article 6(2) which

---

[18] See further: Á Ryall, "Implementation of the Århus Convention through Community Environmental law" (2004) 6 Env. L. Rev. 274.

provides that in addition to administrative review, the Member States must ensure that an aggrieved applicant has access to judicial review *or* review before an independent and impartial body established by law. Article 6(3) goes on to provide that any final decisions taken pursuant to Article 6(2) are to be binding on the public authority concerned. Where a decision is taken to refuse access under this Article, then reasons must be provided in writing.

The net result of the obligation created in Article 6(1) is that once the date for transposition of the Directive has passed (February 14, 2005), it is no longer open to Member States to rely exclusively on existing (and often inaccessible) judicial review procedures to satisfy the remedies requirement. Effective administrative review procedures must also be put in place. As noted above, the Member States enjoy considerable discretion as to the precise form of administrative review to be adopted, subject to the basic parameters set down in the Directive. Even though Article 6(2) provides the Member States with alternative options for implementing the second stage of the review process (*i.e.* judicial review or review by an independent body established by law that is not a court), the overarching principle of "effective judicial protection" developed by the European Court of Justice (ECJ) mandates that judicial review must be available to ensure that decisions involving alleged breach of Community law rights are (ultimately) subject to judicial control. So, where a Member State provides for review by an independent body established by law, decisions taken by any such body must still be amenable to judicial review.

In line with Article 9(4) of the Convention, the mechanisms adopted to give effect to Articles 6(1) and (2) of the Directive must be "equitable, timely and not prohibitively expensive." These conditions also apply to judicial review proceedings. Ensuring that judicial review proceedings involving disputes over access to information are timely and not prohibitively expensive is one of the most difficult aspects of implementation for the Member States. It is interesting to note that the obligation to "consider" the introduction of measures "to remove or reduce financial and other barriers to access to justice" set down in Article 9(5) of the Convention is not mentioned at all in Article 6 of Directive 2003/4/EC. If remedies are to be effective, then the various bodies charged with review must be provided with trained personnel and sufficient resources to ensure the delivery of high quality decisions in a timely fashion.

On a related issue, Directive 2003/4/EC does not address publication of decisions taken by review bodies. Article 9(4) of the Convention requires the publication of decisions taken by courts. Beyond this specific obligation, it is submitted here that publication of the most significant decisions taken by review bodies (other than courts) is essential in order to ensure the consistent application of rules on access to information within the national system. The publication of decisions would also enable individuals and NGOs to monitor the operation of the Directive in practice and would facilitate comparative research across the Member States. It is therefore disappointing to find that the Directive itself is silent on this issue.

It is clear that the Member States retain considerable discretion as to the manner in which they opt to implement the new remedies provision at local level. This discretion is not unlimited, however, and must be exercised in a manner consistent with the underlying objective of the Directive. This is expressed in Article 1(a) as being "to guarantee the right of access to environmental information." The ECJ has kept a tight rein on the discretion enjoyed by the Member States when implementing the requirements of the original Access to Information Directive (Directive 90/313/EEC). For example, the Court interpreted the discretion to levy charges pursuant to Article 5 of that Directive in a restrictive fashion in order to ensure that charges were not deployed to undermine the effectiveness of the right of access.[19] A rigorous approach to the requirements of Directive 2003/4/EC can therefore be expected. It is likely that the ECJ will draw on the text of the Aarhus Convention, and its strong recitals, to support a robust approach to the recent EC Directives designed to implement Convention obligations, including Directive 2003/4/EC. Article 6 of Directive 2003/4/EC provides the ECJ with a strong basis on which to further develop the concept of "effective judicial protection" in the specific context of the Community law right of access to environmental information.

---

[19] See Case C-321/96 *Wilhelm Mecklenburg v. Kreis Pinneberg-Der Landrat* [1998] E.C.R. I-3089 and Case C-217/97 *Commission v. Germany* [1999] E.C.R. I-5087.

ACCESS TO ENVIRONMENTAL INFORMATION IN IRISH LAW

A number of diverse sources of rights fall to be considered in the Irish context: First, planning and environmental protection legislation provides for extensive rights of access to environmental information in specific contexts (*e.g.* documents relating to planning applications pursuant to the Planning and Development Act 2000 and Regulations made thereunder; and applications for various licences such as IPPC licences and waste licences, etc.). Secondly, the European Communities Act 1972 (Access to Information on the Environment Regulations) 1998[20] purport to implement the requirements set down in Directive 90/313/EEC. These Regulations supplement the specific rights of access found in planning and environmental protection legislation. There is no express reference to the Directive in the text of the 1998 Regulations and it is fair to say that the Regulations adopt a minimalist approach to the requirements of the Directive. To date, there have been very few cases where the 1998 Regulations have been considered by the (Irish) courts.[21] This state of affairs reflects the very real barriers to access to justice created by the high costs and unpredictability associated with instituting judicial review proceedings in the High Court.

Beyond the specific rights of access set down in planning and environmental protection legislation and the general right of access found in the 1998 Regulations, the Freedom of Information Act 1997 as amended by the Freedom of Information (Amendment) Act 2003 (FOI Act), provides for a right of access to records held by specified public bodies, subject to certain exemptions. Government Departments, local authorities, An Bord Pleanála and the Environmental Protection Agency (EPA) are among the public bodies covered by FOI. Prior to the amendments introduced via the 2003 Act, no fee applied in respect of FOI requests. However, section 47 of the Act (as amended) now provides for an up-front fee of €15 for making a request for access to non-personal records.[22]

---

[20] S.I. No. 125 of 1998.

[21] See, for example, *Lowes v. Coillte Teo.*, unreported, High Court, Herbert J., March 6, 2003 and *Lowes v. Bord na Móna*, unreported, High Court, Murphy J., March 27, 2004 (both judgments available on the First Law database).

[22] Freedom of Information Act 1997 (Fees) Regulations 2003 (S.I. No. 264 of 2003). Reduced fees apply in the case of requests submitted by medical cardholders and their dependents.

Separate fees have also been introduced in respect of an application for internal review (€75) and a review by the Information Commissioner (€150). It should be noted that the FOI fee was modelled on the €20 planning participation fee introduced in March 2002 (which is currently the subject of Article 226, EC infringement proceedings and a challenge by way of judicial review in the Irish courts).[23]

Where access is refused under the 1998 Regulations, or where a person is dissatisfied with any charge proposed to be levied by a public authority, s/he may complain to the Ombudsman where the public authority in question falls within the Ombudsman's remit.[24] Otherwise, the only available remedy is judicial review in the High Court. Note too that the *Guidance Notes on Access to Information on the Environment* published in 1993 indicated that refusals should not be made without an internal review procedure.[25] Further, at paragraph 3.3, the Guidance Notes provided that:

> "In the event of a refusal of information it will be open to an aggrieved applicant to ask the public authority to undertake a further review of its decision."

Note, however, that this is only an administrative guideline; there is no express provision for internal review in the 1998 Regulations. Contrast

---

[23] See Case C-294/03 *Commission v. Ireland* [2003] OJ C 213/19 and *Friends of the Irish Environment and Lowes v. Minister for Environment, Heritage and Local Government, Ireland, the Attorney General and Galway Co. Co.,* unreported, High Court, Murphy J., April 15, 2005 [2005] I.E.H.C. 123. This decision is currently under appeal to the Supreme Court. See further Á. Ryall, "The EIA Directive and the Irish Planning Participation Fee" (2002) 14 J.E.L. 317, where I argue that the legality of the fee under the EIA Directive and the Aarhus Convention is doubtful.

[24] See, for example, the case noted in the *Annual Report of the Ombudsman 2003* at 35 concerning Louth County Council and access to a report prepared by the Council into allegations of environmental pollution and illegal waste disposal.

[25] At para 2.15(e). These Guidance Notes relate to the original regulations purporting to implement Directive 90/313/EEC—the Access to Information on the Environment Regulations 1993 (S.I. No. 133 of 1993). These regulations were revoked and replaced by new regulations in 1996 (S.I. No. 185 of 1996) which were, in turn, subsequently revoked and replaced by the 1998 regulations.

the review mechanisms available under FOI (formal internal review and the possibility of further review by the Information Commissioner).[26]

DIRECTIVE 2003/4/EC BEFORE THE NATIONAL COURTS[27]

In the absence of national implementing measures, the question now arises as to whether or not Directive 2003/4/EC may be invoked directly against the State and/or emanations of the State[28] now that the February 14, 2005 deadline for implementation has passed? It is instructive to consider the following formulation of the direct effect doctrine in Case C–236/92 *Difesa della Cava*:[29]

> "... wherever the provisions of a directive appear, as far as their subject-matter is concerned, to be unconditional and sufficiently precise, those provisions may be relied upon by an individual against the State where the State fails to implement the directive in national law by the end of the period prescribed or where it fails to implement the directive correctly.
>
> A Community provision is unconditional where it is not subject, in its implementation or effects, to the taking of any measure either by the institutions of the Community or by the Member States ...
>
> Moreover, a provision is sufficiently precise to be relied on by an individual and applied by the court where the obligation which it imposes is set out in unequivocal terms...".

---

[26] An administrative review procedure for bodies falling outside the Ombudsman's remit was promised in *Access to Information on the Environment: A Review* (Department of the Environment, 1995), 9.

[27] See, generally, J. Gaffney, "Pleading EC Law in Irish Litigation: A Case Study" (2005) 1 *Judicial Studies Institute Journal* 153.

[28] See Case 103/88 *Fratelli Constanzo v. Comune di Milano* [1989] E.C.R. 1839; Case C-188/89 *Foster v. British Gas* [1990] E.C.R. I-3313; and Case C-157/02 *Rieser* [2004] E.C.R. I-1477 at paras. 23–24.

[29] [1994] E.C.R. I-483 at paras. 8-10

Where a person seeks to invoke the right of access conferred by Directive 2003/4/EC directly against the State and/or an emanation of the State, it is necessary to work through the text of the Directive and examine whether each provision of the Directive on which an applicant seeks to rely is sufficiently clear, precise and unconditional (in the sense that it is not contingent on any discretionary implementing measure)[30] to be applied by the national court or competent authority as the case may be. The obligations set down in Articles 3, 4 and 5 of Directive 2003/4/EC appear to be sufficiently clear, precise and unconditional for the purpose of being invoked directly against the State and/or an emanation of the State. Furthermore, the Directive expressly confers a *right* of access to environmental information held by public authorities, subject to certain exceptions. The position regarding Article 6 on "access to justice" is more complex. This provision clearly contemplates national implementing measures. Given the level of discretion that is left to Member States as to how they go about implementing this requirement in the national legal system, this provision is not unconditional. Its practical operation clearly depends on discretionary implementing measures. Therefore, Article 6 does not meet the requirements for direct effect. However, apart from the specific obligations articulated in Article 6 concerning "access to justice", it must be recalled that national courts are under a general Community law obligation to provide "effective judicial protection" for the rights conferred by Directive 2003/4/EC.[31]

Beyond the question of direct effect, the doctrine of consistent interpretation is very relevant as a further mechanism for ensuring effective local enforcement of unimplemented or incorrectly implemented Directives. It is a well-established principle of Community law that the national courts are under an obligation to interpret national law in

---

[30] Case C-44/84 *Hurd v. Jones* [1986] E.C.R. 29 at para. 47 cited in A.M. Collins and J. O'Reilly, *Civil Proceedings and the State* (2nd ed, 2004, Thomson Round Hall, Dublin), para. 10.09.

[31] Case 222/84 *Johnston v. Chief Constable of the Royal Ulster Constabulary* [1986] E.C.R. 1651. See further Case C-186/04 *Housieaux* [2005] E.C.R. I-0000 and Joined Cases C-397/01 to C-403/01 *Pfeiffer* [2004] E.C.R. I-8835 (Grand Chamber) where the ECJ confirmed that:

"It is the responsibility of the national courts in particular to provide the legal protection which individuals derive from the rules of Community law and to ensure that those rules are fully effective" (at para. 111).

conformity with the provisions of Directives, at least in so far as this is possible.[32] This obligation also falls on the competent authorities. Note too that Directive 2003/4/EC falls to be interpreted in light of the text of the Aarhus Convention.

FUTURE DIRECTIONS?

It remains to be seen how Ireland will attempt to implement Directive 2003/4/EC within the domestic legal order. Article 6 of the Directive on "access to justice" poses the greatest challenge for the Irish authorities. Streamlining the distinct access regimes should be a priority with a view to making the various statutory frameworks transparent and user-friendly. If and when implementing measures are put in place, the Irish authorities should publish detailed guidance notes for competent authorities together with explanatory leaflets outlining the main elements of the implementing measures in an accessible style and using plain language.

Postscript

Since this chapter was submitted for publication, the European Parliament and the European Council reached agreement (in conciliation) on the text of a Regulation applying Aarhus requirements to Community institutions and bodies (this text myst still be formally adopted by both institutions).[33]

In response to a Dáil question on May 4, 2006, the Minister for the Environment, Heritage and Local Government revealed that he had invited the Information Commissioner to act as "Appeal Commissioner" under the Access to Environmental Information regime and that the Commissioner has accepted this role. There is no further detail available at present regarding the structure and mechanics of the proposed appeal system.

---

[32] Case 14/83 *Von Colson* [1984] E.C.R. 1891 at para 26; Case C-62/00 *Marks and Spencer* [2002] E.C.R. I-6325 at para 24; and Joined Cases C-397/01 to C-403/01 *Pfeiffer* [2004] E.C.R. I-8835 (Grand Chamber), paras. 113-116. For a recent example of the doctrine in action in the Irish courts see *Eircom Ltd. v. Commission for Communications Regulation (Comreg)*, unreported, High Court, July 29, 2005, McKechnie J., para. 35.

[33] See PE-CONS 3614/06, June 20, 2006.

CHAPTER 8

Openness, Transparency and Accountability

ESTELLE FELDMAN*

"FOI has inherent characteristics which limit its impact. It is a form of accountability that governments automatically dominate, even if they do not fully control it. The duty of enforcement is up to citizens. The individual citizen engages through the Act with agencies, which are practised at dealing with requests. Collective action is largely precluded, and applications are made on an individual basis. FOI is not a procedure whereby success by one applicant necessarily increases access to like material for all. It operates on the basis that citizens must rely upon their government to agree to the terms of its being policed. Governments must be relied upon to record decisions and reasons, and to produce them when requested. FOI is founded upon distrust in government, yet it does not escape the need to trust government."[1]

---

* Research Associate, School of Law, Trinity College and Lecturer in Constitutional Law, Portobello College, Dublin. This chapter is an amalgam of papers prepared for the TCD School of Law Annual Conferences on Freedom of Information 2002 to date as well as papers specifically tailored for the Primary and Post-primary sectors, for the Higher Education Authority, for Local Government and for the Northern Ireland Civil Service. In addition it draws on material originally published in "Information Law" subsequently "Information Law and the Ombudsman" in R. Byrne & W. Binchy eds., *Annual Review of Irish Law 1999* to date and with Oran Doyle "Constitutional Law" in *Annual Review of Irish Law 2001* to date (Thompson Round Hall, Dublin), hereafter *Review* for year indicated.
[1] Terrill, "The Rise and Decline of FOI in Australia" in McDonald and Terrill eds., *Open Government, Freedom of Information and Privacy* (MacMillan Press, London, 1998), pp.89-115, p.111.

INTRODUCTION

A public body holds the information in its possession in trust for the
public. As such the public body is not the owner of the information;
rather it is the custodian. Thus, it has a responsibility to ensure that the
information is not freely available to any one who does not have a proper
interest in receiving it. On the other hand, it has an equal, if not greater
responsibility to ensure that any one who does have a proper interest in
receiving it may do so with the minimum of fuss.

In analysing the freedom of information regime, this chapter draws
on the application of common sense and sound management practices.
Hence, it presents a perspective from a management viewpoint as well as
a legal one. The backdrop for this perspective is various court judgments,
various reports and deliberations of the Information Commissioner and
of the Ombudsman, as well as varied material accessible on the Internet.[2]
It must be borne in mind that the fact base of a particular court judgment
or Information Commissioner's review may not immediately appear to
have direct relevance to a reader's own particular situation. Each case
does vary and, during review, it is clear that the Information Commissioner
is at pains to allow for these variations. However, general principles of
importance may be drawn from these reported decisions and it is these
principles that this chapter seeks to highlight. They tend to illustrate why
the Freedom of Information Act is something to be viewed as a positive
opportunity rather than as a troublesome if not a dangerous burden.

It is also intended to highlight some of the key reasons why freedom
of information is advantageous for public bodies, why much of what is
said against freedom of information is nonsense, and why freedom of
information officers who might feel caught between a rock and a hard
place should courageously pursue implementing the practice and spirit
of the Freedom of Information Act.

Three year Administrative Budgets were introduced for civil service
Departments and Offices and a start was made in providing incentives
for good performance. An Efficiency Audit Group was set up with private
sector involvement and amending legislation was passed which, inter

---

[2]   An example is the Central Policy Unit of the Department of Finance website at
www.foi.gov.ie

alia, extended the role of the Comptroller and Auditor General to value for money auditing.

Improving public service management

In the context of developing public administration a bundle of measures was initiated within the public service in the 1990s under the broadband titles of the *Strategic Management Initiative* (SMI) and *Delivering Better Government* (DBG). Two of the legislative measures passed as integral parts of the bundle are the Freedom of Information Act 1997 (FOI[3]) and the Public Service Management Act 1997 (PSMA) A new civil service culture was also conceived and nurtured within the context of developing public administration.

Certainly, with the introduction of SMI and DBG a new age in acronyms was born. It remains to be seen whether there was a twin birth of a new culture of public service. This new culture must be consistent with the declared objectives of openness, transparency and accountability, the only culture in which the aspirations of genuine freedom of information, the *sine qua non* of healthy democracy, can flourish.[4]

NAVIGATING THE FREEDOM OF INFORMATION ACT

The Principal Act of 1997

The Long Title of the Freedom of Information Act describes it as: "An Act to enable members of the public to obtain access, to the greatest extent possible consistent with the public interest and the right to privacy,

---

[3] The acronym, FOI, is the universally accepted abbreviated term to describe freedom of information.

[4] For a deeper analysis of the requirements of openness, transparency and accountability see Feldman, "Open Democracy Legislation ... Implementation Policies and Possibilities" in J. Sarkin and W. Binchy eds. *Human Rights the Citizen and the State. South African and Irish Perspectives* (2001, Round Hall Sweet & Maxwell, Dublin), pp.220-234. This developed research first published in R. Martin and Feldman *Access to Information in Developing Countries* (1998, Transparency International Berlin). Also an Internet publication: www.transparency.de/documents/work-papers/martin-feldman/index.html

to information in the possession of public bodies" These words should
be very familiar to anybody involved with the Act. However, how many
are aware that this appears to be the only Act on the Statute Book that is
directed at "members of the public" and that has as its express object "to
enable members of the public"? Consequently, anyone who is unfamiliar
with the Act might reasonably expect it to be in fairly clear and simple
terms, even, perhaps, in a form that is accessible and transparent to those
who are not experienced administrative and constitutional lawyers. Indeed,
in a public statement at the time of the introduction of the Bill the
sponsoring Minister stated: "I appreciate that navigating a legal text of
some complexity is not always easy for those of us who are not lawyers."[5]

In defence of the Act, it was drafted at a time when openness,
transparency and accountability were only beginning to be spoken of as
the desired culture of the public service. Nevertheless, for all its positive
points, one cannot escape the fact that in some respects the text is
extraordinarily convoluted, *e.g.* section 25 dealing with the procedures
for Ministers to issue certificates exempting records, and section 34
dealing with the Information Commissioner's review of decisions on
appeal. In these two sections, approximately seven pages of a 63-page
Act, there are 85 cross-references to other sections, subsections or
paragraphs of the Act. It might be argued that all these cross-references
are necessary. However, for an Act that was heralded as a culture change
in the openness of the public service, clarity of exposition in its drafting
does not appear to have been a priority.

Freedom of Information (Amendment) Act 2003[6]

Adding the 2003 Amendment Act into this mix does not facilitate
understanding. For instance, section 10(b) amends section 15(6)(d)(ii)
of the Principal Act in the following terms:

> "(*b*) in subsection (6), in paragraph (*d*), by substituting the
> following subparagraph for subparagraph (ii):

---

[5] Eithne Fitzgerald, *The Irish Times* letters column, January 4, 1997.
[6] For comprehensive analysis M. McDonagh, *Freedom of Information (Amendment) Act 2003*, I.C.L.S.A.; Feldman, chapters on Information Law and the Ombudsman, and Constitutional Law in *2003 Review*.

'(ii) the period of 12 months or of such other length as may be determined beginning on the expiration of the period aforesaid and each subsequent period of 12 months or of such other length as may be determined beginning on the expiration of the period of 12 months or of such other length as may be determined immediately preceding.'''

These are the terms of an Act that was drafted in 2003 subsequent to several initiatives within the legal sphere calling for plain language.

An example of the problem of the opaque language in action is the following extract from a judgment of a High Court appeal against the Information Commissioner: "A decision specified in subsection (1) includes a decision under section 14 which includes, at section 14(1)(f) a decision under section 18 in relation to the contents of a statement furnished under subsection (1) of that section or to refuse an application under that subsection."[7]

Hence, because the Act is so complex and abstruse it is all the more important that it is administered in a spirit of openness, transparency and accountability and by an organisational culture that reflects those values. Otherwise, of what use is this legislation to an ordinary member of the public if it is necessary to hire an expert or invoke the watchdog Information Commissioner in order to follow through a request for information from one of the prescribed bodies?

INFORMATION COMMISSIONER AND OMBUDSMAN COMPARED

It is generally recognised that an independent oversight regime is necessary to monitor freedom of information legislation. Under the Freedom of Information Act[8] the Ombudsman was appointed Information Commissioner.[9] Further, the Director of the Office of the Ombudsman

---

[7] *Killilea v. Information Commissioner* [2003] I.E.H.C. 63.
[8] No.13 of 1997, Pt IV.
[9] Mr. Kevin Murphy, second Ombudsman, was appointed first Information Commissioner.

also performs the function of Director of the Office of the Information Commissioner.

Early Ombudsman reports[10] reflect the fact that whereas there are many, many members of the public service who deal with the public in a frank and cooperative manner, this was not the general culture. Nevertheless, a hallmark of the Irish Ombudsman's function is a patient and intensely thorough investigative culture combined with a pervasive and persuasive capacity for encouraging settlement between a complainant and a public body. The Office of the Information Commissioner could draw on the experience of the Office of the Ombudsman and develop from a shared culture. In essence, the new Office of the Information Commissioner knew from the outset how to conduct investigations and what barriers to progress might be encountered on the way.

Administrative accountability

Both the Information Commissioner and the Ombudsman deal with matters of administrative accountability. In the *Report of the Constitution Review Group*[11] this is described as: "the process of ensuring that public service activities and, in particular, the exercise of decision-making powers, whether discretionary or otherwise, are carried out not only in a proper legal manner but fairly and consistently with good administrative practice."[12] The current office-holder, Ms Emily O'Reilly, has succeeded Mr Kevin Murphy as incumbent in both functions. It can be noted that this dual-role combination continues to be mutually advantageous. Indeed, in the first annual report of the Information Commissioner, the Commissioner noted:

> "I have commented publicly on the complementary nature
> of the Information Commissioner and Ombudsman offices
> despite their separate statutory identities. Perhaps this
> complementarity is best illustrated by one of the three new,
> legal rights created under the Freedom of Information Act,
> *viz.*, the right of members of the public to be given reasons

---

[10] Mr Michael Mills was appointed the first Ombudsman in 1984.
[11] *Report of the Constitution Review Group,* Pn 2632, May 1996.
[12] *Ibid.,* p.426.

for decisions affecting themselves. I have said several times that lack of information and failure to give proper reasons is at the heart of many complaints against public bodies which I receive in my capacity as Ombudsman." [13]

The Commissioner noted further that an important part of the statutory functions of the Information Commissioner is to foster an attitude of openness among public bodies "by encouraging the voluntary publication by them of information on their activities which goes beyond what they are obliged to publish under the Act. It is a function which sits very well with that of an Ombudsman investigating complaints of maladministration." [14]

Painstaking investigation process

Any investigation conducted by the Information Commissioner or the Ombudsman is a thorough process. It involves close examination of all files and scrutiny of all records. It may involve interviews. In the *1992 Annual Report of the Ombudsman*, ninth report of the first Ombudsman, Mr Michael Mills, the Ombudsman referred in the Introduction to his staff being specially prepared for the "long and painstaking process" of examining files. When a case which had remained unresolved for six years "was brought to the attention of my Office, and the files were examined, it emerged that one crucial piece of evidence had been overlooked throughout the period. When this evidence was pinpointed the case was quickly resolved."[15]

Access to environmental information[16]

The *Ombudsman's Annual Reports for 1994 and 1995* (first and second reports of Mr Kevin Murphy) gave examples of investigations under the Access to Information on the Environment Regulations 1993, which specify a two-month time limit within which information must be made

---

[13] *Annual Report of the Information Commissioner 1998,* p. 2.
[14] *Ibid.*
[15] *Annual Report of the Ombudsman 1992,* p.1.
[16] *Infra,* see chap.7.

available. In a 1994 investigation the Local Authority concerned in the investigation of a complaint gave 14 reasons for its refusal to make requested information available, the main reason being "the alarmist use to which they feared the information would be put".[17] In the 1995 investigations the Ombudsman reported inordinate delays experienced by his Office after initiating requests for information; these were in addition to the delays experienced by the complainant:

> "I also found that the delay which my staff experienced in their dealing with the Council and its failure to reply to specific queries were not consonant with the degree of cooperation I should receive...The information was released 16 months after the date of the original request and 13 months after I first contacted the Council."[18]

Differences between the Information Commissioner and the Ombudsman

It should, however, be noted that there are significant differences in the statutory role and responsibility of each Office not least of which is the confusion for the general public that, of the increasing number of bodies that now come within the Information Commissioner's ambit, many remain outside the purview of the Ombudsman.

Differences in jurisdiction

Extension of the Ombudsman's jurisdiction to match more closely that of the Information Commissioner thereby facilitating public understanding of, and access to, the distinct but complementary offices is long promised and as long awaited. In particular, the Government's declared intention to extend the Ombudsman's remit to the public voluntary hospital sector and to other voluntary health agencies is only on the cusp of being fulfilled. The Ombudsman's jurisdiction is limited to maladministration in the case of complaints relating to medical, nursing or para-medical issues; in other

---

[17] *Annual Report of the Ombudsman 1994*, pp. 45 *et seq.*, and quotation at p. 49.
[18] *Ibid.*, p.22.

words, the Ombudsman may not become involved in strictly clinical matters.

Differences in powers

The Information Commissioner's decisions have binding effect, subject solely to an appeal to the High Court on a point of law. This is in contrast to the Ombudsman who is governed by the Ombudsman Act 1980, and whose recommendations need not be accepted. However, as the Ombudsman noted in her most recent Annual Report: "Where I find evidence of maladministration and where some form of redress is merited my Office relies on persuasion, criticism, publicity and moral authority to have its recommendations implemented."[19] In the exceptional event that this high regard in which the Ombudsman is held does not obtain the required result, the Ombudsman may have recourse to her statutory powers to issue special reports to the Oireachtas.[20]

The Ombudsman's moral and persuasive authority[21]

Since 1999, the Ombudsman has published a number of special reports on systemic issues arising from the investigation of complaints from aggrieved members of the public: *Non-Payment of Arrears of Contributory Pensions* (March 1997); *Provision* of *School Transport for a Child with Disabilities* (February 1998); *Lost Pensions Arrears* (June 1999);[22] *Local Authority Housing Loans – Overpayments* (June 2000); *Payment of Nursing Home Subventions by Health Boards* (January 2001); *Tax Relief for Passengers with Disabilities* (August 2001), and *Redress for Taxpayers* (November 2002). With regard to *Redress for Taxpayers*, the Ombudsman

---

[19] *Ibid.,* p.7.

[20] S.6, Ombudsman Act 1980. (No.26 of 1980).

[21] For further discussion on the Ombudsman special reports see the relevant *Ombudsman Reports* and relevant chapters/years of the *Annual Review of Irish Law*. These reports are available in hard copy and at www.irlgov.ie/ombudsman

[22] This was a s.6 report developing the findings of the March 1997 special investigation. For comprehensive analysis Feldman, "The Ombudsman: Redressing the Balance for Older People" in O'Dell (ed.) *Older People in Modern Ireland Essays on Law and Policy.* (First Law, Dublin, 2006), pp.327-352.

took the unprecedented step of issuing a special report to both Houses of the Oireachtas in accordance with section 6(5) as well as section 6(7) of the Ombudsman Act. Section 6(5) states:

> "Where it appears to the Ombudsman that the measures taken or proposed to be taken in response to a recommendation [as a result of an investigation] are not satisfactory, he may, if he so thinks fit, cause a special report on the case to be included in a report under subsection (7) of this section."

As a consequence a Joint Oireachtas Committee on Finance and the Public Service intervened; subsequently, all the Ombudsman's recommendations were implemented and the Minister for Finance amended the Finance Acts accordingly.

DEVELOPING PUBLIC SERVICE ACCOUNTABILITY

Following the implementation of the Freedom of Information Act two investigations were carried out within the public service. The first of these, conducted by the Information Commissioner in 2001 in accordance with section 36 of the Act,[23] examined the practices and procedures adopted by public bodies generally for the purpose of compliance with the Act's provisions. This report is now somewhat out of date, especially since the 2003 Amendment Act has come into effect. It may be noted that the Amendment Act has effectively embedded an almost blanket exemption of records of central government without possibility of exercising discretion thereby negating much of what the Commissioner recommended in the relevant section of his report. Nevertheless, it is informative to consider to what extent central government had adapted to this legislation the object of which is to ensure accountability of public service.

The second, a consultants' report published in 2002, is entitled

---

[23] *Annual Report of the Information Commissioner 2001*, chap.6. Full report on Information Commissioner's website at www.irlgov.ie/oic.

Evaluation of the Progress of the Strategic Management Initiative/ Delivering Better Government Modernisation Programme.[24]

The Information Commissioner's investigation into compliance by public bodies

This Commissioner's investigation, which had to be carried out not later than three years after the commencement of the Act, was based on an examination of 12 public bodies spread across the civil service, local authorities and health boards, concentrating for the most part on those bodies which had received the largest number of requests for access to records since the commencement of the Act.

Openness and transparency

The Commissioner concluded that generally the Act had brought about major gains in terms of greater openness and transparency notwithstanding a high rate of refusal of requests. He found the level of refusals a little surprising in the context of a regime, which is designed to give access to information to the greatest extent possible subject to the requirement of the public interest and the right of privacy. He also found an unnecessary use of exemption clauses having examined specifically section 19 (meetings of the Government); section 20 (deliberations of public bodies); and section 26 (information obtained in confidence).

> "It is possible to make a prima facie case for exemption under these or other provisions in relation to many records but whether it is worth doing so, in some cases, is an entirely different matter. In my view the cause of greater openness is not served by trying to rely on an exemption to refuse information simply because the exemption is there or because, while the record sought is innocuous, it is feared that release will, from the public body's point of view, create an unfortunate precedent."[25]

---

[24] PA Consulting Group 2002. Public Service Modernisation website:www.bettergov.ie/index.asp?lang=ENG.

[25] *The Freedom of Information Act–Compliance by Public Bodies*, Office of the Information Commissioner, July 2001, p.5.

The Commissioner discovered widespread failure, when refusing information, to give reasons which meet the requirements of the Act as required by section 8(2)(d). As already mentioned, the Act is intended to provide access to information held by public bodies to the greatest extent possible consistent with the public interest and the right to privacy. Thus, release should be the norm, refusal the exception. In this context, it was, according to the Commissioner, hardly too much to expect a public body which is refusing access to go to the trouble of properly documenting that refusal.

Effectiveness of internal review

In practice, based on figures supplied by all public bodies for 2000, about 7% of initial decisions proceeded to internal review. However, that internal review was not fully effective in many public bodies. Some of the internal review decisions examined in the course of the investigation bore all the hallmarks of rubber-stamping – there was no evidence of independent consideration of the issues and little or no attempt to improve the explanations given to the requester. A significant number of the internal review decisions examined in the course of the investigation, almost 40%, did not meet the full requirements of the Act in terms of quality of response. Without wishing to overstate the problems in this area, the Commissioner expressed concern that on a second attempt and even with the input of a more senior official, some public bodies were failing to accord requesters their full statutory rights by either releasing the information requested or providing clear and comprehensive explanations for not doing so.

Failure to give reasons and prepare schedules of records

The Act generally obliges a public body which is refusing a request whether wholly or partly, to give the requester a statement of the reasons for the refusal. Where information is refused, statements of reasons which fail to meet the requirements of the Act are reasonably common. The sample would suggest that such failures occur in about 50% of cases. Without a proper statement of reasons a requester cannot make an informed decision as to whether to seek a further review. There was clear evidence that unnecessary reviews by the Commissioner were being generated as a result of the failure to give proper statements of reasons.

The Commissioner notes that the Central Policy Unit of the Department of Finance, which was responsible for training personnel in freedom of information procedures, had advised public bodies that a statement of reasons should show a connection, supported by a chain of reasoning, between the decision and the decision maker's findings on material issues. It had also strongly recommended that, other than in cases involving no more than a few records, decision makers should prepare a schedule listing the records sequentially by number and containing the following information: the date of the record; the title of the document or the name of its author or addressee; a brief but sufficient description of the record or its contents to show a *prima facie* claim for exemption; the exemption claimed; and where the claim relates to parts of a record, a clear indication of the parts involved.

In the case of the Department of Justice, Equality and Law Reform, where adequate explanations had not been given in a number of the cases examined, two particular problems were noted. The first was a tendency to rely on an exemption but to give no indication as to why it was appropriate in the particular case. The second was failure to provide a schedule of the records at issue. The failure to provide a schedule meant that in some cases the requester had no indication of how many records were being refused and often was given little real information about the nature of the records held by the Department.

Records management

The Act does not impose specific requirements on public bodies in relation to records management. It is, nonetheless, clear that proper records management is vital to the success of the Act. Unfortunately, on the basis of the current sample, the Commissioner found that record keeping in public bodies was not of a particularly high standard.

Failure to meet time limits

With a few exceptions, the Commissioner found that procedures adopted for the processing of requests under the Act had been satisfactory. This conclusion was based on the findings that most public bodies processed most requests within the statutory deadline (not later than four weeks).

Failures which went beyond the occasional breach were noted in the case of three public bodies - the Department of Education and Science, the Department of Health and Children and, to a lesser extent, the Department of Justice, Equality and Law Reform. In the case of the Department of Health and Children, failure to take the initial decision within the deadline appeared to happen often enough to give the Commissioner cause for concern.

Records for industrial schools

The most serious problem was in the Department of Education and Science. It is of interest to note that the Department has records of over 41,000 former residents of 59 industrial and reformatory schools of which about 13,000 are specific personal files: of the 230,000 documents held by the Department in relation to these institutions, 100,000 documents relate to these individual personal files. As a consequence of the search and retrieval issues arising from about 1,400 requests under the Act and a number of High Court actions which involved the release of these records, the Department moved in August 1999 to scan all the records on to a computer database. However, in relation to other requests, unconnected with industrial schools, deadlines were not met by significant margins in about half the cases examined.

Exemptions and failure to exercise discretion

The Commissioner expressed concern following examination of exemptions claimed under section 19 (meetings of the Government) that this exemption which was clearly intended to be applied with discretion, was regarded, in practice, as mandatory. Further, the refusal of access to records the contents of which are already largely in the public domain was not an encouragement to the creation of a more open public service. The exercise of the exemption appeared to place the emphasis on finding the correct "technical" basis for refusal rather than making information available "to the greatest extent possible consistent with the public interest and the right to privacy". The Commissioner noted that such a minimalist approach could easily spill over into the use of other exemptions resulting in an overly cautious approach to the release of other information.

The Commissioner found that, in practice, it appeared that decision makers rarely, if ever, consider exercising their discretion to release. This had resulted in situations in which decision makers appeared to feel obliged to refuse access to Government memoranda even though their contents had already been released in their entirety by way of press release.

Tactical refusals of records of deliberative processes

In considering section 20 (deliberations of public bodies), the Commissioner found that some decision makers displayed a basic misunderstanding of the nature of the public interest test which section 20 requires, confusing it with the public interest balancing test contained in sections such as 21(functions and negotiations of public bodies); 26 (information obtained in confidence); and 27(commercially sensitive information). Further, a number of reviews conducted by the Information Commissioner had been settled on the basis that by the time the review came to be dealt with the information had been released because the deliberative process had concluded. He noted that this gives rise to suspicion among some users of the Act that refusals under section 20 are tactical. In other words, he was of the opinion that some decision makers act on the basis that the deliberative process will run its course during the period for review so that, in effect, they are using elements of the Act to defer rather than as legitimate refusals.

Information obtained in confidence

The Commissioner noted that section 26 (information obtained in confidence) is a complex exemption and it would appear that many decision makers experience difficulty in applying it correctly. In some cases the exemption was invoked in circumstances where it was inappropriate to do so. In some cases what the public body sought to protect is the identity of the person who has provided information to it in confidence, as opposed to the contents of the information. In such cases, access may more appropriately be refused under sections 23(1)(b) or 46(1)(f) which provide that access may be refused if it could reasonably be expected to reveal or lead to the revelation of the identity of a person who has given information in confidence to a public body in relation to the enforcement or administration of the civil law or in relation to the enforcement of the criminal law.

A second set of circumstances in which it may not be appropriate to invoke section 26 is where the information at issue is intended to influence policy making or legislation. In such circumstances, it is most unlikely that a legal duty of confidence is owed to the provider of the information. However, public bodies may feel that refusing to treat such information in confidence will reduce the flow of information to them. The Information Commissioner is of the view that:

> "this is a consequence which must be suffered in the interests of democracy. The alternative is to permit policy to be formulated and legislation to be enacted on the basis of secret representations - something which is wholly at odds with the concepts of openness and transparency which the FOI Act was intended to foster."[26]

Consultants' progress report on public service modernisation programme

More open and accountable civil service

In March 2002, PA Consulting Group presented their report on *Evaluation of the Progress of the Strategic Management Initiative/Delivering Better Government Modernisation Programme.*[27] The central question addressed by the Review Team was: "What impact did the application of SMI/DBG have across the civil service, and has the service received by the customer improved as a consequence?"

One of the most positive findings of the *Evaluation* is that there is little doubt that the civil service is more open and accountable than it was a decade ago. "If nothing else, the FOI and PSMA [Public Service Management Act] innovations of 1997 have underpinned these changes."[28] Moreover, valuable networks were created for sharing

---

[26] *The Freedom of Information Act–Compliance by Public Bodies, op. cit.*, p.32.

[27] *Evaluation of the Progress of the Strategic Management Initiative/Delivering Better Government Modernisation Programme* (PA Consulting Group 2002). The full report is available on the Department of Finance, Central Policy Unit website.

[28] *Ibid.*, para.3.3.

experience and supporting Departments/Offices in implementing initiatives, particularly in relation to Quality Customer Service and freedom of information.[29]

Positive impact of FOI

Chapter 5 is titled, "Openness, Transparency and Accountability" and the principal finding is that the Freedom of Information Act "has had far ranging and largely positive effects upon the civil service."

> "Almost every senior manager with whom we spoke acknowledged the role of the Act in generating a greater transparency around the conduct of government business, and in promoting a sense of accountability to the public served. This was also confirmed by the survey findings which indicated that 60% of respondents felt that their Department/ Office had become more open in its dealings with customers and stakeholders.
>
> The degree of openness achieved under FOI is such that in many cases information is now routinely available to the public without any recourse to the Act - the regular publication of Strategy Statements on departmental web sites serves as an example in this regard. This achievement however is not resource free. Considerable administrative costs are inevitably involved in processing information requests under the Act. Given that the primary production resource in the civil service is staff time, the deployment of staff in responding to FOI requests necessarily deflects these resources from service delivery elsewhere.
>
> While some concern has been expressed at the willingness of the civil service to document all aspects of its work in a post-FOI environment, there is no doubt that FOI has been a notable success of DBG. It is appropriate at this point also to advert to the report in July 2001 of the Information Commissioner in relation to the practices and procedures

---

[29] *Ibid.*, para.4.3.

adopted by public bodies under FOI. In his report the Information Commissioner concluded, 'the Act has brought about major gains in terms of greater openness and transparency', although he also noted the resource implications of this achievement when he observed that 'the processing of FOI requests can impose a formidable administrative burden on public bodies'."[30]

Human resources

As part of the *Evaluation* a survey was conducted by means of a questionnaire which was circulated to 30,000 civil servants resulting in a 14% response.

Uniformity v one-size-fits all

The authors of the *Evaluation* noted the range of diversity that is the civil/public service and expressed concern that inherent in the desire for modernisation was a danger of imposing uniformity, a one-size-fits-all approach, which would be inappropriate to cope with this diversity.

Change champions

The *Evaluation* noted the necessity for champions of change to ensure the further development of the civil service and the achievement of the SMI/DBG strategies.

Management Report shelved?

In 2002, when first commenting on the low response rate to the survey in the *Evaluation* the author noted as follows:

> "In terms of culture change this raises questions regarding the attitude of the vast number of non-replying civil servants who ought to appreciate that the findings of this survey would play a significant part in decisions made on the future

---

[30] *Ibid.*, paras.5.4 – 5.6.

development of the service. Furthermore, some of the survey findings on attitudes to performance feedback may give cause for concern." [31]

In relation to change champions this was the comment:

"At a public level, surely the most important change champion is the Information Commissioner. Internally, the Central Policy Unit of the Department of Finance plays a significant role. It is interesting to note that the Ombudsman has never been given a real opportunity to take on this role in an effective manner even though everything published by the Ombudsman is about good administrative practice."[32]

Maladministration

Some four years later it may be remarked that, like so many other reports commissioned on behalf of the public service, the *Evaluation* Report was probably shelved. Why else would it not have featured even as a footnote in the *Travers Report* into the role of the Department of Health and Children[33] following the public outcry over the unlawful imposition of nursing home charges?[34] This might be considered all the more surprising given that *Travers*, whilst acknowledging improvements attributable to the then Secretary General, referred to the need for internal reorganisation of the Department in the following terms:

"There is a widespread perception both within the Department

---

[31] *Freedom of Information: The Challenge of a New Management Culture* presented at the first Annual Freedom of Information Conference, Trinity College, Dublin, 2002.

[32] *Ibid.*

[33] Oireachtas Joint Committee on Health and Children *Interim report on the Report on Certain Issues of Management and Administration in the Department of Health and Children associated with the Practice of Charges for Persons in Long-Stay Care in Health Board Institutions and Related Matters* (Pn A5/0363) March 2005 hereinafter *Travers* (J Travers is author of the original report).

[34] For comprehensive analysis, see E. O'Dell ed. *Older People in Modern Ireland Essays on Law and Policy, op. cit.*

of Health and Children and external to it that the MAC [Management Advisory Committee] of the Department of Health and Children has for various, mainly historic, reasons been dysfunctional in many respects for some time. This is an untenable situation within a Department that is now responsible for policy (and previously for operational issues) that directly affects the lives of every citizen in this country."[35]

On the other hand, parallel findings were the subject matter of the Cromien Molloy report into maladministration in the Department of Justice[36] some six years earlier. It might be presumed that this report would have even greater relevance to an inquiry into maladministration in the Department of Health and Children. It, too, went unreferenced.

Thus, it is hardly a surprise that the findings of the *Evaluation* that the Freedom of Information Act "has had far ranging and largely positive effects upon the civil service" were equally ignored when the 2003 Amendment Act was forced through the Oireachtas.

FREEDOM OF INFORMATION (AMENDMENT) ACT 2003

The Freedom of Information (Amendment) Act 2003 passed into law on April 11, 2003. In total, 30 sections of the Principal Act have been amended, some in a most significant manner and others purely for technical reasons. It has been generally accepted that the purpose of the Amendment Act was to restrict ease of access to information held by central government. This has been achieved in a number of ways e.g. by extending the definition of Government in section 19 to include an ill-defined "committee of officials"; by conferring on Secretaries General of Departments the right to exempt records from access by issuing final

---

[35] *Travers, op. cit,* n.33, p.84.

[36] S. Cromien and E. Molloy *Inquiry in the Department of Justice into the Delisting of Judge Dominic Lynch from the Special Criminal Court Panel.* November 18, 1996 (Pn.3254) Government Publications. For comprehensive analysis Feldman, "Accountability – A Case Study" *Studies;* Vol.88; No.50; (Summer 1999), pp.140 – 153.

certificates not amenable to review by the Information Commissioner, section 20; and most particularly, by introducing compulsory fees for requests, internal appeals and appeals to the Information Commissioner, section 47. The Irish Current Law Statutes Annotated (I.C.L.S.A.) version of the 2003 Amendment Act clearly and comprehensively outlines the amendments, the reasons given for their introduction and the likely effects where known. The I.C.L.S.A. also gives some detail about the controversy surrounding the introduction of the Amendment Act.[37]

FOI controversy[38]

The whole process whereby the Bill came to public notice was objectionable. First, for some weeks prior to the introduction of the Bill there were a series of deliberate leaks regarding the proposed changes. Secondly, the Bill was seen as the result of secretive meetings between five Secretaries-General without any input from the one expert in the country, the Information Commissioner, let alone from any of the users of the Act.[39] The media, of course, was in full cry. Given the concurrent proliferation of requests for public submissions from all quarters of government when conducting reviews of policy, failure to request consultation about a review of the Freedom of Information Act was, understandably, seen as a sinister and retrograde development. Nevertheless, it is common knowledge among those who use the Act that in its early years there has been a chilling effect on expressions of opinion and on the keeping of records especially minutes and other recognised forms of note-keeping.

Wholesale amendments

Most early discussion on the proposed amendments centred on the

---

[37] McDonagh, I.C.L.S.A., *op. cit.,* n.6.

[38] For a comprehensive and robust analysis, see *2003* R*eview* p.374 *et. seq.*

[39] The Information Commissioner's commentary on the operation of the Principal Act, arising from his powers under s.39, *The Application and Operation of Certain Provisions of the Freedom of Information Act, 1997* was greeted with extraordinary antagonism, indeed, a direct personal attack on the Commissioner, under the guise of Dáil privilege. See *2003 Review* p.380.

provision for an increase in the exemption period for release of cabinet records from five to ten years. This was not an unreasonable proposal and section 19, meetings of the government, now represents a significant reduction from the original 30-year rule for release, albeit an increase over the Principal Act's five years. Of less validity were the amendments to ensure that communications between Ministers and officials on matters relating to Government business are protected. The proposal regarding total discretionary power for Secretaries General is quite probably unconstitutional as is the extension of the definition of government to include a "committee of officials".[40] On the positive side, the Information Commissioner's powers in respect of appeal have been strengthened in some areas as have the time limits available to her. Of considerable importance is the removal of the statutory barrier hitherto preventing appeals from the High Court to the Supreme Court. This will ensure a consistent legal approach to the interpretation and administration of the Act which has been notably absent. Most controversially, as has already been noted above, was the Minister for Finance's proposal to introduce mandatory fees for the processing of freedom of information requests including appeals.

MANDATORY FEES

As a consequence of the 2003 Act, section 47(6A) provides that the appropriate prescribed fee shall be paid at the time of the making of the request and that "if it is not so paid, the head [of a public body] or, as the case may be, the Commissioner shall refuse to accept the request or application". The Regulations[41] provide that no fee is to be charged for requests for personal information, section 7; nor for applications for reasons for decisions, section 18; nor for requests to amend records, section 17. Additionally, the fee varies depending on whether the requester does or does not hold a medical card. A fee of €15 must accompany the initial request, €75 must accompany a request for internal review, €150 must accompany an appeal to the Information Commissioner. For medical

---

[40] *Ibid.*
[41] Freedom of Information Act 1997 (Fees) Regulations 2003 (S.I. No.264 of 2003).

card holders these fees are respectively €10, €25 and €50. The fee for both medical card and non-medical card holders is €50 if a third party wishes to appeal to the Information Commissioner in a section 29 case.[42] Section 29 allows a third party to a request who is the person who provided the information or is a person named in the record to object to release of the record in cases of information obtained in confidence, section 26; commercially sensitive information, section 27; or information that will be released in the public interest, section 28.

Administration of fees exceeds fee income

The Government claimed that fees were being introduced as a positive measure to defray the costs of administering the FOI regime. However, many commentators correctly predicted that far from making a positive contribution to freedom of information, the fees as statutorily imposed would cause insoluble difficulties for those charged with administering the Act. Indeed, the Information Commissioner noted that his Office might face procedural as well as administrative difficulties.[43] In the subsequent *Review of the Operation of the Freedom of Information (Amendment) Act 2003* the Commissioner stated that to end-March 2004 the amount received by her Office in application fees totalled €15,125. The Office's costs in setting up the scheme were "far in excess of this figure."

Confusion inevitable

With regard to procedural difficulties, in the *2003 Annual Report* the Commissioner commented as follows:

> "While it may appear that the intention of the 2003 Act is that there be no fees for 'personal information', the wording of the regulations has presented difficulties for my Office in determining whether a fee is applicable to a particular request or application. The phrase that is used in the Act for a request or application to be exempt from a fee is that it 'contain only

---

[42] No clue is given as to why a third party in a section 29 case who has the misfortune to be a medical card holder is not given a discount: See *2003 Review* p.375.

[43] *Commentary of the Information Commissioner on the Freedom of Information Act 1997* on s.47. www.oic.gov.ie/24d6_3c2.htm

personal information relating to the requester'. The phrase
'...relating to...' is open to varying interpretations which can
raise a variety of scenarios. In particular, does the Act require
the payment of a fee where the requester is the parent or
guardian of a minor and the records sought are those of the
minor? Or is payment required where the requester is the
spouse or next of kin of a deceased person and the records
sought are those of the deceased person? Secondly, does the
legislation require the payment of a fee where the requester
is seeking records which constitute personal information
relating to both the requester and another individual or
individuals?"[44]

Defining personal information

In essence, an FOI Officer on receipt of a request must now decide the
precise nature of the records requested BEFORE the request can be
formally treated as an FOI request. Not only is more than one page of the
Principal Act devoted to the interpretation of "personal information" but
it includes 14 positive sub-clauses and three negative sub-clauses. It is
doubtful that an FOI Officer, let alone a requester, is conversant with
these subtle complexities; moreover, the Information Commissioner has
ruled that personal information is something that may be implied in a
record.[45] Probably the only certain way to establish whether a record is
personal or not is to examine the record. Does this mean that all
applications must have an accompanying fee to enable the request to
proceed in order to ascertain whether the information is personal or not
thereby deciding whether or not a fee is required? If that is the case,
assuming the information is deemed personal the fee would have to be
returned. If the records to be accessed are a mix of personal and other
information should the fee be adjusted pro rata?[46]

---

[44] *Annual Report of the Information Commissioner 2003*, p. 11.

[45] Case 000365 – *Ms ACH and Others and the Department of Education and
Science*, October 16, 2001.

[46] Whereas the Regulations preclude such action, two points of legal significance
should be borne in mind (i) proportionality is a well-established legal principle
in Irish law: (ii) these regulations are secondary and not primary legislation and
may, thus, be more susceptible to challenge.

Predicted decline of requests

The Information Commissioner published a *Review of the Operation of the Freedom of Information (Amendment) Act 2003*. The starkest finding of the *Review* was the significant decline in FOI requests for non-personal information. The Commissioner went on to note that it would be wrong to conclude that the Act no longer functions in any meaningful way. She noted that many, many people continue to use the Act to access personal information which does not attract an upfront fee. With regard to non-personal information, the media, in particular, are still securing and publishing a significant amount of public interest information. The Commissioner also points out that, despite the amended Act, FOI continues generally to embed itself in the wider administration, from government departments through to health boards, local authorities and public bodies. Her investigation shows that, by and large, the officials charged with executing FOI requests do so in a fair and responsible manner. In addition, there is evidence to show that more information is being released outside of Freedom of Information.

Restoring deficient public accountability

In summary, the Amendment Act, notwithstanding the few positive changes, has resulted in a retrograde step of draconian proportions with dangerous ramifications for open and accountable government.[47] The following might best sum this up:

Thought for the day pre-2003 Amendment Act

> "[Senior management should] encourage a proactive approach to the release of information and a positive standpoint which asks the question on every occasion: *"why can the records requested not be released?"*[48]

---

[47] See *2003 Review.*
[48] From: Outline Action Plan on FOI Compliance Report of the Subgroup of the Inter-Departmental Working Group p.8, 2002.

Thought for the day post-2003 Amendment Act

> "The request itself should be refused under section 10 on the
> grounds that a fee payable under section 47(6A) has not been
> paid."[49]

FOI: GENERAL PRINCIPLES FOR GOOD PRACTICE

Liability of the freedom of information officer

Unfortunately, freedom of information decision-makers may well find
themselves out on a limb within their organisation in relation to how to
apply the spirit of the Freedom of Information Act. Moreover, especially
with regard to government departments and offshoots, in addition to more
senior staff to whom they are responsible, there is a direct political
dimension and oversight to FOI activities. Questions are regularly asked
at the TCD School of Law conferences regarding the possibility of being
sued for misapplication of the rules. It needs to be remembered that before
there can be any action in tort, the supposedly injured party must show
that a duty of care was owed, that there was negligence in exercising that
duty of care and that directly as a result of that negligence harm was
suffered. In the normal operation of the freedom of information regime it
is difficult to conceive of any situation where a freedom of information
officer acting reasonably and in good faith within their function could be
held liable in tort.[50] Certainly, if there is any concern, reassurance can be
found in the opinions regularly expressed by judges and by the Information
Commissioner.

Nevertheless, if a disaffected requester were to pursue a complaint
against a freedom of information officer, it is quite possible that the officer
will be named as a principle against whom legal action is being taken.
Again, in a well-managed organisation this should not be any cause for

---

[49] From: *Information Note Freedom of Information (Fees) Regulations 2003*,
Department of the Taoiseach, July 2003. Found on the Internet during research
for paper presented at 2003 Annual FOI Conference.

[50] S.45, FOI Act provides for immunity from legal proceedings where actions are
properly taken in accordance with the terms of the Act.

concern as the legal representation for the employer will automatically look after the interests of the named individual. It is well-established that providing there is no mal fides on the part of the officer, the courts will take the view that the freedom of information officer was acting bona fide in the course of duty on behalf of the employer. This was the judgment of Barr J. in *MQ v. Gleeson, and City of Dublin VEC and Chance and the Eastern Health Board*[51] in relation to the named officials of each organisation despite the fact that the judge found that the second-named defendant had made some mistakes in carrying out his duties.

Sound management practice

It cannot be overstressed that if an organisation is already well-managed, application of freedom of information will merely reinforce sound practices.

FOI guidelines and guidance notes not law

One of the pitfalls facing FOI decision-makers is that they may feel constrained to exercise the black and white letter of the Freedom of Information Act rather than follow common sense. As described, a great deal of the Act is not only obscure but, overall, it requires an extraordinary skill in mental gymnastics to keep all the sections and subsections and amendments in mind. Thus, there is a considerable danger that, in practice, guidelines and guidance notes written in plainer English will replace the Act as the easier option for understanding. These helpful hints, perhaps at times even policy statements, issued by various Ministers and other heads of public bodies, including the Central Policy Unit of the Department of Finance, are not law. Moreover, there is a mistaken belief among many practitioners that the responsible Minister[52] has issued guidelines on the Act. In relation to guidelines suggested in the Regulations[53] dealing with requests for personal information of minors and the deceased the High Court noted that "[i]t has been acknowledged

---

[51] [1998] 4 I.R. 85.
[52] The Minister for Finance is responsible for public service matters.
[53] Freedom of Information Act, 1997 (Section 28 (6)) Regulations, 1999 (S.I. No. 47 of 1999).

that no guidelines of the kind contemplated in the Regulations have been drawn up or published". [54]

An example of policy purporting to be law was the information note from the Department of the Taoiseach on the application of the new fees. It stated in the final line: "Fees are not refundable if a decision is varied or annulled at internal or external review stage." Such a statement is not included in the Amendment Act nor in the Regulations on Fees. The validity of the statement as a policy guidance is, therefore, questionable.[55]

Qualitative decision-making

In well-managed organisations decision-makers are conscious that their actions have qualitative consequences; thus, as a matter of course they keep their staff informed and ensure that anyone affected by an institutional decision is made aware of the rationale underlying such decisions. For such organisations having to comply with the Freedom of Information Act holds little fear. Staff are already aware of any information retained about them and these and other records are well maintained to facilitate tracking decisions. Staff members who request their personnel files will not have to make a freedom of information request to access files pre-1995.[56] Staff members will participate in regular evaluations and will have the confidence and backing of their superiors when applying for promotional opportunities. In well-managed organisations individuals who are affected by institutional decisions are not obliged to make a section 18 freedom of information request to know why decisions affecting them have been taken. These are qualitative, not quantitative dimensions of sound management practice.

---

[54] *NMcK v Information Commissioner* [2004] 1 I.R. 12.

[55] *Information Note Freedom of Information (Fees) Regulations 2003*, Department of the Taoiseach, July 2003. This note disappeared from the Internet subsequent to the TCD School of Law Annual Conference 2003 at which it was highlighted by the author.

[56] S.(6)(5), FOI Act excludes right of access to personnel records of public bodies which were created more than three years before commencement of the Act (i.e. pre-1995) if that record "is not being used or proposed to be used in a manner or for a purpose that affects, or will or may affect, adversely the interests of the person." (S.(6)(5)(c). See *Minister for Agriculture v. Information Commissioner* [2000] 1 I.R. 309 considered in chap.5 *infra* and below at n.103.

Consistency of procedures

In a 2003 High Court judgment in an appeal against a decision of the Information Commissioner, the appellants claimed *inter alia* that the Information Commissioner had failed to give them an opportunity to reply to a letter thereby failing to adopt fair procedures and appropriate principles of natural and constitutional law and justice. Mr Justice Quirke found for the Information Commissioner as follows:

> "I am satisfied that it has become the practice of the respondent, when notifying *'relevant'* persons such as the appellants of his intention to comply with a request for a review to deliver to such *'relevant persons'* a copy of the guidelines on the adequacy of search records together with other relevant information as to how the review is to be conducted. I am satisfied that this procedure was followed by the respondent in the instant case". [57]

Good administration

Over the years of dealing with the civil and public service, the Ombudsman has developed responses to recurring problems and given guidance to public bodies in the manner in which they conduct their affairs. Two of these are *The Ombudsman's Principles of Good Administration* and *Public Bodies and the Citizen – The Ombudsman's Guide to Standards of Best Practice*.[58] In addition, the Information Commissioner has given important guidance in appeal decisions.

Records Management

Accurate record-keeping and sensible procedures

The Act does not impose specific requirements on public bodies in relation to records management. It is, nonetheless, clear that proper records

---

[57] *Ryan v. Information Commissioner*, (H.C. 2002 N0.18 M.C.A.), unreported, High Court, May 20, 2003, Quirke J.
[58] Available on the Ombudsman's website.

management is vital to the success of the Act. Indeed, whether subject to the Act or not, to be effective, organisations of all kinds require accurate record-keeping and sensible procedures which are applied in a consistent manner across the board. These are the principles that are stressed time and time again by judges and by information commissioners in all jurisdictions.

In a 2001 decision the Information Commissioner stated:

> "I take the view that the FOI Act imposes on public bodies a duty to ensure that their record management systems are capable of enabling them to meet their obligations under the Act. In my view, public bodies should have stated record management policies which set out the standards in relation to the creation, maintenance and destruction of physical and electronic records. Destruction should only take place in accordance with a clearly stated destruction policy and in compliance with the provisions of the National Archives Act 1986 in the case of those public bodies which are covered by that Act."[59]

Claims that files do not exist or cannot be found upheld

A substantial proportion of reviews conducted by the Information Commissioner involve refusals by public bodies on the ground that the records do not exist or cannot be found after all reasonable steps to locate them have been taken.[60] The issue which she must address in such reviews is whether the public body's decision is justified.

> "Occasionally, requesters may expect me or my officials to carry out a search for the records in question. While it is open to me to enter the premises of any public body during the course of a review, my role in these cases is normally one of reviewing the decision of the public body and deciding whether that decision was justified. This means that, as in any other review, I must have regard to the evidence available

---

[59] *Case 99265 – Mr X and the Eastern Health Board,* June 18, 2001.
[60] S.10(1)(a), FOI Act.

to the decision maker and the reasoning used by him or her in arriving at the decision. I must then decide whether the decision maker has had regard to all the relevant evidence and, if so, whether he or she was justified in coming to his/her decision in the case."[61]

The Commissioner's approach to such cases was endorsed by Mr Justice Quirke in *Ryan v Information Commissioner*.[62]

Claims that files do not exist or cannot be found rejected

While in the majority of reviews the Commissioner is satisfied that the public body has taken all reasonable steps to locate the records sought, in two cases during 2003 further records were located following the intervention of her Office. In one case the requester's solicitors sought all records held by the Southern Health Board relating to the requester, who had been in an industrial school between 1975 and 1988:

> "As the file was not located in the areas where it should have been, my Office sought further information and directed that further searches be carried out including a search by all social workers in the relevant community care area of all files held by them or in their offices/work areas. The file concerned was located within the relevant social work department of the Board. Given that the file existed and ought to have been found, my Office was thus justified in directing these further searches. In this particular case it proved useful to direct that the social workers themselves become involved in the search."[63]

In another case the requester had sought a review of the decision of the Department of Justice, Equality and Law Reform when it was unable to locate a file which it held containing information relating to the requester's application for citizenship.

---

[61] *Annual Report of the Information Commissioner 2003*, p.34.
[62] Unreported High Court, May 20, 2003.
[63] *Case 030382, Annual Report of the Information Commissioner 2003*, p.34.

"Having regard to the evidence provided by the Department
to my Office and the fact that the file in question had been
mislaid a short time previously, my Office was not satisfied
that all reasonable steps had been taken to locate it. Therefore,
I was not in a position to find that the Department's decision
was justified. I asked the Department to carry out further
detailed searches of all its premises where the missing file
might have been located. ... The Department was also
reminded that, in the event that the missing file was not found
following further detailed searches, my staff would be visiting
the Department for the purposes of reviewing the recorded
step-by-step details of the additional searches carried out."

Within four working days the Department informed the Commissioner
that the missing file had been located.[64]

Files destroyed

The Commissioner has had to deal with several cases where files had
been destroyed. She commented that doubt and confusion can arise in
the mind of a requester where a public body cannot say with certainty
whether a particular file or record sought has been destroyed.

"Such lack of precision can create suspicion among some
requesters that the file has been deliberately hidden or
misplaced in an effort to frustrate the requester. The drawing
up and implementation of a proper records management
policy which provides guidelines on when and what type of
records should be destroyed, together with a record of the
records or files which have been destroyed, provides
confidence in the public body's decision and reduces the
amount of administrative resources involved in responding
to requests under the Act and to subsequent reviews by my
Office."[65]

---

[64] *Ibid.*, pp.34-35.
[65] *Case 020445, Annual Report of the Information Commissioner 2003*, p.34.

Manner of access to records

The Information Commissioner has noted that public bodies may consider refusing access to records because they are concerned that parties other than the requester could have access to those records. She points out that there is no specific exemption in the Act for refusal on this basis and recommends that in such cases public bodies should consider granting, and where appropriate should grant, access in a different manner, e.g. by way of inspection of the records.

> "For instance, in one case I found that access to certain records would involve the disclosure of personal information of third parties. However, I found that the public interest in the request being granted outweighed the right to privacy of the third parties. In many ways disclosure of records under the FOI Act can be disclosure to the world at large. Providing the requester with photocopies of the records in this case could potentially, have led to individuals other than the requester having access to the records. In order to reduce the disclosure of personal information of the third parties to a minimum, I directed that access be granted by way of inspection of the records. I should state that, in this case, I was satisfied that access to the records would involve only a minimal impact on the third parties' privacy.
>
> I recognise the practical difficulties involved for public bodies in arranging and supervising access by inspection. Likewise, I recognise that access in this manner will not always be suitable for the requester. For example, the requester may only have an opportunity to inspect the records once and in most cases would be unable to transcribe or take notes while inspecting the records. However, such an approach was obviously envisaged by the Oireachtas and is consistent with the overall aim of the Act to grant access to the greatest extent possible consistent with the public interest and the right to privacy."[66]

---

[66] *Annual Report of the Information Commissioner 2003*, p.23.

FOI and Data Protection

Concerns are regularly expressed by FOI officers regarding the relationship of Data Protection issues with FOI. While Data Protection is outside the scope of this book some comments of the Information Commissioner are instructive.

Nexus of Freedom of Information and Data Protection

In the 2003 Annual Report, the Information Commissioner considered the nexus of the Data Protection (DP) and FOI regimes which look at information from two different perspectives The essential principle of DP is the protection of individual privacy and the putting in place of safeguards where personal data is collected, processed or transferred to other bodies and/or other countries. On the other hand, the essential principle of FOI is that there should be access to records held by or under the control of public bodies to the greatest extent possible consistent with the public interest and the right to privacy. While it applies only to public bodies as defined in the FOI Act, it encompasses records containing personal and non-personal or official information.

As the Commissioner stated: "[FOI] is driven by a desire to make government more open, transparent and accountable and by a desire to strengthen the democratic right to freedom of expression which is automatically restricted once access to information is restricted."[67]

INSTITUTIONAL BARRIERS TO RELEASE OF INFORMATION

There is universal acknowledgment that there must be some limits on access to information, e.g. state security, commercial and trade secrets.[68] However, whenever an exemption to the right of access is warranted it should be narrowly defined, in precise and specific language. Clearly, this is not the case with the Irish freedom of information regime especially since the Amendment Act came into force. In any situation where the

---

[67] *Annual Report of the Information Commissioner 2003*, p.22.
[68] See chap.6, *infra.*

exemption is not mandatory and crystal clear in its application, the public body should be tending towards release.

Official Secrets Act

The culture of secrecy in the civil service is attributable to the Official Secrets Act 1963. During the passage of the Freedom of Information Act 1997 a large part of the legislative debate in the Dáil condemned the Official Secrets Act and there were calls from both sides of the House for its repeal rather than its amendment in the Freedom of Information Act.[69]

Self-protection of organisation

Quite irrespective of the Official Secrets Act, many organisations exercise inordinate control over the information they possess in a desire for self-protection or self-perpetuation. An example is the continuing refusal of some health authorities to release individual patient's medical records outside the freedom of information regime. One of the reasons behind this refusal is the fear that the patient will use the contents of the records to pursue litigation against the medical practitioner or health provider. This is not a legitimate reason. If litigation occurs, records will be subject to a discovery order and will inevitably become available to the patient. To be successful in litigation the patient needs to prove negligence. In the absence of negligence any suit will fail. If negligence did occur, it has been found on many occasions that what is required is an apology and failing receipt of an apology the patient becomes much more aggrieved and pursues the suit relentlessly. In summary, any system that hinders the release of medical records on foot of a reasonable request by the patient or the patient's lawful representatives is in error.[70]

---

[69] Considered further at n.119.

[70] FOI and health issues are dealt with in chap.2 *infra*. Examples of health decisions are Cases 99189 – *Mr. X and a Health Board* December 12, 2000 (access to medical records); 99125 – *Mr X and the Mid-western Health Board* (whether private patients' records are accessible); *020220- Mr X and the Southern Health Board* August 12 2002 (amendment to personal information). For FOI and litigation see chap.4 *infra*.

Over-zealousness

There can be occasions when, due to over-zealousness, information which ought to be available to individual requesters or to the world at large is retained. It should be remembered that requests for information need not be made under the freedom of information regime. For instance, as already noted, legislation covering information relating to the environment has always required timely release. Nevertheless, the main reason given to the Ombudsman to justify a Local Authority's refusal to make requested information available was "the alarmist use to which ... the information would be put".[71]

Knowledge is control

It is a well known axiom that knowledge is power: the person who holds information is in a position of control over those without it. The following example of a case dealt with by the Ombudsman illustrates this point.

Failure to indicate where parking discs may be purchased

Drogheda Corporation had rejected an appeal against the imposition of a parking fine by a stranger to the area who did not know where parking discs could be purchased. During the Ombudsman's investigation the Corporation agreed with the complainant that there were no signs on display indicating where parking discs could be obtained. The point was made that the onus was on the Corporation to provide the necessary information to enable the general public, particularly those unfamiliar with the area, to buy parking discs. As a result the Corporation refunded the costs of the parking fine and gave a commitment to put up signs indicating where parking discs could be purchased.[72]

Belittling the other person

Most of us have experienced an officious public servant. It seems as if

---

[71] *Annual Report of the Ombudsman 1994*, p.49. Above at n.17.

[72] *A Digest of Cases: A selection of significant cases completed by the Ombudsman in 2000-2001*, p.38. Also available at www.ombudsman.gov.ie/en/Publications/ CaseDigests/

their sole role is to magnify their own self-importance to the detriment of everyone else including the member of the public whom they are supposed to assist. Even in the absence of such people, it can often happen that systems of administration assume a knowledge on the part of the other person that does not exist i.e. that the member of the public is as informed of the intricacies of various schemes as is the public servant administering the scheme. An example of this behaviour was highlighted by the Ombudsman in the special report on the overpayment by tenant purchasers of local authority housing loans. He noted that in some local authorities it was a requirement of audit to issue a refund to a borrower only on the receipt of a written application from the borrower.

> "However, no evidence was presented to me to suggest that the local authorities concerned actually notified the borrowers that they were due a refund. In these circumstances, for such a policy to be justified, it is important that the borrower be informed of the existence of such a credit and also be notified of the audit requirement."[73]

Lest anyone might consider that it is overstating the case to headline this as "Belittling the other" the following may be noted. The Ombudsman's investigation as outlined in the special report, *Local Authority Housing Loans,* revealed 6,411 accounts, involving refunds of approximately IR£547,000 (€694,547), ranging from IR£1 to approximately IR£3,500 (€4,444) in individual cases. One local authority made refunds totalling IR£122,823 (€155,953); one local authority had a credit balance remaining on an account for almost 19 years and one borrower made 46 consecutive monthly instalments on a fully paid up loan. Seven local authorities reported no overpayments.[74]

Legal excuses to justify refusal to release of records

Refusal to waive discovery undertaking

A freedom of information request for records held by the Eastern Health

---

[73] *Local Authority Housing Loans* p.13
[74] *Ibid.,* p.2.

Board was partially refused on the basis that the records had been furnished to the requester on foot of the discovery process in the course of High Court proceedings between the requester and the Board.

> "While I affirmed the decision of the Board in this case, a question arises, in my view, as to the reasonableness of a public body's refusal to waive an undertaking in these circumstances. A public body, in making a decision under the FOI Act, must give the reasons for its decision including, in particular 'the findings on any material issues relevant to the decision'.[75] While it is not for me as Information Commissioner to decide on the reasonableness of the Board's decision in this matter, I pointed out in my decision that there may be other avenues open to the requester in this case including, for example, a complaint to the Ombudsman. I would also add that I would generally expect a public body which refuses to waive an undertaking in these circumstances to provide reasons for its refusal to do so in its decision."[76]

Individual cases modify institutional actions

Precedent value of decisions

In recognition of the importance of freedom of information decisions to all users of the regime, the Information Commissioner also comments on the value of an individual decision for the benefit of all.

> "Many of the letter decisions have precedent value and some can also be complex in developing positions on issues not previously considered. For this reason, I have continued to add a significant number of letter decisions to my Office's website (www.oic.ie) during 2003 so that, in addition to all of the "long form" decisions, there are now over 100 letter decisions accessible by reference to the relevant section of

---

[75] S.8(2)(d)(ii) of the 1997 Act as amended.
[76] Case 99276; *Annual Report of the Information Commissioner 2003*, p.40.

the Act or otherwise. I would hope that public bodies and FOI users find this resource useful."[77]

INSTITUTIONAL MECHANISMS FOR POSITIVE CONTROL OF INFORMATION

Releasing records outside the FOI regime

If it were possible to compare public body websites from a few years ago with today's websites the sheer volume of information, previously restricted, that is now freely available to the public would become evident. Some health providers release medical records outside the Act.[78] It is probable, however, that many organisations still have a long way to go to satisfy the Ombudsman based on her comments in the 2003 Annual Report:

> "...I believe it is of paramount importance that public bodies should deal openly with people by disclosing information available to them to the public with the minimum of restrictions and in a prompt manner, unless there are valid statutory or other grounds for restricting or refusing the information. I would be very concerned if a pattern emerges of public bodies becoming less open by insisting that members of the public use FOI requests to obtain information which should be made available without recourse to the FOI Act. This is of even more importance since the Freedom of Information (Amendment) Act 2003 enabled the introduction of fees for non-personal information requested under the Act."[79]

These comments of the Ombudsman were made in relation to the policy of the Department of Justice, Equality and Law Reform of not disclosing reasons for refusing an individual a certificate of naturalisation. Failed applicants were advised to apply for access to their records by means of

---

[77] *Annual Report of the Information Commissioner 2003*, p.16.
[78] But see above at n.70.
[79] *Annual Report of the Ombudsman 2003*, p.34.

a FOI request. The Ombudsman noted that it appears that the policy had ceased and that reasons are now normally given for refusals.[80]

Another investigation to which these comments of the Ombudsman applied was the examination of a planning enforcement case against Louth County Council. When the complainant sought a copy of the Council's report on its investigations into allegations of environmental pollution and illegal waste disposal, the Council wrote to her and informed her that she would have to submit an FOI request.

> "I could see no valid reason why the document could not have been given to the complainant outside of the Freedom of Information Act 1997 and there was no evidence to suggest that the Council had considered this option. When my staff conveyed my concern to the Council the document was released, free of charge, to the complainant."[81]

Failure to create records

Since the introduction of FOI public bodies and those dealing with them have legitimate concerns that all their dealings will be made public. This has resulted in a disinclination to prepare written notes of meetings be they mere conversations or more formal gatherings. In relation to central government, the Information Commissioner has commented on the great loss to the National Archive and future historians that would result should this continue. For those involved at any level in committees this loss is already apparent. For example, where it is still acknowledged that there is a requirement to maintain minutes of meetings, these have become so truncated as to render meaningless their value as a true and accurate record of proceedings. It needs to be stressed that behaving in this manner is a failure to understand the protections contained within the Act.

Scrutiny of the Information Commissioner

Even a cursory analysis of decisions of the Information Commissioner demonstrates the diligence in protecting public bodies, requesters and

---

[80] *Ibid.*, pp.34-35.
[81] *Ibid.*, p.33.

third parties. The decisions, which are easily accessible on the Information Commissioner's website are comprehensive and cover a wide range of issues that might be of general interest such as release of evaluation and marking systems or of job interview records;[82] statement of reasons for unsuccessful candidate;[83] unsuccessful candidates' places in order of merit;[84] amendment to marks awarded and opinions expressed by an interview board;[85] shortlisting of candidates;[86] protection for third parties when records are released;[87] confidential enquiries on foot of complaints.[88]

SELECTION OF INFORMATION COMMISSIONER'S DECISIONS

A sample of Information Commissioner's decisions is presented below. The examples are mainly derived from requests following interview boards; nevertheless, they illustrate how general principles of importance may be drawn that apply in multiple situations. It is clear that the constant required from the public body is a fair and reasonable process which is applied in a consistent manner to all concerned. There is also every reason to anticipate that the Information Commissioner will not second-guess the judgement of a properly constituted and balanced interview or

---

[82] For example Case 98187 – *Ms. ABH and the Office of the Local Appointments Commissioners*, March 30, 1999; Case 98082 – *Mr. ABD and the Office of the Local Appointments Commissioners*, February 11, 1999. See also Case 98020 - *Mr. AAF and the Office of the Civil Service and Local Appointments Commissioners*, October 12, 1998.

[83] Case 98095 – *Mr. AAV and the Department of Social, Community and Family Affairs,* January 15, 1999; Case 98187 - *Ms. ABH and the Office of the Local Appointments Commissioners,* March 30, 1999.

[84] Case 98187 – *Ms. ABH and the Office of the Local Appointments Commissioners,* March 30, 1999.

[85] Case 020362 – *Ms X and the Central Statistics Office (CSO),* October 9, 2002.

[86] Case 98082 – *Mr. ABD and the Office of the Local Appointments Commissioners,* February 11, 1999. See also Case 98020 - *Mr. AAF and the Office of the Civil Service and Local Appointments Commissioners,* October 12, 1998.

[87] Case 000365 – *Ms ACH and Others and the Department of Education and Science,* October 16, 2001.

[88] Case 98169 – *Ms ABY and the Department of Education and Science,* July 6, 2000.

examinations board. It should be remembered that each case does vary and, during review, it is clear that the Information Commissioner is at pains to allow for these variations.

Interview procedures and evaluation systems

As any skilled manager knows who has experience of staff evaluations and interview panels, be they internal for promotional or disciplinary purposes or external for staff appointments, decisions are often intuitive and not readily amenable to in-depth analysis. Similarly, academics may have concerns about being required to specify precisely how students are evaluated and marks are allocated. There is a fine borderline between the different grades of honours and pass, and a decision to give a high 2.1 or a 1 class honours grade is not always readily open to quantifiable scrutiny. There is always, nonetheless, some rationale that is capable of explanation.

Criteria and benchmarks for awarding marks

An unsuccessful candidate for promotion sought a statement of reasons for the decisions to award him the scores noted in a superior's assessment form. The form was intended to assess the applicant under the eight headings of knowledge, judgement, creativity, analysis of issues, initiative, reliability and output, assertiveness and planning. There were five possible ratings in respect of each heading ranging from "poor" to "exceptional". The assessor indicated choice of rating by ticking the appropriate box on the form. During the course of this section 18[89] review, the Commissioner commented on the public body's concerns about the difficulty of giving a written explanation of what are subjective ratings:

> "I accept that there are practical limits to the degree of explanation which can be given as to why a particular subjective judgement was made. However, in this instance the task does not appear to be an impossible one. For example, it is reasonable to expect that in making the kind of assessment

---

[89] Under s.18(1), FOI Act a person affected by the act(s) of a public body has a right to be given reasons for the act and any findings on any material issues of fact made for the purposes of the Act.

which has given rise to the present review, an assessor will have regard to certain criteria or benchmarks which will enable him/her to judge the most appropriate rating for each party being assessed. In deciding how a particular candidate measures up to those criteria and benchmarks, s/he will presumably have regard to certain facts about the individual or his/her work performance. I would suggest that a public body should be in a position to explain to such an individual what the criteria and benchmarks are and what facts were taken into account. In my view this is what section 18 requires."[90]

Unsuccessful candidate seeks another candidate's marks

An unsuccessful candidate in a competition run by the Local Appointments Commissioners (LAC) sought access to the notes of the interview board regarding her interview. She also sought reasons for the decision to award another candidate a higher place on the order of merit and asked for details of the marks of the other candidate.

"I have decided that there is a significant risk in this case that releasing the order of merit, even with the deletion of the names, will reveal the marks of some candidates. In any event Ms ABH has made it clear that her primary interest is in discovering the marks of a particular candidate. It is true that the information sought in this case might not be considered particularly sensitive by some. On the other hand, many candidates may feel that how they fared in a competition of the kind in question is a private matter between themselves and the LAC. Revealing their marks could expose them to comments, judgements and inferences of all kinds from work colleagues, acquaintances or unsuccessful candidates. Successful candidates may feel that, having satisfied the LAC about their suitability for a post, they should not have to run

---

[90] Case 98095 - *Mr. AAV and the Department of Social, Community and Family Affairs*, January 15, 1999.

the risk of being called upon to justify their performance again to other parties who might take a different view of the matter."[91]

Inconsistent marking scheme

In the same case the Commissioner noted that the marking scheme devised by the interview board could be criticised as not being totally consistent with the requirements it had indicated.

> "One might expect that the marking scheme would allocate 50 marks in respect of the basic entry qualification as set out at (A) above (as opposed to 50 marks for a primary degree) and additional marks for other qualifications. However, any such perceived deficiency in the marking scheme is not a matter for me as Information Commissioner. My sole concern is whether the marking scheme set out above, which the LAC disclosed to Ms ABH, was adhered to by the board.[92]

Degree of judgement and subjectivity in any interview board

The requester was interviewed for a position with the Central Statistics Office. She subsequently applied under section 17 to have an amendment made to the marks awarded to her at the interview and the comments made by the interview board on her performance. The Commissioner commented that generally speaking, he would be slow to disturb the marks awarded and comments made by an interview board in the absence of strong evidence that such decisions or comments are somehow flawed. The Commissioner was satisfied that an explanation given by the CSO to Ms X addressed an apparent contradiction between some of the marks awarded and comments made. He also accepted that there is a degree of judgement and subjectivity in the decisions of any interview board.[93]

---

[91] Case 98187 - *Ms. ABH and the Office of the Local Appointments Commissioners,* March 30, 1999.

[92] *Ibid.*

[93] Case 020362 - *Ms X and the Central Statistics Office (CSO),* October 9, 2002.

Release of interview boards' deliberations

The requester wrote to the Office of the Local Appointments Commissioners (LAC) asking why he had not been shortlisted for the post of Senior Engineer and sought "all the reasons for the decision that denied me the right of an interview". The Commissioner varied the decision of the LAC and directed that the requester be given access to that part of the shortlisting board's report which contained his name and associated hand-written comments. He noted that during the course of attempts on the part of his staff to arrive at a settlement in this case, the LAC argued strongly that members of shortlisting and interview boards had, prior to the commencement of the FOI Act in 1998, a reasonable expectation that their deliberations would be maintained in confidence. The LAC argued further that interviewers for professional positions such as the one in question are drawn from a relatively small pool. It argued that prospective interviewers would be unwilling to serve on interview boards if they felt that comments recorded in the course of selection processes could be revealed to candidates at a later date. It argued that the willingness of such interviewers to act again would be affected either out of a general sense of grievance that comments which they believed were confidential had now been released or because in specific cases they would be unwilling to interview candidates again about whom they have made unfavourable comments.

The Commissioner did not find it reasonable to expect that the likelihood of and scale of any challenges which might emerge as a result of release in this and similar cases would be such as to have a significant adverse effect on the ability of the LAC to recruit suitable interviewers in future competitions.[94]

Implicit confidentiality

All communications with a public body may come under scrutiny for the purposes of the Act. This includes notes taken of telephone conversations. In the course of dealing with a request regarding a complaint against a

---

[94] Case 98082 - *Mr. ABD and the Office of the Local Appointments Commissioners* February 11, 1999. See also Case 98020 - *Mr. AAF and the Office of the Civil Service and Local Appointments Commissioners* October 12, 1998.

teacher, the Department of Education and Science agreed to release a hand-written note of a telephone conversation between an official of the Department and the Chairman of the Board of Management concerning, *inter alia*, a meeting of the Board. The last three lines were withheld as it was claimed these contained information which did not relate to the requester. The Information Commissioner upheld the decision of the Department making the following comments, *inter alia*:

> "Where, as in this case, there is no express understanding of confidentiality between the parties but it is alleged that confidentiality is implicit, then it is legitimate to look at the nature of the relationship between the parties, the content of the information and the practice of the public body in relation to such communications."[95]

Section 18 request for reasons

Limited to public body, not applicable to every individual involved in decision-making

The requester applied to University College Dublin (UCD) for a statement of reasons for the decisions of each member of UCD's Examination Appeals Committee that marks claimed by him were not due.

> "In this case I found that section 18 requires the head of a public body to provide a statement of reasons which adequately explains why <u>the body</u> acted as it did and that it does not require each and every member of staff who might have contributed to or been involved in the decision making process to provide an account of his/her reasons for every action he/she carried out during the course of the body's decision making process. I further found that even if the Committee had taken separate decisions in relation to each of the 19 points raised by the requester in his examination appeal, as suggested by the requester, those "secondary"

---

[95] Case 98169 -*Ms ABY and the Department of Education and Science*, July 6, 2000.

decisions, of themselves, would not have resulted in the withholding or conferring of a benefit. This was notwithstanding the fact that they would have informed the overall decision making process and the ultimate outcome which resulted in the conferring or withholding of a benefit."[96]

Section 21 decisions

Section 21(1)(a) of the Freedom of Information Act provides that access to a record may be refused if, in the opinion of the head of the public body, access could reasonably be expected to "prejudice the effectiveness of tests, examinations, investigations, inquiries or audits conducted by or on behalf of the public body concerned or the procedures or methods employed for the conduct thereof."

Section 21 (2) provides: "Subsection (1) shall not apply in relation to a case in which in the opinion of the head concerned, the public interest would, on balance, be better served by granting than by refusing to grant the request".[97]

Requirement to identify potential harm that might arise

Section 21 exemption was relied on by the Department of Education in refusing a request from the Principal of St. Catherine's College of Education for Home Economics for records relating to a consultant's report and the Ministerial decision to close the College. The Information Commissioner, in finding for the applicant, *inter alia* noted the following:

"In arriving at a decision to claim a section 21 exemption, a decision maker must, firstly, identify the potential harm to the functions covered by the exemption that might arise from disclosure and, having identified that harm, consider the reasonableness of any expectation that the harm will occur.

---

[96] Case 031015. *Annual Report of the Information Commissioner 2003*, pp.37-38. Underlining included.

[97] S.21(1)(b) refers to significant adverse effects on management functions and s.21(1)(c) refers to disclosure of negotiating positions.

The test of whether the expectation is reasonable is not concerned with the question of probabilities or possibilities. It is concerned simply with whether or not the decision maker's expectation is reasonable." [98]

Public interest test ensuring value for money

The Commissioner also considered the public interest test with particular reference to the circumstances of the decision to close the College.

"There is a significant public interest in members of the public knowing how a public body ensures that its decisions are predicated on ensuring value for money; in members of the public knowing how a public body performs its functions particularly in a context where a decision has consequences for existing employees and their families and, in ensuring openness, transparency and accountability in relation to the expenditure of public money. The Commissioner found that the records sought concern a decision to close a third level college and it is a decision which has very significant implications for existing staff and for potential future students; and is a decision, also, which seems likely to have significant financial implications into the future for the Exchequer."[99]

Access refused to internal audits of Government Department

Section 21 exemption was also relied on to refuse Deputy Enda Kenny access to reports of internal audits undertaken by the Department of Education and Science between January 2000 and March 2003. The grounds for the refusal included, *inter alia*, that disclosure could result in harm to the capacity of the Internal Audit Unit to discharge its functions, disclosure could damage the existing expert/client relationship between the Internal Audit Unit and its clients and disclosure could result in

---

[98] Case 031109 - *Ms. Madeleine Mulrennan and the Department of Education & Science,* August 10, 2004.
[99] *Ibid.*

destabilisation and circumvention of existing accountability arrangements."[100]

In overturning the Department's decision the Commissioner commented:

> "Internal audit reports have been released by other Government Departments in the past and I am not aware of any suggestion that their release has resulted in any of the harms envisaged by the Department in this case. Further, it is clear that some other Government Departments did not anticipate that release of audit reports would have the prejudicial effect on the audit process anticipated by the Department in this case.
>
> The fact that accountability arrangements may already exist in respect of audit reports is not grounds for refusing access under the FOI Act. Further, I do not accept that the work of the Office of the Comptroller and Auditor General, and/or others involved in scrutinising audit reports, would be prejudiced or compromised by the release of such reports under the FOI Act. Although the Department has argued that release of the records would prejudice the procedures and methods which it uses in carrying out such audits, it has not detailed specifically which procedures would be prejudiced or how they would be prejudiced. The Department has also argued that release of the records would impair the existing expert/client relation between the Internal Audit Unit and its clients. I do not accept that release of these records would lead to the Department's Internal Audit Unit staff being perceived as anything other than honest, objective and professional. As the Department has pointed out, some audit reports are already made available to the Public Accounts Committee without any apparent prejudice to the relationship between the Internal Audit Unit and its clients. Furthermore, it is reasonable to assume that all staff of public bodies will co-operate with audit inquiries where such inquiries relate

---

[100] Case 030693 - *Deputy Enda Kenny and the Department of Education and Science*, May 24, 2004.

to their work areas or functions. I consider that it is not sustainable that anything other than full co-operation would be given by public employees to the Department's Internal Audit Unit."[101]

SELECTION OF COURT JUDGMENTS[102]

Consideration of Court judgments arising from the Freedom of Information Act equally illustrates how general principles of importance may be drawn from particular situations.

Withholding personnel files

The first freedom of information case considered by the High Court, *Minister for Agriculture and Food v. Information Commissioner,*[103] was about a refusal to grant access to a personnel file.[104] The withholding of personnel files suggests an organisational difficulty with relinquishing control. It is a surviving vestige of the master/servant era of personnel administration in which there is a vested interest in keeping subordinates in their place. It is nurtured by civil service minds developed in an extremely hierarchical tradition and once this mindset is entertained it seems to take on a life of its own without consideration of the cost in human or real terMs Whom does it harm to release personal information to an employee? Either the file contains records that are already known to the individual in question, or it contains records that should not be retained.

---

[101] *Ibid.*

[102] See chap.5 *infra*. All court judgments are accessible on the Information Commissioners website www.oic.gov.ie. For more general legal analysis Feldman, Information Law in *Review 1999* to date *op. cit.*

[103] [2001] 1 I.L.R.M. 40. See *Review 1999*, p.354 *et seq*; *Review 2000* p.274, and *Review 2001* p.396 *et seq.*

[104] S.(6)(5) FOI Act excludes right of access to personnel records of public bodies which were created more than three years before commencement of the Act (i.e. pre-1995) if that record "is not being used or proposed to be used in a manner or for a purpose that affects, or will or may affect, adversely the interests of the person." (S.(6)(5)(c). See *supra* n.56.

The first matter to consider is the restrictive clause that denies pre-April 1995 files to staff of public bodies. Why is this enshrined in law? During the Seanad debates on the Freedom of Information Act the sponsoring Minister, Ms Eithne Fitzgerald, provided the answer:

> "A civil servant may look for his or her personnel file and if there is anything on the file which has obstructed his or her promotion, he or she can see the full file, otherwise the files go back three years. This was included at the request of Government Departments for the purpose of managing personnel files created before thought was given to freedom of information. If there was anything on the file which might be inappropriately used, the whole file becomes available."[105]

This explanation raises the question: why would anything on a personnel file be refused to the person whose file it is unless it was intended to be used to that person's detriment? That implied motivation was denied by the Department when required to explain its refusal. Nevertheless, the behaviour of officials in the Department of Agriculture as described by the Information Commissioner in his deliberation, and quoted by Mr Justice O'Donovan in his judgment, is somewhat astonishing. Bear in mind when considering the following that this all took place post-Freedom of Information Act:

> "[O]n the 27th of October 1998, which was well after Mr G's request for a 'sight of my entire personnel file' a total of 16 of the 41 records, which the respondent [Information Commissioner] noted on Mr G's personnel file, were placed by the Department of Agriculture and Food in a sealed envelope to which was attached a notice signed by the personnel officer in the said Department in the following terms, namely;
>
> *Please note that the records contained in the sealed envelope attached are to be regarded as closed records and, to ensure that they are not used in any manner or*

*form which might adversely effect Mr G's interests, are
not to be consulted in the future.*"[106]

In Mr Justice O'Donovan's view:

"[G]iven that the personnel file relating to Mr G which was
submitted to the respondent by the department does not appear
to have been complete, given that only some of the records
on Mr G's personnel file had been placed in a sealed envelope
and not only had that sealing taken place after Mr G had
requested access to them, but it took place after the respondent
had commenced his review, and, *given that the sealed
envelope was permitted to remain in Mr G's personnel file
so that its mere presence, with a note attached to it that it
was not to be consulted in the future, is more likely than not
to excite the curiosity of anyone who consulted the file; so
much so, that such a person would be tempted to open the
sealed envelope, in which event, its contents might well be
used to Mr G's detriment* and I think that those are reasonable
grounds for doubting the stated intention that it was not
proposed that the records would be used in a manner which
might adversely affect Mr G's interests. This is all the more
so when regard is had to the fact that the note attached to the
sealed envelope is only signed by the personnel officer and,
therefore, is unlikely to be perceived as having binding effect
on a superior officer or even an officer of equal rank and, in
any event, the respondent was entitled to ask himself *why
was the file being maintained at all, if it was not proposed to
use it? Is not its continued maintenance a statement of intent
to use?*"[107] (emphasis added)

When an employee requests his personnel file, how can whatever potential
hassle that might ensue at an industrial relations level by granting the
request in any way match the time and energy required to challenge the

---

[106] [2001] 1 I.L.R.M. 40 at 46.
[107] *Ibid.*, p.48 *et seq.*

Information Commissioner in the High Court? Did anybody in the Department of Agriculture consider the impact in cost/benefit terms of denying the requested files?

School league tables or the clash of the Acts

Minister for Education and Science v. the Information Commissioner,[108] was a High Court appeal against the Information Commissioner's decision directing the Minister to give *The Sunday Times*, *The Sunday Tribune* and *The Kerryman*, access to certain records held by the Minister concerning the results of the Leaving Certificate Examinations held in 1998. The substantive matter was already moot by the time of the High Court hearing in July 2000. In other words, whatever way the High Court decided, the timeliness for the media of publication of the Leaving Certificate results was long past its sell-by date. Known popularly as the *School League Tables* case, the circumstances of the Information Commissioner's review and the High Court action caused public furore.

Denying parents information

The Minister and his advisers could have chosen one of two approaches to the requests by the media: be secretive or be open. Sadly, they took the first route apparently deciding that parents, although products of our educational system, are unable to handle critically the implications of school league tables published in the media that are of a uni-dimensional character, *i.e.* based solely on Leaving Certificate results. The Department and Teachers' Unions could have taken a more generous approach whereby a comprehensive body of information could be released regularly indicating factors such as class sizes, remedial classes, sports curricula, involvement in debating societies, theatrical productions, chess clubs, social and charitable activities, etc. The reasons for a choice of school encompass a variety of factors, not least location and family connections, and if there are parents who select a school solely based on the criterion

---

[108] [2001] I.E.H.C. 116. See *Review 1999* p. 354 *et seq*; *Review 2000* p. 274, and *Review 2001* p.396 *et seq*.; for broader analysis see Feldman "Balancing Education and Secrecy" in D. Glendenning and W. Binchy eds., *Litigation Against Schools* (Firstlaw, Dublin, 2006).

of academic results in the Leaving Certificate surely that is their right so to do.

The decision of the Minister to appeal the Commissioner's determination was deplored in an editorial of *The Irish Times* in the following terms: "There is a sense in which the Minister, with the support of the educational establishment, is turning his face against the principles of openness, transparency and accountability which are now a routine part of some other aspects of public administration."[109] Bearing in mind that this decision was, indeed, taken by the then Minister for Education and Science in the supposed new era of freedom of information, it is instructive to note that the Department took even more draconian action in favour of secrecy.

Legislative opportunism[110]

Section 53 of the Education Act 1998 confers discretion on the Minister in relation to examinations, to refuse access to any information which would enable the compilation of information (that is not otherwise available to the general public) in relation to the comparative performance of schools in respect of the academic achievement of students, notwithstanding any other enactment. Section 53 is in direct contradiction to section 8(4)(b) of the Freedom of Information Act that requires that any belief or opinion of the head of the public body as to what are the reasons of the requester for the request shall be disregarded. The timing of the amendment introducing section 53 coincided with the process of the requesters' appeal against the refusal by the Department of Education and Science to provide information relating to examination results. The consequence was that when the Information Commissioner's decision to release the records was appealed by the Minister, the High Court decided that section 53 overrode the FOI Act.

Primary school league tables

The case of *Sheedy v Information Commissioner*[111] is also about the

---

[109] *The Irish Times,* November 3, 1999.

[110] See also at n.137 below.

[111] [2004] I.E.H.C. 192, [2004] 2 I.R. 533, [2005] I.E.S.C. 35, [2005] 2 I.R. 272.

clash between Section 53 of the Education Act 1998 and the terms of the Freedom of Information Act, this time in respect of the possibility of primary school league tables. The High Court affirmed the Information Commissioner's decision to release a primary school inspection report but this judgment has been reversed on appeal to the Supreme Court. This was the first opportunity since the Freedom of Information Act was passed for the Supreme Court to adjudicate the Act's terms; the appeal judgment centred on whether or not section 53 of the Education Act trumped the Freedom of Information Act. A majority of the court, Mr Justice Kearns, Ms Justice Denham assenting, held that it did.

Presumption of secrecy displaced by openness

Mr Justice Fennelly dissented. He considered that the Freedom of Information Act holds special significance.

> "The passing of the Freedom of Information Act constituted a legislative development of major importance. By it, the Oireachtas took a considered and deliberate step which dramatically alters the administrative assumptions and culture of centuries. It replaces the presumption of secrecy with one of openness. It is designed to open up the workings of government and administration to scrutiny. It is not designed simply to satisfy the appetite of the media for stories. It is for the benefit of every citizen. It lets light in to the offices and filing cabinets of our rulers."

Consequently, he did not agree that section 53 ought to be applied in order to deny disclosure of the information requested.

Separated parents' rights of access to records

NMcK v Information Commissioner[112] allowed an appeal of a separated parent against a decision of the Information Commissioner that affirmed the refusal of a hospital to grant access to medical records relating to his

---

[112] [2004] 1 I.R. 12; [2006] I.E.S.C. 2. See *Review 2004* p.321 *et seq.* for High Court judgment.

daughter. This judgment, both in the High and Supreme Courts, has significance for any body holding children's records. This case involved consideration of the Freedom of Information Act 1997 (section 28 (6)) Regulations 1999.[113]

Strained family relationship irrelevant

The background to the case is that during separation proceedings between the applicant and his wife, an allegation was made that the applicant had sexually abused his daughter. He vigorously denied and still denies this allegation and the Gardaí, having investigated the allegations concluded that there was "no evidence to warrant a prosecution". The applicant was granted supervised access to his children. Subsequently, the wife died and by agreement the two children of the marriage went to live with the late Mrs McK's brother and his wife, with whom Mr McK had a strained relationship. It was agreed, *inter alia* that they and the applicant would be appointed as joint guardian of the two children. In January 2000, the daughter, then aged 12, was admitted to hospital. The applicant had failed in his appeal to the Information Commissioner following the hospital's refusal to grant him access to his daughter's records and he had then appealed on a point of law to the High Court.

With regard to the applicant's history, Mr Justice Quirke stated:

> "Although a complaint has in the past been made about the appellant, it remains unsubstantiated and the appellant comes before this Court enjoying the presumption of innocence which is enjoyed by every citizen of the State. The evidence indicates that he is concerned with the welfare of both of his children and avails of his rights of access to them in a conscientious fashion."

Mr Justice Quirke rooted his judgment in the Supreme Court judgment of Mr Justice Hardiman in *North Western Health Board v. H.W.*[114] which

---

[113] S.I. No.47 of 1999. These Regulations are considered in Chapter 1 *infra* and in *Annual Review of Irish Law 2005* (forthcoming).

[114] [2001] 3 I.R 622.

declared that any legislation vindicating and defending the rights of children must be interpreted in the light of the Constitution particularly Article 41 (The Family) and Article 42 (Education). He found that there is a presumption of parental entitlement to a minor child's medical information.

Supreme Court Appeal

The Supreme Court judgment,[115] which both affirmed and varied the High Court decision, was delivered by the presiding judge, Ms Justice Denham, Justices McGuinness, Hardiman, Geoghegan, and Fennelly assenting. The Supreme Court held that the error of the Commissioner was in not presuming that the parent was entitled to the child's medical records. Based on that presumption the Commissioner should then proceed to consider "any evidence which exists addressing the issue that it would not be in the minor's best interests that the parent should be furnished with such information." However, the Supreme Court remitted the matter to the Information Commissioner for review in accordance with the correct test and in light of all of the circumstances.

Request remitted to Information Commissioner

Having specified the correct test that the Commissioner must use in deciding whether or not a minor child's medical records should be released to a parent, Ms Justice Denham remitted the matter for decision to the Commissioner. This remittal was consequent on three factors: the delay, the circumstances of the case, and "especially the age of the minor [nearly 18 years of age], whose views now are very relevant".

Missed opportunity

The importance of the *NMcK* case was signified by the number of judges sitting in judgment, a bench of five rather than three. It was not unreasonable, therefore, to anticipate some significant judicial comments on Articles 41 and 42 of the Constitution, which deal with the rights of

---

[115] [2006] I.E.S.C. 2, [2006] 1 I.L.R.M. 504.

the family and the right to education. In particular it was hoped that the court would comment on the rights of children to preserve confidentiality of information as against the rights of parents as enshrined and inferred in the Constitution and from earlier court judgments. It is to be regretted that there was no expansion on the clear declaration that a child has rights within the family unit.

The judgment is a disappointment in these respects; moreover, nothing of great import was said about the Freedom of Information Act itself. Thus, despite the welcome amendment, which opened the way for appeal to the Supreme Court,[116] in the two judgments to date whereby eight opportunities were afforded to members of that court to comment on the Act, on only one occasion, the dissent in *Sheedy*, was that opportunity seized.

UNDERSTANDING REALITIES

Corporate image and the citizen

As noted, in the *Evaluation of the Progress of the Strategic Management Initiative/Delivering Better Government Modernisation Programme*[117] concern was expressed that the desire for modernisation has the danger of imposing uniformity, a one-size-fits-all approach, which would be inappropriate. Nevertheless, to the consumer, to the member of the public who has to deal with government bodies, it is all one, a monolith.

Some years ago, it used to be that every letter began "A chara" and ended "Mise le meas" with an indecipherable mark masquerading as a signature. You knew where you were: a supplicant who had been honoured with a letterhead that you carried around in your pocket to show your friends. Now, with all the advances in technology, if you want to know something you are supposed to link into a website: no two departmental web sites appear to be the same; no two links to freedom of information pages appear to be the same. In hard copy the story is no different: no two section 15 publications[118] appear the same.

---

[116] S.42, FOI Act as amended by s.27 FOI (Amendment) Act 2003. See at n.40.

[117] PA Consulting Group 2002, *op. cit.* at n.27, *supra.*

[118] S. 15, FOI Act requires publication by a public body of a wide range of information

For the member of the public that means that every time a website or publication is approached it is a new learning experience. To say that this is frustrating is an understatement. There is no corporate image to provide a backdrop against which to develop individual departmental images. Is this view prescriptive, yes? Is it one-size-fits all, no? It is a plea to get some order into a mass of organisational detail that is supposed to be informative. Further, use of jargon and code is a barrier to genuinely free exchange of information.

Data v information

The speed with which technology is impacting on communication is, in effect, a two-edged sword. There is an increasing amount of data being conveyed on the information highway but the extent to which this amounts to "information" is questionable. Public bodies need to be conscious that a real problem confronting most members of the public is that they may not be able to formulate their requests so as to elicit the information they seek. This is the case whether or not the Freedom of Information Act is brought into play.

Consider for example:

- When a student queries her marks in an exam, perhaps what she wants is not to query her mark but to have someone she trusts go over her paper and point out where she went right and wrong;

- when a hospital patient requests his medical records perhaps what he wants is not to query the medical competence of his doctor but to have someone explain in simple terms and away from the stress of illness, what exactly was the nature of the ailment;

- when a member of staff queries why they were not promoted, perhaps what they actually want is not to question the dubious antecedents of the interview board and the general incompetence of the Secretary General/ Chief Executive/School Principal and every member of senior management in sight. It is possible that what is wanted is an intelligent conversation with somebody trustworthy and a genuine appraisal of

including description of its structure and organisation, functions, powers and duties, any services provided for the public and the procedures by which services may be availed of by the public.

her career prospects and whether or not she should continue in current employment or look for transfer or exit.

In such scenarios the requester of information does not set out to be a troublemaker. Unfortunately, all too often that is how they are treated and with certain predictability that is what they become.

Secret v confidential

One of the great fallacies permeating both the public and private sector is that there are "secrets". This false presumption leads to the situation where information is withheld on a blanket basis. There is a necessity in all walks of life to maintain confidentiality but that is quite different from the presumption of secrecy. The terms of the Amendment Act appear to take little account of this. On the other hand, a serious flaw in the Freedom of Information Act is that it gives little discretion for public bodies to retain the confidentiality of the early stages of policy innovation or other pre-decision deliberations. There is no denying the chilling effect in a situation where anything that is said or done may find its way into a newspaper headline. There are very real negative effects to openness if every one on a committee feels constrained to talk in code and minutes are truncated so much that they are no longer a true and accurate record of proceedings.

Some further thought to these issues, coupled with in-depth training, is required. In these respects, following the law rigidly and in an extremely formalistic manner only serves to increase a secrecy culture.

RENEWING AND REVIVING THE OFFICIAL SECRETS ACT 1963

Culture of secrecy

The culture of secrecy in the civil service is attributable to the Official Secrets Act 1963, which was reviewed in January 1997 by the Oireachtas Select Committee on Legislation and Security. The Select Committee recommended repeal at the earliest possible date. During the legislative debate on the Freedom of Information Act the sponsoring Minister, Eithne Fitzgerald, noted that:

"section 4 of the Official Secrets Act, which causes most grief and sets out the presumption that all information is secret — when I joined the Civil Service 27 years ago I was obliged to sign the Official Secrets Act and give an undertaking not to park my bicycle at Government Buildings[119] — will be made redundant by section 48 of the Freedom of Information Bill in respect of information made available under the terms of the new legislation....

[If the Official Secrets Act were repealed] a vacuum would remain with regard to unauthorised disclosures which could put the security of the State at risk at a time when there is armed conflict on one part of the island. It would be prudent to wait until the legislative framework, the preparation work for which I have asked the Minister for Justice to expedite as quickly as possible within her Department, is in place."[120]

Recent prosecutions under Official Secrets Act

The most recent known prosecution under the Act was that of Liz Allen, the journalist, and Independent Newspapers, in 1995 for disclosing an internal Garda memo alerting the force to a major robbery prior to the Brink's-Allied robbery. Prior to that, the Official Secrets Act had been invoked against Susan O'Keefe, the journalist instrumental in disclosing irregularities that led to the Beef Tribunal. In the latter case the prosecution failed on a technicality.

Reviving the Official Secrets Act in 2004

In 2004 it was reported that prison doctors were being required to sign up to the Act for the first time as part of a newly negotiated contract following a prolonged dispute. Concern has been expressed that the purpose of this provision is to prevent the doctors from talking freely and openly about prison conditions.[121] According to the Irish Prison Service, the Official

---

[119] Included as it would be a shame to leave this gem mouldering undiscovered in libraries or electronic files. It also indicates the relative importance of the Official Secrets Act.

[120] 476 Dáil Reports col.755.

[121] *Irish Medical News,* September 13, 2004.

Secrets Act will not be used to "gag" prison doctors: rather it is a condition of employment for all civil servants; this contractual provision will allow the doctors the benefit of the non-contributory pension and other benefits agreed with the Irish Medical Organisation and the doctors cannot stand for election while working for the service.

Since doctors are already subject to a very strict code of medical ethics and confidentiality, one can only wonder why, seven years after the Oireachtas not only recommended repeal of the Official Secrets Act, but also passed freedom of information legislation, prison doctors come within its ambit. Surely there were other ways to provide pension and other benefits for the doctors? Moreover, notwithstanding the fundamental importance of an independent, objective and non-politicised civil service, why should a prison doctor be precluded from standing for election? Finally, what has any of this to do with the Official Secrets Act?

Reviving the Official Secrets Act in 2005

Most recently, the Minister for Justice and Law Reform invoked the Official Secrets Act during the debate on his revelations under parliamentary privilege about Mr Frank Connolly, Chief Executive, and the Centre for Public Inquiry.

> "I have been advised that it is my legal right and my constitutional duty to make public information which is given to me in my role as Minister for Justice by An Garda Síochána acting as one of the intelligence services of the State when, in my judgement, the public interest so requires.
>
> My legal authority for disclosing information in such circumstances is clearly set out in section 4 of the Official Secrets Act 1963.[122] It is not qualified or abridged in any

---

[122] S.4 Official Secrets Act. Disclosure of official information: "(1) A person shall not communicate any official information to any other person unless he is duly authorised to do so or does so in the course of and in accordance with his duties as the holder of a public office or when it is his duty in the interest of the State to communicate it.(2) A person to whom subsection (1) applies shall take reasonable care to avoid any unlawful communication of such information. (3) A person shall not obtain official information where he is aware or has reasonable grounds

way by the terms of the Garda Síochána Act recently enacted by the Oireachtas. Nor do the provisions of the Data Protection Act in any way effect data kept for the purpose of safeguarding the security of the State."[123]

Leaks: deliberate or inadvertent?

Experience shows that even where there is rigid application of secrecy provisions leaks either deliberate or inadvertent cannot be ruled out. The first knowledge the public had of the impending amendments to the Freedom of Information Act in early 2003 was through a series of deliberate leaks from senior levels of central government. The Flood, now Mahon, and Moriarty Tribunals of Inquiry have been plagued by constant leaking of confidential information.[124]

Sir Humphrey reigns

At the same time the Freedom of Information (Amendment) Act 2003 was killing access to central government information, the Department of Health and Children, presumably with Cabinet acquiescence, judiciously leaked elements of the Health Reform Policy to journalists. The *Prospectus*[125] and *Brennan*[126] reports, supposedly about re-organisation and value for money respectively, filled pages and airwaves in the media long before they were ever properly published let alone made available

---

for believing that the communication of such information to him would be a contravention of subsection (1). (4) In this section 'duly authorised' means authorised by a Minister or State authority or by some person authorized."

[123] *Statement [to the Dáil] by Minister in regard to information now in the public domain reflecting on the probity, past conduct and fitness to hold office of the Chief Executive of the Centre for Public Inquiry* December 13, 2005.

[124] See McGonagle, *Media Law*, 2nd ed. (Thompson Roundhall, Dublin, 2003), p.196.

[125] *Audit of Structures and Functions in the Health System*, Prn 170, 2003. Commissioned consultants, Prospectus.

[126] *Commission on Financial Management and Control Systems in the Health Service*, Pn 12935, Jan 2003. Chairman, Prof. Niamh Brennan.

[127] "This Chapter should be read in conjunction with the detailed analysis in Appendix 7". *Prospectus,* Chapter 4: *Audit of Governance and Accountability Arrangements*, p. 59.

to the public, never mind to the health professionals most directly affected. Moreover, *Prospectus* is a report in two hefty volumes, the primary content in one and the appendices in the second; readers are specifically advised to read the two in conjunction with each other[127] yet the appendices volume was not published on the internet nor available in hard copy until many weeks after the first volume. So much for encouraging informed debate!

Not so secret secrets Irish-style

With regard to freedom of information requests, a classic example of the inability to prevent certain specified information being made available to the public are the circumstances around school league tables.[128] The fact that the Department of Education and Science won its first case against publication of information that might be used to present league tables became irrelevant in September 2002 with the publication of details of numbers of university entrants from specified schools. These were first published in *The Irish Times*[129] and, subsequently, the *Farmers Journal*[130] and in other newspapers. Ironically, the information had been obtained through the exercise of the Freedom of Information Act.

Such was the interest in this latter publication that some Dublin city centre newsagents were sold out of copies by lunchtime on the first day of sales, and this stock-out resulted in some newsagents in the outlying urban areas failing to receive any copies.[131] The very situation that the Department of Education sought to avoid, namely uni-dimensional school league tables, is now a matter of media record and, since the request for information went directly to the Universities, which in the intervening time[132] became subject to the Act, the Department was and is powerless to prevent its release. This particular debate is now over since the Minister

---

[128] See *School League Tables* case at n.108.
[129] September 17, 2002.
[130] *Farmers Journal*, January 25, 2003.
[131] The author had to go directly to the publisher to obtain a copy following a fruitless search within the dense farmlands of Dublin 2 and 24.
[132] The FOI Act allowed for staged inclusion of public bodies of which approx. 500 are now subject to Act.

exercised her discretion under section 53 of the Education Act 1998 and is publishing school inspection reports on the Internet.[133]

Not so secret secrets UK-style

A parallel exercise in the futility of trying to keep public information secret is highlighted by the two-year correspondence of the UK Campaign for Freedom of Information with UK government departments requesting information about the identity of individuals seconded from the private sector. Eventually this information was released subject to the consent of the secondees whose wishes are respected "regardless of any public interest in openness and regardless of whether there is any affect on their privacy." The Campaign highlights that the shortcomings of the approach are revealed by the fact that some of the staff who have refused to be named are already publicly identified on related web sites.[134]

UNFINISHED BUSINESS

Repealing the Official Secrets Act

As noted,[135] the Oireachtas Select Committee on Legislation and Security, meeting in 1997, recommended repeal of the Official Secrets Act at the earliest possible date.

Access to past records

Again, as has been noted, as a general rule access to personal files pre-April 1995 is denied under the Freedom of Information Act. It was intended that access to past records should be provided on a rolling basis. The Minister stated:

> "Access would apply initially to all personal information of
> the requester, all current files subject to security, etc.

---

[133] Discussed in "Balancing Education and Secrecy" *op. cit.,* n.108.
[134] See www.cfoi.org.uk/secondees.html. Quote from letter of November 11, 2002.
[135] See at n.69.

exemptions and any related historical records needed to understand current files. Access to past records would then be provided on a rolling back basis – first two years, then four years, then six years, etc. ... ...

I hope it will not be too long before this process meets the 30 year rule under the National Archives Act, so that we will have full access."[136]

To date there is no real indication that either of these promises will be met in the foreseeable future.

Call for Non-Disclosure Act

The Information Commissioner advocates the creation of a new Non-Disclosure Act which would accommodate all non-disclosure provisions[137] currently housed in individual enactments. This call arose from the Commissioner's section 32 report[138] to an Oireachtas Committee in which she regrets the growing number of non-disclosure provisions in individual pieces of legislation, the reported number of which is in excess of 150. Of the 78 non-disclosure provisions recommended by government ministers for exclusion from reference in the FOI Act, 29 were enacted since 1997; Ministers recommended 34 provisions for inclusion in the FOI Act of which 23 were enacted since 1997. The Commissioner found that around one third of all existing non-disclosure provisions were introduced in an FOI environment. "This shows that a culture of secrecy continues and there can be no doubt but that it hinders the achievement

---

[136] Eithne Fitzgerald, 150 Seanad Report col. 92.

[137] S.53 of the Education Act 1998 is an example of a legislative non-disclosure provision passed without reference to the Freedom of Information Act. It was found by the courts in the *School League Tables* cases that this provision trumped the provisions of the FOI Act and blocked release of information on schools, see Chap.5 *infra* and at n.108.

[138] S.32 of the FOI Act refers to non-disclosure enactments that are not included under any other section of the Act. Access shall be refused to any record whose disclosure is prohibited, or whose non-disclosure is authorised in certain circumstances, by statute (including statutory instrument). In circumstances where such a statute is listed in the Third Schedule to the Act, the disclosure of records is assessed solely by reference to the other provisions of the FOI Act.

of a simple, transparent and consistent approach to the treatment of information in public bodies".[139]

Trojan Horse effect

Writing about these issues in the *Annual Review of Irish Law 2004* the author commented on the disregard by the Oireachtas of the principles underlying the FOI Act when enacting non-disclosure provisions in legislation. "In the absence of Oireachtas scrutiny of secrecy provisions as required by statute,[140] it remains to be seen what other non-disclosure provisions of legislation [apart from section 53] lie in wait to render the openness of freedom of information of null effect."[141] Regrettably, this was a prophetic comment.

Covert amendments of FOI Act

> "[I]n mid September 2005, my Office became aware that the FOI Act had been amended by the Safety, Health and Welfare at Work Act 2005 which had commenced on 1 September 2005. This information was given to one of my staff by a member of the public while dealing with an enquiry. The effect of the amendment is that, for all practical purposes, the Health and Safety Authority is no longer subject to the FOI Act. While I, as Information Commissioner, have no statutory entitlement to be consulted in relation to amendments to the FOI Act, it would seem sensible (and indeed many would assume this would happen) that some such consultation should take place. I think it is undesirable that the FOI Act should be amended in a piecemeal fashion;

---

[139] *Report to the Joint Oireachtas Committee on Finance and the Public Service for the purpose of Review of Non-Disclosure Provisions in accordance with The Freedom of Information Act 1997 [section 32]*, Office of the Information Commissioner, December 22, 2005. Hereafter *Section 32 Report*.

[140] S.32 obliges Ministers to report to the Commissioner and the Houses of the Oireachtas on all non-disclosure provisions related to that Ministers' functions on a regular basis.

[141] *2004 Review*, p.320.

such an approach tends to favour the sectional interests of particular public bodies over and above the purpose and principles of the FOI Act generally."[142]

Legislation by stealth

As a matter of policy it is disturbing that any Minister can effect legislation which contravenes both the literal intent and the spirit of an earlier statute without reference to that statute. This is particularly so in the case of the FOI Act which is directed at increasing openness and transparency of government.[143]

FREEDOM OF INFORMATION REGIMES COMPARED

Comparing Irish and UK FOI Acts

UK Act omits "access"

Many public bodies subject to the Irish FOI regime have contacts either directly or indirectly with Northern Ireland and the United Kingdom. For this reason, and also on the basis that there is always somebody worse off than you are, it might be some consolation to consider the UK Freedom of Information Act. It is beyond the scope of this chapter to compare the differing Irish and UK freedom of information regimes in any detail: there are significant differences and some similarities. Suffice it to say that the spirit and thrust of the Irish Act, irrespective of recent adverse developments. is to enable members of the public to *access* information. The Scottish Act has a similar thrust thanks, no doubt, to following the advices received from the Irish Office of the Information Commissioner.

In a concentrated effort to try to understand the UK Act[144] and background advices including a great deal of material on the Campaign for Freedom of Information web site,[145] the author had extreme difficulty

---

[142] *Section 32 Report* pdf. version p.10.
[143] For fuller discussion of these issues see *2005 Review* (forthcoming).
[144] The Act that applies in Northern Ireland.
[145] www.cfoi.org.uk

in finding any unqualified aspiration to that effect; it seems to be more concerned with restrictions and refusals and exemptions and charges.

It appears that the primary consideration in setting up administrative procedures to implement the Act are procedures that "include *arrangements for refusal of requests* and consideration of the public interest."[146] Even reading about Publication Schemes it was soon discovered that these are about publishing information about information, not releasing the information itself. Despite being passed in 2000, the Act did not facilitate requests for information from the public until 2005.

Data protection or FOI?

Much of the success in opening up the secret culture of the Irish civil service is attributable to the decision to make the Ombudsman the Information Commissioner. The oversight scheme in the UK made their Data Protection Commissioner the responsible person. It may be remembered that the FOI regime should be about disclosure of information; a data protection regime is about privacy and restricting disclosure. It remains to be seen whether the UK Commissioner, immersed in Data Protection, will be as effective as the Irish counterpart.

Persuasive not coercive oversight

A further contrast with the Irish Commissioner is that the UK Information Commissioner has been given persuasive rather than coercive authority. The Lord Chancellor's office, charged with responsibility for the Act in place of the Home Office, has estimated that there are more than 100,000 public authorities to come within the ambit of the Act. One wonders at how effective enforcement will be with these thousands of public authorities the Commissioner has to regulate.

Obscurity in drafting

The UK Act is so convoluted that by comparison the Irish Act, obtuse as it is, seems to be an exercise in clarity. Criticism of drafting complexities

---

[146] Lord Chancellor's Report, Nov. 2001. Emphasis added. www.dca.gov.uk/foi/imprep/annrep01.pdf

in the legislation features strongly in a comprehensive legal publication about the UK Act. For the authors this difficulty is most pronounced in relation to section 40, legal personal information, which is exempt from access under the 2000 Act. They comment: "Frankly, mud is as a mountain spring compared with these provisions".[147]

UK Official Secrets Act

Overshadowing everything to do with access to information in the UK is the Official Secrets Act (OSA); its malevolent shade permeates all public service activity even to the extent that the power of the OSA has in no way been diminished by the Public Interest Disclosure Act 1998 (PIDA): PIDA purports to give protection to bona fide whistleblowers.[148]

Secrecy and fear of reprisal

Official secrecy permeates the UK scene in a manner unknown in the Irish jurisdiction. The UK Official Secrets Act 1989 is the trump card that defeats any bid for open expression. The culture of secrecy and fear of reprisal that this legislation has engendered is all pervasive. For instance, Lord Justice Phillips, when he opened the BSE (Mad Cow Disease) Inquiry, advised that the Head of the Civil Service had given an assurance that civil servants would not be disciplined for giving evidence or help to the inquiry.[149] Surely one is entitled to expect that, of all people, civil servants would be under a duty to cooperate fully with any judicial inquiry and be subject to disciplinary procedures for failing to do so. Given that the BSE crisis is arguably one of the most damaging events of recent years in respect of public health and of the UK economy, the remarks attributed here appear utterly at odds with the aspirations of the Public Interest Disclosure Act the purpose of which is to protect bona

---

[147] *"The Law of Freedom of Information"* MacDonald and Jones eds. (2003, Oxford University Press) reviewed by Feldman, *Irish Jurist* (n.s.) (2004) Vol.xxxix 371.

[148] For analysis of whistleblower legislation, Feldman, "Whistleblower Protection: Comparative Legal Developments." *Irish Law Times.* Vol.17; No.17; (November 1999); 264 –272.

[149] "Inquiry Opens with Chairman Seeking to Reassure Whistleblowers." *The Financial Times,* January 28, 1998.

fide whistleblowers. It remains the case that no considerations of public interest can be balanced in defence of a breach of the Official Secrets Act which protects information relating to security, international relations, defence and criminal investigations. "[O]nce the necessary degree of harm is proved, no amount of public benefit can be taken into account and weighed against it. For example, if disclosure was likely to jeopardise United Kingdom interests abroad, it could not be argued that it was nevertheless justified because it prevented loss of life at home."[150]

Public right to information

The public's right to information in the UK did not come into effect in January 2005 giving ample time for government departments and public bodies to develop an accessible system for their records or, alternatively, to destroy or secrete away information which they considered inappropriate for public consumption. The big question is whether these organisations, so accustomed to the protection of secrecy, really can and really will embrace a policy of openness. The corollary is to ask whether the British public can appreciate that they have become entitled to access information from great ministries of state, from local government and from hitherto secretive quangos.

Comparing FOI regimes in Australia, Canada and New Zealand

A 1999 publication in Britain, *Open Government, Freedom of Information and Privacy*,[151] reviewed the access to information provisions in a number of other common law countries including Australia, Canada, New Zealand and Ireland.

Right to personal information v right to privacy

A constitutional policy expert highlighted the difficulties lately being experienced at the national or federal level in countries that have had

---

[150] Lewis, *Whistleblowers and Job Security*. (1995) 58 Modern L. Rev. 208 at p.214.
[151] A. McDonald and G. Terrill eds. *Open Government, Freedom of Information and Privacy* (MacMillan Press, London, 1998).

access legislation since the early 80s, particularly at the nexus between the right to personal information and the right to privacy.

> "The main hinge between FOI and privacy lies in the definition of personal information. It is a fundamental definition for privacy legislation which determines its scope. It is a key exemption provision in FOI legislation which may protect from disclosure personal information about third parties. Whether privacy is the dominant value will depend on the breadth of the definition of personal information, whether its release is subject to any public interest test and by whom the definition is interpreted."[152]

Thwarting FOI in Canada

Aspects of the Canadian experience are of particular interest. A number of high profile incidents were recorded which centred on attempts to thwart access to government information through the destruction of or tampering with records. These included altering the records of peacekeeping activities in Somalia by the Department of National Defence in 1995. The following year a senior manager in Transport Canada ordered the destruction of all copies of an audit report to ensure the suppression of criticism of departmental management.[153] Also in 1996 it was discovered that in the 1980s records of the Canadian Blood Committee were destroyed so that the information would not become public and be used in any legal actions involving tainted blood and blood products.[154]

Improved accountability and decision making in New Zealand

A senior public servant in New Zealand recorded that the Act has enhanced accountability. Moreover, the openness ensuing from its implementation may have improved the quality of advice and of decision-making. With

---

[152] Hazell, "Balancing Privacy and Freedom of Information" in McDonald and Terrill *ibid.* pp.67–85, at p.80.
[153] Gillis, "Freedom of information in Canada" in McDonald and Terrill *op.cit.* pp. 143-166, at p.149.
[154] *Ibid.*, p.156.

open government came wider participation in decision-making. It was highlighted that to achieve this, information needs to be made available and interpreted to the general public or special interest groups in a form that enables them to express opinions or take action. In this regard, the media have a major responsibility to discover information and to disseminate it objectively in a way that will throw light on government.

The early Irish Experience

This use by the media has been the experience of the Irish regime since its introduction.[155] What is of most interest in the contribution of the two Irish civil servants to this published debate on privacy and freedom of information, is their frank and informative assessment of the lessons learned during the implementation of the Freedom of Information Act 1997. They helped steer through the legislation and reflect that the single critical factor that they overlooked is that freedom of information was a change process, not just a legislative matter.

> "In a democracy profound change such as FOI requires a lot of time for consultation and information-giving across parliamentary, administrative and public forums….This was a learning experience, not just for others but also for ourselves. Their perspectives and concerns helped us crystallize issues and develop our thinking. However this process of telling, selling and learning meant a daily struggle to ensure that time was actually spent on progressing the legislation itself.
>
> Because of the nature of the legislation and its lack of congruence with existing culture and practice there were strong reservations about the measure. These found expression in a number of ways: outright opposition on the

---

[155] Media requests under the Freedom of Information Act have led to significant public debate on such issues as the manner in which parliamentarians' expenses are used; the extent and nature of information which should be made available to the public about schools by the Department of Education; the behind the scenes decision-making processes regarding major planning decisions and the drafting of certain pieces of legislation.

grounds that FOI was unworkable; a view that it was not in the public interest that it should apply in a particular area; assertions to the effect that FOI proposals were highly laudable but required far greater consideration and development before matters could proceed further; and official silence, complemented by discreet efforts to build alliances against the measure."[156]

The authors considered that three key factors contributed to smooth the implementation of the cultural change in the Irish public service from secrecy to freedom of information. As with the New Zealand experience, access to information was introduced as part and parcel of much wider changes in an effort for greater openness and accountability in government. Perhaps, as a consequence, there was in place an informal network across the senior levels of administration who were well-informed and highly effective in encouraging wider support. However, deemed of vital significance was "ongoing direct access to officials abroad who had practical experience of FOI for over a decade and a half, and were able rapidly to provide answers to many hard questions."[157]

Training

"Any law, no matter how well intentioned requires implementation. Where the law is going to effect the operations of government and its administration at every level, such implementation requires considerable training. Little attention has been paid by legal commentators to the training aspect of laws imposing duties to provide information. Legal objectives are not made effective by simply placing words on paper. Skill and expertise are required, as well as financial resources.[158]

---

[156] G. Kearney and A. Stapleton, "Freedom of Information Legislation in Ireland", in McDonald and Terrill *op.cit.* pp. 167-179, at p. 177.

[157] *ibid.,* p.178.

[158] Birkinshaw, *Freedom of Information: The US Experience*, Studies in Law, Hull University (1991).

Irrespective of the oversight regime, the significance of training should most definitely not be underestimated. The New Zealand States Services Commission carried out intensive training for all public servants when the Act was introduced to make them aware of their obligations and responsibilities. Combined with public confidence in the enforcing authority, the New Zealand Ombudsman, these two factors were critical to the Act's smooth implementation.

In Ireland during the lead in period, i.e. a twelve-month period prior to the full implementation of the Act, there was extensive training for personnel in the public bodies affected by the new legislation including implementation of and training in new methods of filing, in retrieval of files and in dealing with requests under the Act.

Disappearance of FOI unit of Department of Finance

Training is an on-going process resulting in a depth of openness and transparency in relation to almost all public bodies which was unexpected given their former secrecy. Unfortunately, one of the consequences evident after the passage of the 2003 Amendment Act was the effective disappearance off the radar of the FOI section of the Central Policy Unit of the Department of Finance. The personnel in this unit had been deeply committed to the development of FOI and were involved in training and advice especially for central government bodies. Pre the 2003 amendments locating them via the Internet was simply a matter of logging on to the Department of Finance's website and following the clear links. Post the 2003 amendments one not only needs to be aware of their existence in advance of trying to locate them, but without their specific web address,[159] searches of the Internet are almost as good as useless.

---

[159] www.foi.gov.ie

Effective record keeping and Freedom of Information

Checklist

- Every record of a public body is subject to a freedom of information request.

- Every record of a public body is NOT subject to release under FOI.

- Records subject to discretionary exemptions under the Act and subject to most mandatory exemptions remain subject to the scrutiny of the Information Commissioner even if deemed exempt by the public body.

- Any communication with a public body which is given in confidence and falls within recognised parameters of confidentiality is likely to remain confidential.

- There is a presumption that an affected third party will be informed in advance of the intention to release a record.

- There is also a presumption that if a party to a communication with a public body considers that publication might reveal commercial or trade secrets, that third party is advised if not consulted before release.

- Representations made by third parties in these cases may not prevent release because of other legislative requirements such as the public interest or harm tests.

- Communications given in confidence should be marked as such.

- When preparing minutes it is acceptable to isolate elements of the record as e.g. deliberative process, commercial secret etc. as appropriate.

- Systems need to be developed in public bodies to ensure that when records are flagged with FOI exemptions as suggested e.g. given in confidence; deliberative process, these records are filed in isolation from other records to avoid accidental release.

- Just because a record is flagged as being exempt does not make it exempt. The content needs to be examined to ensure that it falls under the exemptions.

It must always be borne in mind that, in general, all records are subject to scrutiny by the Information Commissioner irrespective of the view of the public body as to content.[160]

No accountability without openness

The issues raised in this chapter are not confined to public service management, but are about a management culture that applies irrespective of the organisation in question whether it be a profit or a not-for-profit organisation and whatever its aiMs What is necessary in all cases is that the organisation becomes wedded to a concept of accountability. There is no accountability without openness.

Of course, if access to information is to operate effectively it should not be necessary to appeal any decisions through national courts. The costs of this are prohibitive and, as is evident from the litigation, the timescales involved are likely to render the information useless if and when it is accessed. What is required is a non-secretive public service. In the case of Ireland, the Freedom of Information Act was introduced at a time when the Strategic Management Initiative, a radical reform of the Civil Service, had already been initiated. In the words of the Information Commissioner in his first annual report "the Act has an important contribution to make to public service reform. If it is used effectively by requesters and operated conscientiously by public servants, it has the potential to bring about significant improvement in the overall standard of public administration."[161]

The key to a successful transition from secrecy to sunlight lies in intent, motivation and training. It is a sad reflection on Irish government that the open intent present in the early years has disappeared in the Freedom of Information (Amendment) Act 2003 and is replaced by a series of draconian measures intent on closing down access. Nevertheless,

---

[160] Under s.20 of the FOI Act as amended, a declaration by a Secretary General of a Department that a record is exempt is final and not subject to scrutiny by the Information Commissioner. However, if challenged to the High Court the manner of these exemptions may well be found unconstitutional, *Commentary of the Information Commissioner on the Freedom of Information Act 1997 op.cit;Review 2003 op.cit.*

[161] *Annual Report of the Information Commissioner 1998*, p. 1.

is to be hoped that public service reform had advanced to a stage whereby it can withstand the retrograde impact of the 2003 amendments to the freedom of information regime.

FOI and Tribunals of inquiry

Finally, a critical question to consider is the extent to which the freedom of information legislation would have obviated the need for recent and on-going Tribunals of Inquiry had it been in effect at the time of all the events in question. In relation to the infection of the national blood supply, the most grievous of all events conducted in secret, it is a matter of record that information held by public bodies was not accessible to the Expert Group[162] in the absence of the powers available to the Finlay Tribunal,[163] namely powers to order discovery and compel witnesses. Where a duly appointed Expert Group of inquiry failed it is hardly likely that a freedom of information request could have succeeded. Hence, the short answer to this important question is that the Act is likely to have made no difference whatsoever.

It is fitting to leave the final word to the Information Commissioner when talking about

> "that grey area where elected politicians and public officials interact and which remains to this day one of the darkest secrets of Irish public administration. And we have been over this course before. First with the Beef Tribunal, which, in itself, created an impetus for an FOI Act. Then came the Moriarty and Flood (now Mahon) Tribunals and the Dáil Public Accounts Committee Enquiry into the evasion of payment of DIRT.
>
> The hope was that the FOI Act, which came into effect in 1998 and in response to past failures to shed light on the workings of Government, would, at last, shed greater light

---

[162] Despite its official status the Expert Group was a failed attempt to discover the causes of infection.

[163] *Report of the Tribunal of Inquiry into the Blood Transfusion Service Board*, Pn 3695, 1997. Sole Member of the Tribunal, Thomas A. Finlay (retired Chief Justice).

on this grey area. And so it did for five years until in 2003 the Government's proposals to restrict the scope of the Act in relation to access to Government Memoranda and the deliberative process and other aspects of Government work were passed by the Oireachtas. In addition, fees for requests and appeals to my Office were introduced which are unparalleled in any other country that has an Information Commissioner. Whose interests does this serve? It seems to suggest that the people are seen as adversaries and nothing more than lip-service is being paid to the principles of open, fair and accountable government."[164]

---

[164] *Address by the Ombudsman and Information Commissioner, Ms. Emily O'Reilly, at the Annual Conference of Assistant Secretaries,* March 3, 2005.

Index